The Cherokee Indians called the place "Eeseeoh,"
which means "River of Cliffs."

RIVER OF CLIFFS

A LINVILLE GORGE HISTORY

CHRISTOPHER BLAKE

Published by The History Press
Charleston, SC
www.historypress.net

Front cover: View from the Chimneys on the Gorge's east rim. The pillar to the left is the Camel and ahead lie, first, Table Rock, then Hawksbill Mountain. Behind the view lie Shortoff Mountain and Lake James. *Ken Thomas, public domain.*
Back cover: *From the editor's archive.*

First published 2017

Manufactured in the United States

ISBN 9781625858849

Library of Congress Control Number: 2017934946

Sacred places are for the most part storied settings:
a little part of some great soul
cleaved to these walls, to these heights

—Louis Aragon, surrealist poet

In our land [Ireland] *there is no river or mountain that is not associated in the memory with some event or legend. . . . I would have our writers and craftsmen of many kinds master this history and these legends, and fix upon their memory the appearance of mountains and rivers and make it all visible again in their arts.*

—W.B. Yeats

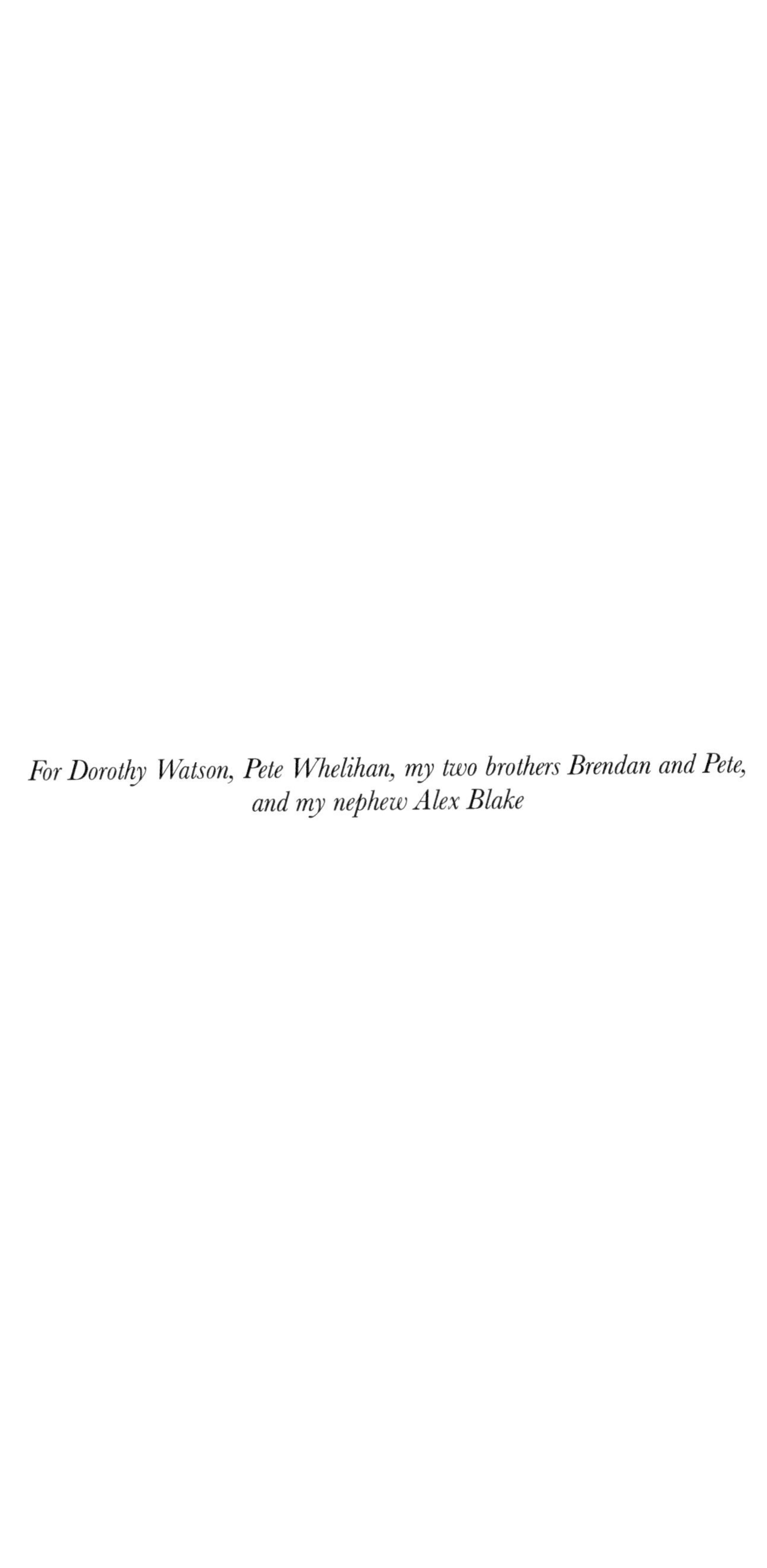

For Dorothy Watson, Pete Whelihan, my two brothers Brendan and Pete, and my nephew Alex Blake

TO THE READER

The popular Linville Falls and the Linville Gorge Wilderness Area have been described dozens of times. Both fictional and historical accounts abound, and we have records of this wild and spectacular place that reflect the interest of botanists, geologists, preservationists, outdoors educators, students of pioneer culture, hikers and climbers and historians. No less valuable have been the creative interpretations of poets, painters, novelists and photographers.

This book offers a rich and representative sampling of these varied perspectives, familiarity with which, it is hoped, will deepen your experience of this exceptional place.

—Christopher Blake

CONTENTS

ACKNOWLEDGEMENTS

For all the help I've gotten along the way, I am grateful indeed. "One book opens another," the old alchemists were fond of saying, and in my searches I found authors like Carolyn Sakowski invaluable in pointing out to me source after source—the Jules Verne connection to Table Rock, for example. Her list of works cited at the end of *Touring Western North Carolina's Backroads* displays all that is best in a thorough bibliography. Much of my own work has involved merely procuring copies of the materials and providing brief introductory notes to them. And so my debts to other writers, curators and archivists are many and obvious. Here I should like to acknowledge assistance of those individuals and institutions that lent me the most support in my work.

For permission to reprint his poem on Bea Hensley, I heartily thank Mr. Jonathan Williams of Highlands, North Carolina. I thank Fred Brown, editor of *Brown's Guide to Georgia*, for the permission to reprint Tom Patterson's 1978 article "Linville." Thanks also to editor Jamie Shell at the *Avery Journal-Times* for letting me include rescue reports from his paper. *River* benefits greatly from the naturalist gorge expertise shared by local biology professor Stewart Skeate and speleologist Dr. Cato Holler.

For her help with statistical information on the Linville Gorge Wilderness Area, I thank Ms. Miera Crawford of the Grandfather Ranger District Office of the U.S. Forest Service, Pisgah National Forest in Nebo, North Carolina. Interpretive specialist for the Blue Ridge Parkway Jonathan Bennet is to be thanked for bringing Lyman Draper's biography of Daniel Boone to my notice.

I am highly grateful for the assistance of former special collections librarian Helen D. Wykle at the D. Hiden Ramsey Library of the University of North Carolina at Asheville. Ms. Wykle helped me obtain analog copies of historic photographs from the Ewart M. Ball Photographic Collection and rights of reproduction for them. Serendipitous was it for me to meet a person so well informed about the travel and tourism literature of western North Carolina.

Ms. Norma Myers, curator of East Tennessee State University's Archives of Appalachia at the Charles C. Sherrod Library, provided me with access to the D.R. Beeson Sr. journal and photographic album record of the trip to Table Rock Mountain that Mr. Beeson made with his friends in 1914. Mr. Beeson's son D.R. Beeson Jr. of Johnson City, Tennessee, has graciously given permission for the publication of his father's journal in this book.

Ms. Andrea Fey, former alumni coordinator of the North Carolina Outward Bound School in Asheville, was instrumental in answering my questions about the early years of Outward Bound at Table Rock Mountain. Ms. Fey also kindly let me make a copy of the promotional film *Solo* (1969), which includes footage of this editor and Anakiwa Crew. Messrs. Dave Mashburn and Jack Shirey were godsends in clarifying certain puzzling references in my Outward Bound 1967 course journal. Ms. Deb Whitmore, program director at Outward Bound, shared valuable insights on the growth of the school over the years since I attended and invited me to tour the much-changed facility.

I thank the staffs of the Carson Library at Lees-McRae College in Banner Elk, North Carolina; the Carol Belk Library at Appalachian State University Library in Boone, North Carolina; and the Burke County Public Library in Morganton, North Carolina. Mr. Keith Longiotti of UNC-Chapel Hill's Wilson Library was especially helpful in locating the photographs among the Hugh Morton Collection. Parkway Publisher's 2005 edition of *River* put me in touch with Linville living legends Bob Underwood and Allen Hyde—and, through them, the very-much-active Gorge Rats (with its Lady Gorge Rats auxiliary) reached at www.linvillegorge.net. They all expanded my consciousness of this "gorgeous" place.

My Friends of Linville Gorge group (FOLG) has no Internet presence, nor much of an organization, but it offers gorge visits to hikers in good condition. Formed in 1993 around guided mushroom walks or forays conducted by fungi expert, or mycologist, Pete Whelihan, the group contracted in 2006 with the Grandfather Ranger District's Adopt-a-Trail Program and undertook trail maintenance training at the USFS training facility in Woodlawn, North Carolina. Program coordinator Pat Wilson taught us the requisite "non-motorized" hand-labor means of maintaining wilderness access. FOLG adopted the Devil's Hole Trail in 2006 and, in 2014, added care of forestry trails on the canyon's west side: Bynum's Bluff, Cabin and Babel Tower Trails, each joined by the main north–south footpath paralleling the river, the Linville Gorge Trail. Many volunteer groups, including scouts, cooperate in keeping these wonderful trails open.

Finally, words fail to describe the magnitude of the debt I owe to my beloved friend and companion Dorothy Watson, with whom I moved to the Falls and Gorge area in 1993. Together, we learned about the birds, trees and wildflowers of the wilderness while exploring its many trails. My best friend, Pete Whelihan, brought his expertise with wild mushrooms to Gorge forays and continues to sell wild species to the chefs of Asheville from his My-Co Gardens farm in Alexander, North Carolina. Ms. Wendy Funk at the Linville Falls Lodge and Spears Restaurant and Ms. Martha Piercy at the Linville Falls General make the little community an especially friendly, hospitable place from which to launch gorge adventures.

My two late brothers, Brendan and Pete, inspired the creation of *River of Cliffs* by their own appreciation for this unique and richly storied wilderness area.

INTRODUCTION

If you put your finger on a map of western North Carolina, and onto one of the oldest mountains in the world, the venerable Grandfather in the Blue Ridge Mountains, you should be able to trace the course of the Linville River southward from its sources as it runs through a plateau of rolling farm country to the small village of Linville Falls. The river flows under the Blue Ridge Parkway at milepost 316, becoming for a short distance a part of the National Park System. Well before this point, it continues to flourish as a popular trout stream. In the Falls park, it twists and almost doubles back on itself, flowing by a campground and a visitor center to a point where its course is parted in two by a midstream rock formation, the "Upper Falls." Suddenly morphing its dynamics (or hydraulics, rather) from placid stream to churning whitewater, it narrows and plummets in two distinct stages to the choppy waters of a circular "Plunge Basin." Here the Linville River earns its Native American sobriquet *Eeseeoh* ("River of Many Cliffs"), as it snakes its turbulent way below sheer precipices and around colossal boulders. And here indeed is a primordial place, where man and his incursions seem puny and fleeting—the Linville Gorge Wilderness Area. For some fourteen miles, the river meanders through a canyon so rugged and hazardous that only a series of primitive trails serves to make the area passable. High over visitors' heads tower the silent sentinels known as Hawksbill and Table Rock. There are also other rock formations (typically of Chilhowie quartzite), such as the Sitting Bear, Wiseman's View, the Chimneys, the North Carolina Wall and Sphynx Rock, terminating to the southeast in Shortoff Mountain, which oversees the Linville's mingling with the waters of the Catawba River in Lake James.

From its origins in the high country of the Blue Ridge to its terminus in the Catawba Valley, the river descends some three thousand feet, and it is this activity that has, over the course of eons, created the gorge. In fact, the Linville Falls area forms what scientists call a "geologic window," through which the actions of plate tectonics millions of years ago can be seen as in a cross-section of the earth's history. The theory has it that the collision of the North American with the African continent thrust older, metamorphic rock over younger, sedimentary rock in a reversal of the normal erosion process. Originally, the Linville River flowed over the edge of the mountains at a point twelve miles downstream; in so doing, it eroded the softer rock beneath the harder, metamorphic layer. This undermining process caused a steady series of collapses as the waterfall gradually moved its way upstream to its present location.

For generations, the Linville Gorge has been a popular destination for sightseers and lovers of the outdoor life, including hikers, campers, painters, rock climbers, hunters and fishermen. University and government scientists have long taken an acute interest in the area, studying its geology, its flora and fauna and even certain mysterious phenomena associated with nearby Brown Mountain. The U.S. Army Special Forces made use of it for a period in the 1960s, as it resembled the Central Highlands of Vietnam. In the early nineteenth century, the Gorge was already well known as an exceptionally wild and romantic spot, "a savage place…holy and enchanted" as the English poet Samuel Taylor Coleridge might have described it. To Native Americans, the Gorge was a favorite summering spot, cool and filled with abundant game animals. Unfortunately, the colorful legend that Table Rock Mountain was Attacoa—the mystic sacrificial altar of the Cherokees—was spun out of the dreams of early travel and tourism promoters. More recently, the spectacular terrain of the Gorge has been featured in a Hollywood movie, director Michael Mann's *The Last of the Mohicans*, based on the novel by James Fenimore Cooper. Today, the area is a base for the North Carolina Outward Bound School, which utilizes the demanding physical challenges of the terrain for intensive outdoors education.

The Gorge is a unique ecosystem, home to an abundance of wildlife and plant species. Heller's Blazing Star and Mountain Golden Heather are but two examples of the rare flora sheltered there. It is also one of the few intact areas of old-growth forest in the eastern United States. Among the rare and endangered species in the Linville Gorge are varieties of chameleons and turtles. Typical among the woody growth are eastern white pine; Carolina hemlock; Fraser magnolia; red maple; red, black and white oak; tulip poplar; flame azalea; rosebay; Catawba and Carolina rhododendron; mountain laurel; and chinquapin. Sand myrtle, turkey beard and blueberry are also abundant. Animal life in the Gorge includes deer, bear, beaver, wild geese, otter and ruffled grouse. In 1987, peregrine falcons were introduced into the high cliffs south of Table Rock and are a protected species there. I have mentioned some of the striking geological formations that give the Gorge its gorgeous vistas. On the canyon's east side, Jonas Ridge runs south from Sitting Bear to Hawksbill to Table Rock and the Chimneys and Shortoff. Each of them presents a distinctive profile, especially when viewed from a distance. On the western rim of the gorge—following the ridgeline formed by Linville Mountain—is a dramatic outcropping just off the bumpy dirt road. Wiseman's View has long been a favorite lookout point from which the famous Brown Mountain Lights are occasionally visible. The forty-one-plus miles of official trails offer access to the river below; their unusual names preserve some of the past history of the Gorge (Spence Ridge, Bynum Bluff, Erwin's View and others). Trails can be steep and demanding, even dangerous in places, and they often present challenges to even the hardiest of hikers. Several of the trails, especially the ones to the views of the Falls, were created in the early years of the twentieth century by a colorful poet and outdoorsman from Charleston, South Carolina, named A.M. Huger, or "Chucky Joe."

In 1950, Linville Gorge was declared a wild area by the U.S. Department of Agriculture. The 7,575-acre tract was officially included in the National Wilderness System in 1964. With the passage of the North Carolina Wilderness Act in 1984, the size of the protected area was increased to its present 12,000 acres. The U.S. Forest Service is the federal agency responsible for the Gorge, actively managing the place to preserve its character as an "untrammeled wilderness" by closing it to logging, road building and vehicular traffic, as well as to any commercial development. In addition, usage in certain areas, such as the peregrine falcon nesting sites, was restricted.

The National Park Service oversees the Linville Falls Recreation Area, about two miles along a paved spur road off the Blue Ridge Parkway. Here there is also a trail system, a visitor center and facilities for camping and picnicking, as well as a series of spectacular overlooks of the Falls. Once a commercial attraction owned by the Hossfield family, the Falls passed into parkway management thanks to a donation made by John D. Rockefeller at the urging of local lawyer and civil libertarian Marion C. Wright.

The wilderness is a world of enchantments, but it can be a highly dangerous place, as well, unforgiving of those who are careless. Accidents, even fatalities, in the area have been many, including two deaths from falls in 2001. The Burke County Emergency Service averages between forty and fifty rescue missions a year in the Gorge. According to a county spokesperson, while fatalities in the wilderness are infrequent, "the number of non-fatal accidents is on the rise." In turn, the increasing popularity of the Gorge has put the area itself at risk (over thirty thousand people a year visit the wilderness). The irresponsible behavior of a growing number of casual visitors, for example, has left some trails badly littered. This is only one of several major problems threatening the area. In November 2000, a fire in the Brushy Ridge area damaged over ten thousand acres in the Gorge—the result of an unattended campfire. Today, a permit system limits the number of overnight summer visitors, but human impact remains considerable. The worst blow dealt the Gorge in recent memory has been the blight of the invasive hemlock woolly adelgid, responsible for the loss of most of the old hemlock giants but not the complete destruction of the species here.

No verbal description can hope to convey the sensations awaiting one who visits the Falls and the Gorge, or even the charming community nearby, which over the years has managed to resist large-scale tourist development to remain a comfortable home base for visitors as well as a place with a distinctive history of settlement and use. In 2015, the Linville Falls General opened its doors to offer food, gear and firewood to a stream of visitors from around the globe. There is an indefinable quality about the Gorge that lures one with a deep sense of connectedness to wild space. A person quietly attentive to its features may come to feel a deep sense of oneness with nature here, as though the forest and peaks had just emerged from the shaping hands of their Creator. The collection of pictures and words I have gathered here do not aim to reproduce that unique authentic experience. Every encounter with the Gorge and the Falls seems to leave me with a welter of vivid impressions:

> *Knobby roots of the rhododendrons clutching the black forest loam. Ripples and slivers of milky quartz undulating through the mossy granite. And the sheer monoliths whose smooth sides glisten with spring water or loom high overhead, speckled with hoary olive lichen.*
>
> *Dense stands or "bays" of dog-hobble swaying along the river banks. The greenbrier vine (smilax) like ripsaw teeth looping the limbs of mountain laurel in the sunless grottoes; "hells" they call them, so close compacted they devour the daylight.*

And from the majestic Hawksbill and her sister peaks the ridgelines are rolling on to a haze of infinity, while far below the silent river glistens like a tinsel strip. As you climb down towards it, the river begins roaring. On the ascent, it dwindles away below to a whisper like the breezes in the hemlocks.

"Hey! Smells like a skunk's been through here" (you pause to snuff the rank odor). "Or it's that old stinkweed," someone ventures. "No. Sorry. You're both wrong. It's galax, its old dry leaves mulching into the duff. And whenever you catch a whiff of that funky fermented odor, look closely by for a patch of these shiny round leaves, with wrinkly edges, sitting low on the ground. That'll be your galax. Deep green in the summer, wine red in the frosty days of winter. Long time collected by the locals in bundles for sale to florists."

And so the experiences engage, entwine, knitting the fabric of vivid memories.

Appreciation for such experiences, however, can be heightened by an awareness of what others have left in the way of testimonial to their wonder and respect for the place. This collection, then, serves as an introduction to and a record of one of earth's enchanted places, forbidding yet delightful: Linville Falls and the Linville Gorge Wilderness Area. The selections gathered for this reader appear in chronological order, from the early days of the 1752 diary of the Moravian bishop August Spangenberg and the *Pennsylvania Gazette*'s report on the Indian attack on the Linville hunting party in 1766 to later fictional uses of the wilderness for settings and the anecdotes of tourists.

I should mention here that in order to preserve the flavor of the original documents, various irregularities in spelling and capitalization have been retained; thus, "Linvill" and "Lynvil" are variant spellings of Linville, and Tablerock is used for Table Rock. We also read "pine blank" for point blank, noting Horace Kephart's gloss on "pint black" in *Our Southern Highlanders* (1913): "Pint blank is a superlative or an epithet, 'We jist pint blank got it to do.'" Some of the anecdotes retailed in *River* bid to become icons: Culgee Watson strutting below the Sitting Bear in his peacock feather costume; Franklin's mad dash up the Gorge in trousers bristling with venomous snakes; the photographs of D.R. Beeson, with their Asiatic landscape painting effects of mist-shrouded peaks with dwarf trees in dawn rain. The cumulative effect is extraordinary and fulfills the Irish poet W.B. Yeats's call for artists who would work in the mind and memory of Nature for their subjects.

It may be remembered that many of the more flowery, even romantic pieces of writing about the area served a commercial agenda. Intended to boost the Southern Highlands not only as a vacation wonderland of scenic beauty, plentiful game for sport and cool elevations "above the sweltering plain," these narrations also promoted the rich timber and mineral resources of the region. A case in point is Shepherd M. Dugger's *Balsam Groves of the Grandfather Mountain*, written for the Linville Improvement Company and plugging the area with unabashed hype. Reading the record in such a historical context needn't spoil the charm of our writer's gushy posturing, for it is balanced with brilliant thumbnail sketches that inform and delight.

My primary goal in selecting materials was to provide the reader with scarce and out-of-print records, with unpublished sources, with old histories and old images. Readily available sources such as hiking and rock-climbing guides would be extraneous here; they can be purchased at bookstores or found online. When readers compare the old-time accounts with their own impressions of the Falls and the Gorge, they will be pleasantly surprised at how the area has managed to retain its power to produce emotions of awe and wonder. Ultimately, that is the wild glory of this place, this Land that Time forgot; its primordial tracts await the explorations of generations to come.

1
THE SPANGENBERG DIARY

In the fall of 1752, the Moravian bishop August Spangenberg received a warrant from Earl Granville, one of the eight Lords Proprietors of North Carolina, to seek out one hundred thousand acres in the vast territory for the brotherhood to settle on. In the company of a surveyor and several Moravian Brethren, Spangenberg traveled west, remarking on the living conditions of the Indians and the white settlers as he passed through. The party passed the sites of present-day Morganton and Blowing Rock before opting for the tract named Wachovia at what is now Winston-Salem. The original Spangenberg papers (twenty-three pages of field notes in miniscule handwriting) reside in the Salem Archives of the North Carolina Office of Archives and History in Raleigh.

Nov. 19th. From camp on the middle river of the three rivers flowing into the Catawba near Quaker Meadows, not far from Table Mountain. We reached here last Thursday, and made our camp, and went out to see the section, riding into the night. We found everything needed for a settlement,—very fertile lowlands, the best we have seen in North Carolina, which can be cultivated year after year without impoverishing them, for they lie at the foot of steep, rich hills, from which the soil washes down, enriching the meadows. Wheat and corn can be grown.

The tract is well watered, with springs, little streams, and creeks, and the water is as beautiful and sweet as one could wish. In the lower part of the tract we have the [Johns] River, which is half as large as the Lecha. Above we have the two branches [Wilson Creek and Mulberry Fork], forming a fork, each being perhaps twice as large as the Manocasy at Bethlehem. They are crystal clear, so that one can see the stones on the bottom even where the water is deep.

There are tall, strong trees; also young growth. There are good meadows for pasturage, and many reeds, which are still green,—otherwise our horses would starve.

Nov. 24th. From camp in the forks of the third river [Upper Creek in Burke County] that flows into the Catawba near Quaker Meadows. Perhaps five miles from Table Mountain. This is the fifth tract that we have selected, and contains seven or eight hundred acres,—a fine piece of land, lying on two creeks.

The land is very rich, and has been much frequented by buffalo, whose tracks are everywhere, and can often be followed with profit. Frequently, however, a man cannot travel them, for they go through thick and thin, through morass and deep water, and up and down banks so steep that a man could fall down but neither ride nor walk!

This tract lies not far from No. 4, perhaps a good mile to the west, and the way is not bad when one knows it.

The wolves here give us music every morning, from six corners at once, such music as I have never heard. They are not like the wolves of Germany, Poland, and Livonia, but are afraid of men, and do not usually approach near them. A couple of Brethren skilled in hunting would be of benefit not only here but at our other tracts, partly to kill the wolves and panthers, partly to supply the Brethren with game. Not only can the skins of wolves and panthers be sold, but the governor pays a bounty of ten shillings for each one killed.

2

ROYAL GOVERNOR TRYON ON THE LINVILLE MASSACRE

In a letter dated July 30, 1766, colonial governor William Tryon relates to his surveyor, John Stuart, the scantily known details of a surprise Indian attack on the Linville hunting party. Most of the letter describes the establishment of boundaries between the Cherokees and the whites, following a royal proclamation of 1763, and is included here as revealing the existing tensions between the indigenous peoples and the colonists.

Brunswick 30th July 1766.

Since my letter to you of the 17th last month I have laid before his Majesty's Council of this province our correspondence on the subject of Indian affairs and the following is a copy of the Resolution of the Council on that business Vidt.

His Excellency communicated to this Board letters of correspondence on Indian affairs from Mr. Stuart, Superintendent of the Southern District with respect to a boundary line between this province and the hunting grounds claimed by the Cherokee Indians, and it is the opinion of this Board that his Excellency direct the Surveyor General by himself or his deputies to run such lines as the Governor shall think proper to quiet the Indians, and secure the western inhabitants in their legal possessions. And as there is no fund approved for this contingency, and that the service may be impeded it is also the opinion of this board, that the Governor may issue his warrants to the Receiver General of his Majesty's quit rents for such sums of money as may be found necessary to carry the above service into execution, and that upon the meeting of the assembly application be made to reimburse the sums so drawn for.

I am sorry to find by the favor of your letter of the 24th of July delivered me by Mr Barnett that you are obliged to postpone your intended visit to me, as I am now anxious to see you and ready to consult with you on the proper measures to be taken relative to the demands of the Cherokees. I shall acquaint the inhabitants of the back country of this province of the hostile disposition of some of the Indian tribes, and the probability of a rupture, at the same time strongly recommend to them to avoid all opportunities of giving them a pretence to commit hostilities and to caution them to be on their guard in case the Indians should make any inroads on them. If the Cherokees permit agreeable to their first talk, the line to be run from Dewis's corner a north course to the mountains, and from thence a strait course to Chiswell's mines, I believe the inhabitants of Mecklenburg and Rowan Counties will be extremely well satisfied and upon the execution of this agreement I am willing to advance £100 for the cost and charges of such presents, as you may think most acceptable to the Cherokee Indians. If the above line could be run by the end of September and you could accompany me, I should not dislike to be present as it might not only prevent any little jealousies that might arise between the settlers, and the Indians but give me an opportunity to take a view of the back country.

I this day received information that one William Linville, his son, and another young man who were gone over the mountains at the head of the Yadkin to hunt, that in the first week of this month they were surprised by the Indians, that Linville and his son were killed, that the young man made his escape wounded to his settlement, where I am informed he is since dead of his wounds. I cannot as yet learn of what tribe or nation these Indians were.

NOTE: It is likely that the Linville party was hunting in violation of the king's proclamation prohibiting whites from entering land west of the Blue Ridge. In 2015, the National Park Service erected a plaque at the Linville Falls Recreation Center on the Blue Ridge Parkway identifying the attackers as Shawnees. The full inscription reads: "*Death on the Long Hunt.* In 1766, along the banks of this river, William Linville and his son were killed by the Shawnee while on a long hunt. The Shawnee, who were on their way to attack the Cherokees, feared that Linville's hunting party would discover their presence and alert the nearby Cherokee. Because the Linville party was on an extended hunt, lasting from six months to a year, they may have amassed a very valuable stash of furs—another likely reason for the attack. Today, this river carries the Linville name."

3

"ATTACK ON THE LINVILLE PARTY"

Appearing in the *Pennsylvania Gazette*, this is the first published notice concerning the Linville Falls and Gorge area. In her history of Linville Falls, Emma L. Franklin gives an account of the Indian attack that varies considerably in important details from the article below. According to Franklin, the Linville party numbered four: William Linville, his son Thomas, Chelsea Dobbs and John Williams. While camping for the night above the Falls, the party was attacked by Indians and both Linvilles were killed. Dobbs and Williams escaped, however. According to historian and North Carolina hiking trail expert Allen de Hart, John Williams alone survived, making a five-day ride to safety with a broken leg. Furthermore, writes de Hart, the scene of the attack is in question: "Folk historians are not certain where the massacre took place because the records show the site was 'below the falls,' or 'in the gorge,' or near the headwaters above the falls." The year after the massacre, the Cherokee and whites agreed to a boundary line following the crest of the Blue Ridge, but in 1777, Colonel Waightstill Avery forced the withdrawal of the Indians from the area.

October 9, 1766. They write from North-Carolina that one William Linvill, his son, and another young man, who had gone over the mountains at the head of the Yadkin River to hunt, were there surprised by some Indians. The father and son were both killed on the spot; the other young man got off, though much wounded, and arrived at his settlement, where he is since dead. No accounts had been received of what tribe or nation the Indians were. But it is thought, the relations of those Cherokees who were killed last year in Virginia, will, according to their inhuman custom, take every opportunity of revenge, at least till they have killed as many as they lost.

The same letters add, that the government of North-Carolina hath agreed, that the line dividing that province from the hunting-grounds claimed by, and reserved to, the Cherokees, shall be immediately run out, as proposed by the said Indians in their talk to the honourable John Stuart, Esq. superintendant of the southern district of America, viz. From the place where the line behind this province terminates on Reedy-River, a north course to the mountains, and thence a direct course to colonel Chiswell's lead mine, on the Great Kannawah, behind Virginia. In consequence of which, orders have been dispatched to Mr. Cameron, the superintendent's deputy in the Cherokee nation, to proceed with such headmen as the said nation shall depute, to meet the persons appointed by his excellency governor Tryon, in order to finish this very important business.

September 16, 1766. By letters from the Cherokee country we are informed that the white people mentioned in our last, were killed by a party of northward Indians, who still continue their excursions against the Cherokees, notwithstanding the steps taken by Sir William Johnson, and Mr. Stuart, to effect a peace between them. The son of Attakullakulla and seven others, his relations, were lately killed by a party who fell upon them as they were picking berries at a small distance from their habitations. Ouconnostota, or the great-warrior, and several other headmen, were lately at fort Prince-George, on a visit to Mr. Price, the commandant, who delivered and explained to them, a talk from the superintendant, relating, among other things, to the war between the Creeks and the Choctaws; Ouconnostota said they were both rogues, and might fight it out between themselves. It appears that the Creeks have been tampering with the Cherokees, in order to induce them to take part with them against the Choctaws.

Note: The Reedy River is a tributary of the Saluda River, about sixty-five miles long, in northwestern South Carolina. It rises in Greenville County in the foothills of the Blue Ridge Mountains some ten miles northwest of Greenville. It drains with the Santee into the Atlantic.

Colonel Chiswell's lead mines were located near present-day Austinville, Virginia, in Wythe County, lying south of Wytheville and north of Hillsville, Virginia. While hiding from Indians in a small cave, Colonel Robert Chiswell discovered a pocket of lead. Later, he dug a twenty-five-foot access tunnel to the lode, "Chiswell's Hole." Because of his Tory sympathies, Chiswell lost his lead lands during the American Revolution.

Attacullaculla ("Leaning Wood") was an English-speaking Cherokee and the youngest chief among the group of seven Cherokee taken to London in 1733 by Sir Alexander Cumings to meet the king.

Fort Prince George was an English trading fort in Oconee County, South Carolina, north of present-day Seneca. It was built after the 1753 conference between South Carolina governor Glen and Cherokee chiefs who wanted protection from hostile western tribes and the French.

Ouconnostota also traveled to London in 1750 and met King George the Second in Whitehall. The Cherokee created a fashionable stir in London, as, no doubt, reports about the Linville Massacre did.

John Stuart remained superintendant of Indian affairs from 1763 until after the Revolution.

4

DANIEL BOONE AND THE LINVILLE MASSACRE

BY LYMAN C. DRAPER

Lyman C. Draper set aside his monumental eight-hundred-page biography of Daniel Boone in 1856. The book was not published until 1998, a result of the labors of editor Ted Franklin Belue. Draper gives the most extensive account of the Linville Massacre, and, among other interesting details, explains how the Boones and Linvilles were related by marriage. To this editor, the text's main attractions are the weighty irony residing in the old captain's intent to go hunting in the mountains to improve his bad health and the premonitory dream he had of the attack seconds before it had begun. Draper sites the "fatal camp" on the east side of the Linville River, near Shortoff Mountain and some ten miles below the falls. Other sources place the camp above or near the great Falls. In a note, Belue identifies the raiders as Shawnee, who often ranged south of the Ohio River on the Warrior's Path to attack the villages of the Catawba and the Cherokee.

Among the Indian troubles of the period may be mentioned that of four traders and a half-breed child of one of them who were killed in the Cherokee country during the month of May 1766—some of whom, it was thought, in retaliation for a chief and four warriors of the Cherokee nation treacherously slain the previous year by a party of lawless Virginians on the frontiers of that province. Such crimes with their bloody retaliations rendered it dangerous for the white hunters to expose themselves too far upon the

Indian hunting grounds; yet some more fearless than others, prompted by their passionate love of the chase, would make the venture.

It has already been mentioned that Linnville Creek, in the valley of Virginia, where the Boones probably tarried awhile on their way to the Yadkin country, was named after a noted border hunter—William Linnville. Among the pioneer settlers of that frontier region of Virginia, his name appears as a militiaman of Augusta County as early as 1742 and two years later a captain. He early removed to the Yadkin Valley and perhaps with the Boone emigration. He married a sister of Joseph Bryan, who, be it remembered, was the father-in-law of Daniel Boone; and about 1763 George Boone, a younger brother of Daniel's, married Nancy, daughter of Captain Linnville. In the summer of 1766 Captain Linnville, being in bad health, thought a hunting trip among the mountains might prove beneficial. Accompanied by his son John and another young man, he passed far beyond the settlements over the mountain ranges at the head of the Yadkin River and pitched his camp upon a very clear and rapid stream, a very considerable branch of the Catawba.

Awakening one morning just before daylight, Captain Linnville aroused his companions, telling them he had just vividly dreamed that they would all be killed by the Indians, and urged them instantly to escape and leave him to his fate—that he was not able to leave. He had scarcely finished his statement when they were fired upon and the old man wounded, when he again begged the young men to make their escape if possible. They sprang to their guns, when a second volley from the Indians killed young Linville and badly wounded the other, having received a ball through the thigh, partially fracturing the bone. He, however, ran off in the dark without being discovered; but unfortunately, after having gone some distance, [he] trod on a stick, which, breaking, in some way caused him to fall and resulted in completing the fracture of his thigh. There he lay in agony, expecting as soon as light should appear to be tomahawked. But at daylight the Indians went to catching the horses and secured all but one, a wild young animal belonging to Captain Linnville, which he had brought out to break into use by packing with the expected proceeds of the hunt. Scalping the unfortunate Linnvilles, the Indians packed up what plunder they desired and left the camp, the young horse following the others.

The wounded young man discovering the departure of the enemy, crawled back to the camp to die beside his friends. He had not been there long when the wild horse returned, went kindly up to the prostrate sufferer, suffered him to put on an old bridle the Indians had left and then get him little by little to a suitable place, where he managed to mount and started for home, sixty miles distant. With his broken leg painfully dangling, when he had gone about a mile, the horse took fright from the broken limb or dripping blood and, throwing the poor rider, ran off.

Despairing of reaching the settlements, he again crawled to the camp amid great suffering, his thigh by this time having become much swollen and very painful. He now discovered the Indians during his absence had returned to camp, probably in quest of the young horse, and failing to find it, had taken off [with] what they previously left. So his absence had saved him from the tomahawk and scalping knife. The wild horse again returned with the old bridle on and suffered the almost helpless cripple to remount and actually succeeded in reaching the settlements without dismounting. He survived his singular adventure and in due time recovered and was presented by Mrs. Linnville with the noble horse which had brought him to the settlement from the scene of carnage. Relating upon his return the particulars of the attack upon the camp, the death of the Linnvilles, and his own remarkable escape, a party of friends went out and buried the dead; and none more likely than Daniel Boone to have headed a mission of humanity like this.

The place where Captain Linnville and his son were unfortunately killed and their companion mortally wounded was on a clear and rapid mountain stream, a considerable branch of the Catawba of about fifty miles in length, in Burke County, North Carolina, which has ever since borne the name of Linnville River to perpetuate the misfortunes of these fearless border hunters. Their fatal camp, it is believed, was located not far from the bluff of the Short-Off Mountain, on the eastern bank of the river and about ten miles below the Falls, a beautiful cascade of from eight to one hundred foot descent. This attack was made by a band of Northern Indian warriors. Nor did the Cherokee fare any better, for a son of old At-ta-kul-la-Kul-la, together with seven of his relations, when engaged in picking berries, were about the same time fallen upon and slain by some of their Northern Indian enemies.

5

WESTERN NORTH CAROLINA: ITS MOUNTAINS AND ITS PEOPLE TO 1880

The Native Americans and white settlers contested bitterly over the Blue Ridge territory, with various worthless and broken treaties assuring the Cherokee of their rights to certain ancestral lands in western Carolina. No signs of Indian settlement appear in or around the gorge; rather, it was a happy summer hunting ground for Catawba, Creek and Cherokee coming up to the Blue Ridge from their rich foothill farm villages. Ora Blackmun conveys a keen sense of the oppression of native peoples by an ever-increasing influx of European settlers. Into this political hotbed trekked the Linville Party with their fatal encounter with invading Shawnee braves.

With the close of the French and Indian War in 1763, representatives of Virginia, Georgia and North and South Carolina met with a group of Cherokee chiefs and explained to them the terms of the peace treaty. A royal proclamation that same year restrained the whites in the two Carolinas from entering or taking up land west of the Blue Ridge, that is, west of the headwaters of streams flowing into the Atlantic Ocean [as the Linville River does via the Catawba and Peedee Rivers]. By this means the king hoped to avoid further border conflicts. The Cherokee were, of course, in no position to bargain to their own advantage. Also that year the native Americans signed a treaty ceding to South Carolina approximately one hundred square miles of their land in that colony, pushing their eastern boundary west to a line running north and south through the colony from a point on the Savannah River and passing near the present Greenville, on to the North Carolina line. Unaffected by the king's proclamation, Virginia gained by a forced treaty all Cherokee lands within the present state of Virginia and West Virginia in 1770 and in 1772 won from the Cherokees all lands east of the Kentucky River.

The Cherokees, scarred by memories of the recent war and fearing the encroachment of the whites, asked for a clearly stated eastern boundary line in the two Carolinas. That request was granted, and by royal order in 1767 North Carolina's Governor William Tryon, accompanied by two surveyors, two regiments of militia, and sixteen servants and aides, made the trip to the Cherokee country. The new South Carolina–Cherokee line was surveyed and a line run from it into North Carolina. But to survey the wild terrain of the Blue Ridge was an impossible feat.

Both Cherokees and whites agreed to a line declared from Tryon Mountain, passing near the present town of Tryon and following the crest of the Blue Ridge in a northeasterly direction to the mines of Colonel Chiswell in Virginia. The Board of Trade also agreed to this arrangement. While later surveys showed that such a line would not pass the designated site in Virginia, the crest of the range provided a boundary sufficiently clear to both races. The Cherokee were to stay west of that line; the whites were to stay east of it. The present Blue Ridge Parkway, along stretches of its North Carolina length, follows that old line of demarcation.

But there were loopholes in this agreement. In the first place, the line did not apply to Virginia. In the second place, it was possible that it would not govern the Lord Granville tract that crossed the Blue Ridge Mountains in the northern part of North Carolina. And in the third place, white men had already looked upon the fair mountain land with covetous eyes, and spirals of blue smoke were already rising skyward from scattered cabins dangerously close to the Blue Ridge. South Carolina traders had entered the Cherokee country under arrangements and could in no way be called settlers, although many of them remained in the territory the rest of their lives. Even though they married Cherokee women and their children were Cherokee, their status remained that of visitors or sojourners. They had no desire to own land, but they adopted the native American way of life, becoming a part of the Cherokee community.

How early, daring hunters and trappers, with only their wits and their guns to protect them from the natives, crept warily over the mountains will never be known, for they were not the type of men to write of their deeds.

But like the traders, they were not settlers and had no interest in owning the land they saw beyond the Blue Ridge. Even before Governor Tryon's line was drawn, a few hardy settlers east of the mountains had begun the practice of taking their cattle over the ranges to the meadows beyond for summer forage. For convenience, some of them had built tiny log shelters. But these men, too, had no intention of settling in this region, and when pasturing days were over, they took their way back over the hills to their cabins to the east.

6

TABLE ROCK DESCRIBED BY ANDRE MICHAUX, JOHN FRASER, ELISHA MITCHELL AND ARNOLD GUYOT ON LINVILLE GORGE

Following on the explorations of natural historian William Bartram, who traveled through the South from 1773 to 1778, was the famous French botanist Andre Michaux (1746–1802). Michaux was commissioned by the French government to collect and send to France the trees and shrubs he found after his arrival in 1785. He established two nurseries, one in New Jersey, the other in South Carolina. After the French Revolution, his funds were cut and his nursery in Rambouillet, France, fell into ruins. Michaux died of sunstroke while working in Madagascar. His earlier travels had brought him to the Blue Ridge Mountains, where he wrongly declared Grandfather Mountain to be the highest peak in eastern America. His field journal for 1794 records a day spent botanizing on Jonas Ridge.

September 6. Visited the cliffs of the mountain called Hock-bill [Hawksbill] and of Table Mountain. These mountains are very barren, and the new shrub (*Leiophyllum)* is the only rare plant found there. It is there in abundance. Slept at a distance of six miles, at Parks.

Note: Michaux refers to *Leiophyllum buxifolium*, or sand myrtle, a low, evergreen shrub resembling boxwood. When it blooms on Table Rock in June, its clusters of thick white blossoms give the appearance of snowcaps. For the mountain novelist Shepherd M. Dugger, the shrub makes a floral love-seat, "a soft, deep, flexible cushion, on which a gentleman may recline at ease, with his lady sitting by him mired to her waist in a girdle of beauty." The sand myrtle is quite delicate, however, and welcomes human backsides no more than it does boot traffic.

We have John Fraser to thank for the name of the popular Blue Ridge Christmas tree, the Fraser fir. This hardy Scotsman botanized seven times in America and on his final trip discovered the rare spring blossom, Fraser's sedge (*Carex fraseri*), "near the Table Mountain: and upon the banks of the Catawba River, in the neighborhood of Morgan-town, North Carolina." Burke County historian Edward Phifer Jr. notes that the plant was named for Fraser in 1811 by Henry Andrews.

Dr. Elisha Mitchell (1793–1857) was a professor of minerology, chemistry and geology at the University of North Carolina at Chapel Hill. In 1835, he made the first attempt to measure the height of the Black Mountains. After a bitter controversy with former pupil Thomas Clingman over whether Mitchell had actually scaled the highest peak, he returned in 1857 to prove his claim but slipped at a waterfall on the mountain that now bears his name and plunged to his death in a pool.

In 1827 and 1829, the state legislature commissioned Dr. Mitchell to conduct a geological survey of the state; this was to be his first visit to the Blue Ridge. The one sentence I reproduce below is taken from his *Diary of a Geological Tour*, published by the University of North Carolina Press in 1905. Writing from Wilkes County on July 20, 1828, Elisha informs his wife, Maria, about his eventful visit to the top of Grandfather Mountain. At that time, the Grandfather was held to be the highest peak in the East, but on this day, Mitchell first records his suspicion that the Black and Roan Mountains are higher. Then he tries to convey a sense of the grandeur of the view from the peak, of just how diminished the Table Rock now seems eleven miles away

The Table rock which appeared as a considerable eminence at Morganton was dwindled down to a Mole Hill.

NOTE: Morganton is the county seat for Burke County, North Carolina, bounding whose northern end is the Linville Gorge wilderness.

Arnold Guyot (1807–1884) was a Swiss American geologist and geographer who measured the mountain peaks of western North

Carolina and explored the eastern Continental Divide in the area near Linville, North Carolina, where the Watauga River flows west to the Mississippi and the Linville River joins the Catawba to flow eastward to the Atlantic. Guyot tells how the Linville has carved out the Linville Gorge, which he deems "a fearful and perfectly impassible chasm...from the plateau of the Grandfather, forming magnificent waterfalls."

7

"SKETCHES OF THE PIONEERS IN BURKE COUNTY HISTORY"

This account of reckless horseplay atop the Table Rock sometime in the years before 1828 first appeared in the old *Morganton Herald* and was published there in 1894. The narrative suggests how popular the distinctive 3,950-foot peak was for nineteenth-century lowlanders. Today, one takes Forest Service Trail no. 242 for 1.2 miles to the flattop—which offers breathtaking views of the canyon and Table Rock's slightly taller sister peak, Hawksbill (4,020 alt.).

Major Brice Collins fought in the Revolutionary War at the Battle of Camden in Baron De Kalb's regiment. Born about 1758 in Maryland, he served in the North Carolina State Legislature eleven times and owned a four-hundred-acre plantation on John's River in Burke County. He married Jemima Moore in 1803, one of whose sisters, Mary (Polly) married Dr. Thomas Bouchelle. He died in January 1829, and was buried on his plantation. In allusion to his bulky, muscular physique, he was known as "Collins Ram," because "He had a head of his own and butted where he pleased."

Mr. Collins was of striking physique, robust and muscular. On one occasion being with a large pleasure party on the Table Rock, Dr. Bouchelle [Collins Ram's smaller brother-in-law] was anxious to take a peep over the awe-inspiring perpendicular precipice 300 feet high and of solid rock, Collins following, seized him by the feet and pushing him over as far as he could reach without losing his balance, called out, "Now you go, you old rascal, I always wanted Polly [the doctor's wife]."

If anyone wants to know exactly how the Doctor felt they will have to undergo the strain upon the nervous system. It is an unquestioned fact that extreme fright will make the hair of the head stand erect "like the quills on the fretful porcupine" and turn white in a few hours. Whether this was the cause of the Doctor's, not only turning white, but his extreme baldness, is a question unanswered. The immense size form and altitude of the Table Rock (5,000 feet above sea level), the magnificent picturesque and extensive view it commands from its summit, has caused the visitations of thousands in the past and doubtless will cause to come to it thousands in all time to come.

8

THE MOUNTAIN PEOPLE AND LINVILLE GORGE

Historian Alberta Pierson Hannum describes Uncle Jake Carpenter's *Anthology of Death* and one of its notables in a chapter of the 1943 book *The Great Smokies and the Blue Ridge*. The Altapass, North Carolina anthologist made entries in his red accounting ledger whenever someone in his Blue Ridge Mountain community died, such as the fellow who maintained four wives and households. One epitaph, with the heading "That Fighting Thing Called Freedom," reads:

> *Wm. Davis age 100.8 dide oc 5 1841 war old soldier in rev war and got his thie broke in last fite at kings mountain he war farmer and made brandy and never had drunker in family.*

Ms. Hannum comments: "William Davis was a Pennsylvanian. During the Revolution he happened to be a part of Washington's troops who got into North Carolina. One day when the camp ran out of food, he was sent out with a foraging group for game. When he got up into the mountains, he thought it was the prettiest country he had ever seen.

I happened to hear this about William Davis at the top of Linville Mountain, with the Linville River too directly below to see and too far down to hear. But the opposite side of the gorge does not drop sheer there. It lies back, full and lush with all the greens there are—wide and spreading with unplungeable depths. And away and beyond reach miles and miles of sun and shadow, with the shadow at some indefinable place becoming blue mountain; blue mountain and blue mountain and gray mountain until it is hard to say which is gray cloud and which gray mountain. There is no one thing the eye can get a hold of. But all the senses grow lulled as you look, and at the same time heightened. I could understand how William Davis had thought it was pretty country.

"Of course," explained the old-timer who was telling me the story, "hit war the b'ar and the deer made hit so purty to him."

9

LETTERS FROM THE ALLEGHANY MOUNTAINS

The travel writer Charles Lanman visited the Linville Gorge area in June 1848, publishing an account of his trip as one of a series of letters (here, letter XVIII) about the scenic attractions of western North Carolina. The term *Alleghany* was once a general descriptor for the Appalachian chain. The high point of the following letter must surely be Lanman's tale of the hermit Culgee Watson. Note that Lanman spells Linville as Lindville.

In coming from Burnsville [Yancey County, North Carolina] to this place [North Cove in McDowell County, North Carolina] I enjoyed two mountain landscapes, which were supremely beautiful and imposing. The first was a northern view of Black Mountain [Mount Mitchell, 7,544 feet] from the margin of the South Toe river, and all its cliffs, defiles, ravines, and peaks seemed as light, dreamlike, and airy as the clear blue world in which they floated. The stupendous pile appeared to have risen from the earth with all its glories in their prime, as if to join the newly-risen sun in his passage across the heavens. The middle distance of the landscape was composed of two wood-crowned hills which stood before me like a pair of loving brothers, and then came a luxuriant meadow, where a noble horse was quietly cropping his food; while the immediate foreground of the picture consisted of a marvellously beautiful stream, which glided swiftly by, over a bed of golden and scarlet pebbles. The only sounds that fell upon my ear, as I gazed upon this scene, were the murmurings of a distant water-fall, and the hum of insect wings.

The other prospect that I witnessed was from the summit of the Blue Ridge, looking in the direction of the Catawba. It was a wilderness of mountains, whose foundations could not be fathomed by the eye, while in the distance, towering above all the peaks, rose the singular and fantastic form of *the Table Mountain.* Not a sign of the breathing human world could be seen in any direction, and the only living creature which appeared to my view was a solitary eagle, wheeling to and fro far up towards the zenith of the sky.

From the top of the Blue Ridge I descended a winding ravine four miles in length, where the road, even at mid-day, is in deep shadow, and then I emerged into the North Cove. This charming valley is twelve miles long, from a half to a whole mile in width, completely surrounded with mountains, highly cultivated, watered by the [North Fork of the] Catawba, and inhabited by intelligent and worthy farmers. At a certain house where I tarried to dine on my way up the valley, I was treated in a manner that would have put to the blush people of far greater pretensions; and, what made a deep impression on my mind, was the fact that I was waited upon by two sisters, about ten years of age, who were remarkably beautiful and sprightly. One of them had flaxen hair and blue eyes, and the other deep black hair and eyes. Familiar as I had been for weeks past with the puny and ungainly inhabitants of the mountain tops, these two human flowers filled my heart with a delightful sensation. May the lives of those two darlings be as peaceful and beautiful as the stream upon which they live! The prominent pictorial feature of the North Cove is of a mountain called *the Hawk's Bill,* on account of its resemblance to the beak of a mammoth bird, the length of the bill being about fifteen hundred feet. It is visible from nearly every part of the valley, and to my fancy is a more *picturesque* object than the Table Mountain, which is too regular at the sides and top to satisfy the eye. The table part of this mountain, however, is twenty-five hundred feet high, and therefore worthy of its fame.

The cabin where I am stopping at the present time is located at the extreme upper end of the North Cove. It is the residence of the best guide in the country, and the most convenient lodging place for those who would visit the Hawk's Bill and Table Mountain, already mentioned, as well as the Lindville Pinnacle, the Catawba Cave, the Cake Mountain, the Lindville Falls, and the Roan Mountain.

The *Lindville Pinnacle* is a mountain peak, surmounted by a pile of rocks, upon which you may recline at your ease, and look down upon a complete series of rare and gorgeous scenes. On one side is a precipice which seems to descend to the very bowels of the earth; in another direction, you have a full view of *Short-off Mountain*, only about a mile off, which is a perpendicular precipice of several thousand feet high and the abrupt termination of a long range of mountains; in another direction still the eye falls upon a brotherhood of mountain peaks which are particularly ragged and fantastic in their formation—now shooting forward, as if to look down into the valleys, and now looming to the sky, as if to pierce it with their pointed summits; and in another direction you look across what seems to be a valley from eighty to a hundred miles wide, which bounded by a range of mountains that seem to sweep across the world as with triumphal march.

The *Catawba Cave* [Linville Caverns], situated on the [north fork of the] Catawba River, is entered by a fissure at the base of a mountain [Humpback], and is reputed to be one mile in length. It has a great variety of chambers, which vary in height from six to twenty feet; its walls are chiefly composed of a porous limestone, through which the water is continually dripping; and along the entire length flows a clear and cold stream, which varies from five to fifteen inches in depth. This cave is indeed a curious affair, though the trouble and fatigue attending a thorough exploration far outweigh the satisfaction which it affords. But there is one arm of the cave which has never been explored, and an admirable opportunity is therefore offered for the adventurous to make themselves famous by revealing some of the hidden wonders of nature.

The *Ginger Cake Mountain* derives its very poetical name from a singular pile of rocks occupying its extreme summit [Sitting Bear]. The pile is composed of two masses of rock of different materials and form, which are so arranged as to stand on a remarkable small base. The lower section is composed of a rough slate stone, and its form is that of an inverted pyramid; but the upper section of the pile consists of an oblong slab of solid granite, which surmounts the lower section in a horizontal position, presenting the appearance of a work of art. The lower section is thirty feet in altitude, while the upper one is thirty-two feet in length, eighteen in breadth, and nearly two feet in thickness. The appearance of this rocky wonder is exceedingly tottleish [tottery], and though we may be assured it has stood upon that eminence perhaps for a thousand years, yet it is impossible to tarry within its shadow without a feeling of insecurity. The individual who gave the Ginger Cake Mountain its outlandish name was a hermit named Watson, who resided at the foot of the mountain about fifty years ago, but who died in 1816. He lived in a small cabin, and entirely alone. His history was a mystery to everyone but himself, and, though remarkably eccentric, he was noted for his amiability. He had given up the world like his brother hermit of the Bald Mountain [David Greer, see note that follows], on account of a disappointment in love, and the utter contempt which he ever afterwards manifested for the gentler sex, was one of his most singular traits of character. Whenever a party of ladies paid him a visit, which was frequently the case, he invariably treated them politely, but would never *speak* to them; he even went so far in expressing his dislike as to consume for firewood, after the ladies were gone, the topmost rail of his yard-fence, over which they had been compelled to pass, on their way into his cabin. That old Watson "fared sumptuously every day" could not be denied, but whence came the money that supported him no one could divine. He seldom molested the wild animals of the mountain where he lived, and his chief employment seemed to be *the raising of peacocks*, and the making of garments for his own use, which were all elegantly trimmed off with the feathers of his favorite bird. The feathery suit in which he kept himself constantly arrayed he designated as his *culgee;* the meaning of which word could never be ascertained; and long after the deluded being had passed away from among the living he was spoken of as Culgee Watson, and is so remembered to this day.

I come now to speak of *the Lindville Falls*, which are situated on the Lindville River, a tributary of the beautiful Catawba. They are literally embosomed among mountains, and long before seeing them do you hear their musical roar. The scenery about them is as wild as it was a hundred years ago—not even a pathway has been made as yet to guide the tourist into the stupendous gorge where they reign supreme. At the point in question the Lindville is about one hundred and fifty feet broad, and though its waters have come down their parent mountains at a most furious speed, they here make a more desperate plunge than they ever dared to attempt before, when they find themselves in a deep pool and suddenly hemmed in by a barrier of gray granite, which crosses the entire bed of the river. In their desperation, however, they finally work a passage through the solid rock, and after filling another hollow with foam, they make a desperate leap of at least one hundred feet, and find a resting place in an immense pool, which one might easily imagine to be bottomless [the Plunge Basin]. And then, as if attracted by the astonishing feats performed by the waters, a number of lofty and exceedingly fantastic cliffs have gathered themselves together in the immediate neighborhood, and are ever peering over each other's shoulders into the depths below. But as the eye wanders from the surrounding cliffs, it falls upon an isolated column several hundred feet high, around which are clustered in the greatest profusion the most beautiful of vines and flowers.

This column occupies a conspicuous position a short distance below the Falls, and it were an easy matter to imagine it a monument erected by Nature to celebrate her own creative power. [Two rock "chimneys" stand on the west side of the gorge below the Falls; one rises beside the U.S. Park Service's Chimney View and the other beside Erwin's View.]

With a liberal hand, indeed, has she planted her forest trees in every imaginable place; but with a view of even surpassing herself, she has filled the gorge with a variety of caverns, which astonish the beholder, and almost cause him to dread an attack from a brotherhood of spirits. But how futile is my effort to give an adequate idea of the Lindville Falls and their surrounding attractions! When I attempted to sketch them I threw away my pencil in despair; and now I feel I should be doing my pen a kindness, if I were to consume what I have written. I will give this paragraph to the world, however, trusting that those who may hereafter visit the Lindville Falls, will award to me a little credit for my *will* if not for my *deed*.

Note: *Culgee* is a Hindi word meaning either the decorative spray of feathers atop a turban or an exotic and richly patterned silk, worn as a turban or sash, and imported from India into England during the eighteenth century. David Greer lived as a recluse on Big Bald Mountain, or Greer's Bald, from 1802. Rejected by David Vance's daughter, he created his own sovereign government for his mountain, lived in a cave and shot at anyone who approached.

On the Gorge's "variety of caverns," see Dr. Cato Holler's "Linville Gorge Caves" (chapter 25).

10

MOUNTAIN SCENERY

THE SCENERY OF THE MOUNTAINS OF WESTERN NORTH CAROLINA AND NORTHWESTERN SOUTH CAROLINA

In the latter years of the nineteenth century, a burgeoning travel and tourism industry launched a prodigious flock of literature touting the natural wonders of the Carolina mountains as both spectacular and healing. Much of the travel writing promotes the expanding railroad service to the high country as well as the popular hostelries in places such as Burnsville (Nu-Wray Inn) and Roan Mountain (Cloudland Hotel). Henry Colton edited the weekly *Asheville Spectator* in the late 1850s.

CHAPTER VII

Morganton and Its Surroundings—The Piedmont Springs of Burke—The Table Rock and the Hawk's Bill

In a ride of about fifteen miles, westward from Morganton, the Piedmont Springs are found. The waters of the springs are sulfur and chalybeate [having an iron taste]. Their somewhat out-of-the-way location has kept them from being much resorted to; but the beauty of the scenery around, and the health-restoring properties of the waters, certainly demand more attention from them at the hands of visitors, than they have heretofore received. Immediately in their neighborhood, the Hawk's Bill and Table Rock are situated. These sublime works of nature have not received the notice which their merits deserve. The Table Rock is a high, bleak rock, rising out of the top of a mountain to the height of over two hundred feet at the south end,—a gradual rise being the boundary on the north side. It can easily be ascended; and there is upon the top about an acre of rock, in a smooth surface. An excellent spring gushes out of a little hollow on one side of the rock, and thus enables the traveller to spend his time comfortably amid the lovely and grand scenes that burst upon his view.

Immediately at the foot of the beholder runs the Linville River, fretting and groaning within its immovable walls. In front rise the towering rocks of the Linville Mount, shutting out from view the lovely farms of the North Cove. On one side is Morganton; on the other, we see the cloud cap of the Grandfather rising from out the Blue Ridge. Behind, far in the distance, and only to be seen of a clear day, the quaint-formed peak of the Pilot attracts out notice. Immediately at hand, and seemingly so near at hand that we might step upon its top, is the peak of the Hawk's Bill. All around the mountains rise, some in the soft beauty of rich verdure, others in the grim grandeur of solid rock, without even a trace of vegetation. But the eye, wherever it wanders, will turn again and again to the awful gulf which yawns beneath us, and we shudder at the thought of what would be out fate were our frail bodies cast into that almost fathomless abyss. There runs the Linville River; and we see it, as the sun glances on its waters, apparently naught but a threadlike, silvery stream; and, almost pitying the trouble that its waters endure, we trace its course until it unites with the noble Catawba, and, with it, sweeps on to lose its purity amid the mud of the lowlands. Taking all things into consideration, especially just at sunset, there are probably few mountains the view from which excel that from Table Rock.

The Hawk's Bill is a bare rock, rising probably to a greater height than Table Rock. The view from it is about the same as from that point, as they are, in fact, but a short distance from each other. It has been but seldom visited. The peak, from a number of points on the road from Morganton to Pleasant Gardens, bears a striking resemblance to the hooked-bill of a hawk.

These two mountains rise out of the valley comparatively alone. They look like twin-sisters, or, as a tourist once expressed it, "like two mighty sentinels guarding the peaceful stillness of the valley," that no intruding hand should break the calm repose of nature. Their formation, and that of the valley of the Linville, afford much fertile study for the geologist. What great convulsion once rent them in twain, and caused the awful chasm in which the Linville pursues its torturous course?

These points can, perhaps, be best visited from Piedmont Springs. Ample accommodations will be found at that place for many visitors; and, as far as the scenery is concerned, no one will ever regret a visit to them.

CHAPTER VIII

Linville Falls

There is, in what might be said to be the vicinity of Morganton, a curiosity of nature, almost unnoticed, which, for its grand sublimity, and that of its surroundings, is, perhaps, equal to anything of the kind in our country. We allude to the Falls of the Linville River, not a great deal more than twenty-five miles from Morganton in a direct line, but more than thirty by an accessible route. The best route by which they can be reached is Carson's on the Catawba [see note that follows]; there taking a road to the little settlement of Childsville, from which place the Falls can be easily visited. The tourist, however, who has his own conveyance, and prefers to do so, can, with ease, go to the same place from Morganton; and from thence, after having visited the Falls, go to Carson's without returning to Morganton; and it is probable that such would be the best and most interesting route. The following, which has heretofore appeared before the public eye, will give an idea of the scenery and the manner of visiting the Falls a year or two ago:

"There are a number of natural curiosities throughout the South which are never seen or heard of except by some adventurous traveller, and known intimately only by the intrepid mountain hunter. Thus, these curiosities remain unnoted, while yearly thousands of our citizens go northwards in search of health or pleasure. Among such may be classed the Falls of the Linville River in Burke County. We doubt not but that numbers of persons in Burke County never heard of them. They are to be found in the northwest corner of that county, near to that famous tree upon which the four counties of Burke, Watauga, Yancey, and McDowell corner, and about nine miles from the Piedmont Springs. [The tree was located at the site of present-day Famous Louise's Restaurant on Highway 221. Three counties meet there now: Avery, Burke and McDowell.] The facilities for getting to them are as yet about no facilities at all, an idea may be formed from our experience:—

"Leaving Childsville on the morning of Tuesday, in company with Col. Childs, we rode within three miles of the Falls, and then leaving our buggy, we went on horse-back to the house of Mr. David Franklin, one mile from the Falls. Mr. Franklin consented to become our guide, and, after a short rest, we moved on to the Falls. Having arrived within half a mile of them, we dismounted and proceeded on foot, being unable to ride on account of the fallen trees. We soon reached the river, the din of the waterfall having been for some time roaring in our ears; we then crossed it, to do so, being compelled to put certain portions of our person in a state of nature. Having crossed, we proceeded down the eastern bank, through a wild and irregular growth of ivy, laurel, and whortleberry bushes. It is rather singular that on the west bank of the Linville, the soil is rich and covered with a most luxuriant growth of trees, while on the east bank, just here, for some distance out, nothing of any worth grows. The river, where we crossed it, has as clear, smooth an appearance as any other mountain stream; it soon becomes agitated by slight rapids, until suddenly it is divided by a huge rock, and dashes over a fall of about twenty feet; it then boils and surges in a most terrific manner for about a hundred yards, the while falling three several times, twisting and turning in every shape that human fancy can imagine.

"Following our guide, we seated ourselves on the top of a rock, around the base of which the river rushes in its wild career. About forty feet below us, on one side, dashed the troubled waters of the Linville; on the other side, these same waters having forced through a passage not more than ten feet wide, made their descent over the last and highest fall. Here, the mist was rising; and the rays of the sun, as it shone through, caused the peculiar view which resembles so much the sulphurous flames, which Bunyon [in *Pilgrim's Progress*] so well describes as arising from a certain dark abode, that it gives the cavern under the lower fall the name of the Devil's Hole. Our position was a commanding one, but not such as a person with weak nerves should seek. As we gazed far down the course of the river, we could see the stream again assume its comparatively placid appearance; but now, instead of banks almost even with its bed, it was locked in by an impenetrable mass of chimney rocks, which continue for miles down its course rising in the most majestic grandeur to a height of one, two, and three hundred feet, and in some places near to a thousand. At one point we are informed the rocks close over the river, and it is easy for a person to jump from one bank to another.

"The grand sublimity of the scenery which is hereabouts presented to the eye, cannot be surpassed by any in the world. Language fails to describe it, and the pencil of the artist can give but a faint conception of its beauty and magnificent grandeur. Here it is that man feels his insignificance, and trembling kneels with awe and fear. We have seen Niagara in all its artistic splendor, and we have seen what was called grand scenery, but never, never, have we seen anything to equal the scenery of Linville Falls, nor do we ever expect to see the like again until we revisit them.

"Ere long the pencil of the artist will trace the rarest beauties, and give them to the world's view. Ere long the spirit of enterprise will make good roads, and build a good house, at which visitors may stop. No place can present the same attractions as a watering-place that Linville can. Its beautiful scenery, that never has been fully explored; its healthful climate, the excellent water of the Rattlesnake Spring, the fertility of the soil, and last, but far from least in the pleasure-seeker's eye, the large quantity of game which is to be found hereabouts.

"Having spent the afternoon at Linville, we returned to Mr. Franklin's house, and there rested for the night. The next day we visited the Gingercake Rock. This rock is a curious formation, resting on a ridge [Jonas Ridge] between Hawk's Bill and the Gingercake Mountain, very near to the latter. It is a high rock, conical in shape, between fifty and seventy feet in height, about six feet through at the base, and rising to a thickness of twenty-five or thirty feet. This rock is flat on top, and covered with gray moss. On one end of its top there is a rock about fifteen feet long and four or five feet wide, with a thickness of about four feet. This rock is, to all appearances, just about to fall. At least ten feet of it is projecting from the edge of the main rock, the whole presenting the appearance of having just been dropped in its place, and lodged for a little while, thus making one of the grandest sights that can exist in nature. Reascending the mountain, we walked over to the Chimney Rocks, and there we had presented to us as beautiful a landscape as can be found in Carolina, unless it be that from the Pilot Knob. The eye has a full open scope from the Grandfather Mountain entirely around the Roan, and even beyond that. The valley of the Catawba is open to the view from its origin to its end, the whole of Turkey and North Coves, with their rich fields of waving corn. In the dim, dark distance, a lone mountain rises to view, which, from its location, we suppose to be the Pilot [2,413 feet, near Mount Airy, North Carolina]. Just as the sun fades beneath the horizon, it casts forth a clear, red light, and you see flashing in its blaze the windows of the houses of Morganton; from the same source, a golden tinge is thrown upon every leaf, and everything is mellowed into soft loveliness in the accomplishment of nature's most splendid creation. Far, far beneath, hid amid a mass of shrubbery and rocks, the Linville finds its way to the Catawba. Turning to our guide, we asked: 'Does the Linville run there?' He replied, 'Yes, and poor thing, it sees troublous times before it gets out of there too.' We have never seen anything which gave one so forcible an idea of man's littleness at this point. The Chimney Rocks of the mountain are about three hundred feet high; from their base the mountain descends with fearful rapidity into the Linville River; how far, it is beyond our power to estimate, but it seems as if it was almost into the bowels of the earth. It seems as if one might fall

'From morn till noon, from noon to dewy eve,'

and but then fathom its depth! We looked, and turning, looked again. Gladly would we have spent hours upon that summit; but nature changes not to suit man's wishes, and days must end upon the mountain top as well as in the valley. We returned to Mr. Franklin's house, thankful for what we had seen, but wishing that we could spend weeks roaming among the beauties of that mountain country."

Lanman, it seems, found this hidden spot, and, in his letters from the Alleghany Mountains, says of it: [here follows Lanman's description of the Falls; see chapter nine].

The Falls are about five miles from Childsville, from which place buggies can go within a half mile of the Falls, but is even best to ride all the way upon horseback. However, before the summer of 1859, a good carriage road will be made entirely to the bank of the river. Very fine views are to be obtained below the Falls from the high bluffs which rise for awhile on both sides, and at one point recede on the east side.

The cliff, at this point, is called Bynum's Bluff, from the Hon. John Gray Bynum. The Hawk's Bill and Table-Rock stand immediately in front, and through the space between them is seen the far-distant prospect, while some twelve hundred feet, perpendicularly below, runs the Linville River. An idea may be formed of the height of these cliffs when it is known that Linville River runs nearly through the center of a mountain of the same name, which is about five thousand feet above the level of the sea. I have never seen any place so well calculated to give one a good idea of height and depth; one seems to look into the bowels of the earth. Far, far down beneath us the eye traces by the rough rocks and want of trees the course of the Linville River, and a spy-glass enables one to see the troublous moving of its waters, but not a sound is heard to indicate the awful whirlpools which exist in the stream as it passes on its rapid source.

Note: The Carson House was a popular McDowell County stage post on the way between Morganton and Asheville. The stage line was discontinued upon the completion of the Western North Carolina Railroad in 1877, though the inn continued to serve travelers to North Cove and Linville Gorge to the north. Today, it is a historical museum and national landmark.

Childsville was a former Mitchell County seat located near present-day Avery County Airport off Highway 19-E. The post office was located on the famous Bright's Trace, a road authorized by the North Carolina State Legislature in 1777 running from Johnson City, Tennessee, to Burnsville, Spruce Pine, Marion, and then Hickory, North Carolina. Albert Childs had his farmstead-plantation here, and Dr. Ebenezer Childs's body was preserved in whiskey upon his death.

The line of verse is from book 1 of John Milton's *Paradise Lost*, line 743.

11

THE HEART OF THE ALLEGHANIES, OR WESTERN NORTH CAROLINA

This 1883 travel book, written by Wilbur G. Zeigler and Ben S. Grosscup, offers vivid descriptions of the area's "topography, history, resources, people, narratives, incidents, and pictures of travel adventures in hunting and fishing." It also relates "legends of its wildernesses" in a further effort to accentuate the picturesque appeal of the Southern Highlands. Interestingly, this pair of travel writers chose to write in the first person, so that the reader wonders which of the duo is speaking. Their account, which repeats the common nineteenth-century misnomer of referring to the Appalachians as the Alleghenies, is typical of the era's promotional literature, intended to lure those suffering in the "sweltering plains" to summer in or at least visit the cool mountain watering spots and scenic attractions.

About an hour before sunset, on that August day, I left Old Fort, by way of a well-traveled road, for Pleasant Gardens [near Marion, North Carolina]. There is many a level stretch for a gallop along this road, and I improved the opportunities afforded for a rapid push on my journey. Through the country I went, with the fields on my right, and the woods of the hills on my left; past large, pleasant-looking farm houses in the midst of ancestral orchards and wide-spreading farm lands. The streams are clear, but slow and smooth-flowing. The number of persimmon trees and hollies along the roadside mark a difference between the woods of this section and those of the higher counties.

It was after one of my easy gallops, that, bursting from a twilight wood, I beheld lying before me a valley scene of striking beauty. A broad and level tract of farming land, covered with meadows, corn and pea-fields, stretched away from the forested skirts of the hill-sides. From my point of observation not a house dotting the expanse could be seen, and not even the sound of running water (a marked feature of the higher valleys) disturbed the evening stillness. A cool pleasant breeze was stirring, but it scarcely rustled the leaves overhead. The dark outlines of Mackey's mountains filled the foreground, making a broken horizon for the blue sky. On the right lay low hills. On the left the summits of a lofty line of peaks, behind which the sun was sinking, were crowned with clouds of flame, while the scattered cat-tails held all the tints and luster of mother of pearl. That night I stopped in Pleasant Gardens, one of the richest and most beautiful valleys to be found in any land. It is miles in extent. John S. Brown was my hospitable and entertaining host. The large, frame house and surroundings vividly reminded me of my native state. Everything showed evidence of thrift and neatness, and withal a certain ancestral air, one that only appears with age, overhung the approach to, and portals of, the mansion. It was built a century ago, but many additions and repairs have been made since the original log-raising. Osage-orange hedges line the path to it under the cluster of noble trees. On the left as you approach, only a few feet from the house's foundation, flows Buck creek with swift, clear waters: a trout stream in a day before civilization had cleared its banks.

Under a clouded sky I mounted my horse on the third morning of my journey and set out from Pleasant Gardens. The fording of a stream is so frequent an occurrence in a trip through the Carolina mountains, that one is apt to have a confused recollection of any one river or creek that he crosses, although few are void of beauty or wildness. Those of the Catawba, as it flows through McDowell County, have lost the characteristics of the mountain ford. Boulders and out-cropping ledges of rock are absent; the rush and roar of crystal waters have given place to a smooth and less transparent flow, or noiseless, dimpled surface; the banks are of crumbling soil, and, instead of rhododendrons and pines, alders and willows fringe the waters' edges.

The great valleys of the Catawba are covered principally with unfenced fields of corn. The road leads through rustling acres, where one's horse, guided with slack rein by absent-minded rider, can, as he walks along, break a green ear of corn from the standing stalk, without stretching his neck over the fence. To prevent cattle running at large through these thickly-planted lands, gates are swung across the roads at the division fence of each plantation, and from necessity, the traveler must open them to ride through; and then, from moral obligation, he must shut them behind him. The farm-houses are home-like in appearance. They denote prosperity, happiness and culture in the families inhabiting them. Many are of antique architecture, and set back on level lawns, under ornamental trees and flourishing orchards.

Toward the middle of the morning, the sharp outlines of the Linville Mountains showed themselves in the east, and after an abrupt turn from the Bakersville road, I struck the North fork of the Catawba, and rode twelve miles along its picturesque course. Its waters have a peculiar, clear, green hue, and speak of speckled trout in their depths and shaded rapids. [Brook trout are native to the area; rainbow and speckled trout have been introduced.] Without a guide, I could have followed up the North fork, under the shadows of Humpback Mountain, and, by a trail, have crossed the ridge to the Linville Falls; but by this route the wild scenery of the Linville canon is lost. Bryson Magee was my guide to the Burke county road along the summit of Bynum's bluff. Just after a slight shower, he overtook me as he was returning from a day's work for a North Fork farmer. He had an open, tanned countenance, fringed by a brown beard, and capped by a head of long hair, hidden under the typical mountain hat—a black, slouch felt, with a hole for ventilation in the center of the crown and minus the band. An unbleached, linen shirt, crossed by "galluses" which held his homespun pantaloons in place, covered his body. He wore shoes and walked leisurely.

"Is there anyone on this road who can guide me up Bynum's bluff?" I asked him, after returning his "howdy."

"Why, some blacks nigh hyar who could do hit, but they're all at work two mile below."

"Anyone else I could get?"

"Not a soul, except—"

"Who?" I asked.

"Wal, stranger—I reckon you's a furriner—I can do hit, but I'm powerful tired: worked all day."

When we arrived at his log cabin, he had definitely determined to go. It was then four o'clock, and clouds were driving thick and dark across the sky. We tied the saddle-bags to the saddle, and then began the ascent. Bryson led my horse; I walked on behind.

Before we had proceeded 100 yards, a light rain began falling. This did not deter us, for Bryson, like all the denizens of the coves, was callous to dampness, heat, and cold, and as for myself, a rubber coat came in play. The flinty ground was set with whortleberry bushes—a true indicator of sterility.

These berries were ripe, and we gathered them, as we trampled along the trail, while the clouds grew heavier around us, and the rain swept in blinding sheets through the scrubby forest. There was no thunder to add variety to the storm, only the moan of the wind, and the sound of tree tops swaying in the gusts. The water poured in streams from my hat, and my legs, to the knees, were soaked from contact with wet bushes; but gradually it cleared over-head, and when we reached the main road, on the summit of the ridge, the clouds had parted, and through their rifts the sun, still an hour high, poured a burning glory over the dripping forests.

Looking southward in the direction the guide pointed, a mighty, rock-topped mountain, lifting itself into the sunlight above the fog, was visible. It appeared like a stone wall rising from the ocean. Squared off in sharp outlines, without trees or lesser visible vegetation on its level summit, it presents a striking contrast to the other peaks of the Alleghanies south. It is the Table Rock mountain, 3918' in altitude. Hawk-bill, a peak named from its top being crowned with a tilted ledge of moss-mantled rock, resembling the beak of a hawk, stood before me as I turned toward the left. Its altitude is 4,090 feet. Both these peaks are accessible for climbers, and are much visited by tourists curious to examine the character of their rock formation.

"We jist hit it," broke forth the guide, "a minute more an' we wouldn't seen 'em. See, the fog's crawlin' up, slow, but shore."

It was as he had said. The massed vapors in the low sunk vales were being driven upward, and a moment later they had enfolded Table Rock and Hawk-bill, and were creeping though the woods around us. I now handed him fifty cents, the price for a day's common labor through that section, and, shaking hands, we separated. It was five miles to the nearest house, and lacked only one hour of sunset. Three miles had been passed over, when a sound, as of some distant waterfall, struck on my ears. It was a soft, steady, liquid murmur. Halting my horse, I sat in the saddle and listened, then dismounted, tied, and walking through the weeds a few steps, reached some broken rocks at the edge of a precipice. Clinging to a tree, I leaned over and looked below through perpendicular space over 1,000 feet. I shouted from the sensations created by the wonderful wildness of the scene.

At first sight down into a canon, that seemed almost fathomless, I saw an inky, black band stretched through the depths, with surface streaked with silver. It was the Linville river, but distance rendered its waters motionless to the vision. A thin mist lent an indescribable weirdness to the scene, and seemed veiling some mighty mystery in its folds. "Wrapping the tall pines, dwindled to shrubs in dizziness of distance," it was being shaken from its foothold by varying breezes, broken into separate sheets of vapor, and pushed upward along the perpendicular walls. It curled and twisted weirdly through the tangled pines, filling black rents in the opposite mountain's face, shielding a ragged, red cliff here and there, but at every moment mounting toward the canon's rim. Soon the profile faces on the upper cliffs jutted out in clear air; the brick-like fronts of rock, in pine settings across the chasm became plainly visible; the lower forests stood free; the dark river, sweeping in an acute angle, within stone drop below, tossed upward its eternal echo; the mists had clustered in thick clouds on the summit of an unknown peak, and then all grew dusky with the approach of night.

A scene is sublime, according to its power to awaken the sense of fear; the more startling, the more sublime. The view of Linville Canon from the Bynum's bluff road possesses, in the writer's opinion, more of the elements of sublimity than any other landscape in North Carolina. The region of the Linville is one of scenery grandly wild and picturesque. The only region that approaches it in wildness and sublimity—being somewhat similar in the perpendicularity and the clearness of its stream, but contrasting by the fertility of its soil and luxuriance of its forests—is the Nantihala River valley.

The Linville range is a spur of the Blue Ridge, separated from the latter by the North Fork valley. It trends south, and for a distance is the dividing line between Burke and McDowell. Its highest altitude is about 4,000 feet. Jonas' Ridge runs parallel with it on the east, and between them, through a narrow gorge, over 1,000 feet deep, flows Linville river. The rocks of these mountains are sandstones and quartzites. The soil is scanty and sterile, and the forests scrubby. The falls are distant from Marion on the Western North Carolina railroad, about twenty-five miles, and reached as the writer has described. From Morganton, on the same railroad, they can be reached by a day's ride in conveyance over the highway on the summit of the mountain. Hickory is also a point from which to start, and one frequently taken by tourists.

That night I dried my clothes at T.C. Franklin's fireside, one mile from the falls of the Linville. Around the crackling logs (this was in August) was a small party, such as is often collected at mountain wayside farm-houses.

[At the fireside, a pair of Philadelphia lawyers relate how they had been mistaken for highwaymen during a recent ascent of Roan Mountain. Two honeymooning couples arrive in the rain, and shortly thereafter, everyone turns in for the night.]

On the next morning, under a clear sky, I wound my way on foot under the limbs of kalmia and rhododendron to the Linville falls. It is a wild approach. Over the hedges tower ancient hemlocks with mossed trunks. The blue-jay screamed through the forest, and around the boles of the trees and along the branches, squirrels, known as mountain boomers, chased each other, halting in their scampers to look down on the disturber of the solitude. Once, a brilliant-breasted pheasant, roused by my footsteps, from a bed of fern-crested rocks, sprung in air close before me, and with a startled whirr, sailed up a shaded ravine. A sportsman, with a shot-gun, could easily have winged the bird in its flight, thereby securing a valuable trophy for the taxidermist. The cock pheasant of the mountains has not a shabby feather on his body. They are found in many sections of the mountains, but not in great numbers. The hollow drum-like sound caused by beating their wings against their bodies, is in most instances their death tattoo. At its sound from the neighboring cove, the hunter takes down his rifle, creeps near the favorite log, and generally makes a dead shot.

An old mountaineer, famous as a narrator of bear and fish stories, was particularly fond of telling one relative to pheasant shooting. One autumn day, having already marked the forest locality from which the drum of a pheasant resounded every morning, he crept near with his rifle. The bird had just jumped in place and was drumming within his sight. He took deliberate aim and fired. On running to the log he discovered a red fox struggling in its death throes on the opposite side of the log, and in his mouth a dead pheasant. Reynard, as the mountaineer explained, had secreted himself close beside it, and, while the mountaineer was aiming, was preparing to seize the bird, and did so at the moment the trigger was pulled.

The heavy thunder of the falls swept through the forest, increasing as I advanced. The path diverged at one point, and, taking the right hand trail, by means of the roots of the laurel, I descended a cliff's face in cool, dismal shade. At the bottom, I came out on a black ledge of rock, close to the river. A stupendous fall was before; stern walls of a rocky canon, 100 feet high, around me, and a blue sky smiling above. I claimed a stair-way of moist rocks, and walked along the path on the cliff's front to a point directly before the fall's face. The great volume of the Linville river, formed from drainage for fifteen miles back to the watershed of the Blue Ridge [near Grandfather Mountain], here at the gap between Jonas' Ridge and the Linville mountains, has cut asunder a massive wall, leaving high perpendicular cliffs towering over its surface, and then, with a tremendous leap, pours its current down through space, fifty feet, into the bottom of the canon. It seems to burst from a dark cavern in the mountain's center. A pool [the Plunge Basin] sixty feet across, looking like the surface of a lake with dark waves white-capped, spreads in a circle at the base of the cliffs. After recovering from the dizziness of its plunge, the river, leaving the piny walls on either side, rushes along in view for a short distance, and then disappears around the corner of a green promontory.

If one, retracing one's steps, takes the left hand trail at the point of divergence, and follows it to the edges of the cliffs, a magnificent downward view will be obtained, both of the foot of the cataract, and above, where its waters race in serpentine course, increased in velocity by the plunge over smaller falls only a few yards up the gorge.

A wilder solitude, a more picturesque confusion of crags, waters, woods, and mountain heights, can scarcely be found. But even here, man once fitted for himself a dwelling-place; for plainly visible across the tops of the trees, was a little cabin on a small, sloping clearing. No smoke curled upwards from its weather-worn roof; its doors had been torn away and chimney leveled. A few cows pastured before it.

Note: Pleasant Garden is today a small community just west of Marion, North Carolina. Later in *River of Cliffs*, we read of adventurers from a Jules Verne science-fiction classic passing through. *The North Carolina Guide* informs us that John McDowell settled down here in a two-room cabin before the Revolution. "He called the tract Pleasant Gardens, and he became known as 'Hunting John' because of his prowess in tracking game in the wild Indian country." Two miles away lies the Carson House, where Henry Colton spent the night. This was the home of Colonel Jonathan Carson. He wed the widow of Colonel Joseph McDowell, John's cousin, and she bestowed the name "Pleasant Gardens" on the Carson House (today a historical monument), and the area roundabouts came to be designated by that name.

The boomer is the Boreal red squirrel (*Tamiasciurus hudsonicus*), endeared to locals for its aerial antics and vivacious nature.

12

"A MOUNTAIN TRAMP FROM BRIDGEWATER TO BLOWING ROCK

SKETCHES OF LINVILLE FALLS AND BYNUM'S BLUFF"

The author of this piece, "V.W.L.," has effectively preserved his or her anonymity, and I have been unable to determine the writer's identity. This article, published in the *Morganton Star* on August 20, 1886, suggests a local author. During the overnight stay at McCall's, the party discusses a Civil War skirmish, famous in the area. Captain George W. Kirk, attached to the Union's Army of the Ohio, had captured East Tennessee, from which he led devastating raids into North Carolina. In June 1864, Kirk captured Camp Vance outside Morganton by a daring mix of guile and deceit; that is, he led a force apparently ready to surrender but which then seized the camp. After his destruction of Camp Vance, he retreated north, up what is now Highway 181, hotly pursued by the Burke Home Guard. The skirmish at Winding Stair Knob was marked by Kirk's heinous war crime of using young captive recruits as human shields and by the death of the outstanding Burke County citizen William Waightstill Avery.

"How shall I spend the summer? Where shall I go? How shall I go?"

These are the questions which hundreds put to themselves every year.

One very pleasant way—and the best way for one not over afflicted with delicate stomach and weak limbs, is to "rough it" through the mountains of Western North Carolina.

A companion and I, wishing to see something of the country, away from railroads and the usual beaten track of tourists, took a most delightful jaunt through parts of Mitchell, Burke and Watauga counties.

After the Black Mountain Assembly was over we went to Bridgewater, a small station near Morganton, and struck out through the country for Linville Falls. We carried no baggage except for a few articles in our pockets. We were in regular tramp costume—big pants, flannel shirt and slouch hat. We made about five miles the first evening and stopped after wading Paddy's Creek up to our knees at McCall's.

Plain fare, but hospitable welcome made our stay very pleasant. Around the fire after summer we smoked and talked of Kirks men and his Morganton raid. Mine host gave us a graphic description of his descent upon Morganton, by way of the Winding Stair, and the capture of Camp Vance.

Sleep came, all too soon, and in the Land of Nod Mr. Kirk and his Tennessee band found no place. Next morning we bade our kindly host farewell and began the climb of Linville Mountain. Soon after our start we left houses, people and civilization behind and for fifteen miles saw not a house or a trace of man. The road was a mountain "ridge road"—simply a bridle path up the Linville Mountain. To our right was Shortoff's Mountain, ending abruptly in a precipice of three or four hundred feet, overlooking the foaming Linville River.

On our way the ferns lay out on each side, acre after acre, growing from one to three and four feet high. The timber too, especially chestnut, was very fine.

All along our way from Short-off to Table Rock there is a canyon cut down by the river hundreds of feet deep. The sides are solid rock, chimney-like in appearance and are insurmountable—there being only one or two places in the whole distance where one can get down into the river bed.

Near Hawksbill and Table Rock we were so fortunate as to fall in with a party of mountaineers, looking for cattle. Numerous were the tales told of bear hunting "around the mountings." "I'll tell ye," said one of these nimrods; "the most ticklish bear hunt I ever had was right up there on Hawks Bill mounting. I went up to that ravine way up near the top and went into a cave, way down under the ground. The first thing I knowed I run right plumb up against a bear's nest, and seed her eyes a-shinin'. You just bet I got out of there double-quick. I went home and got my Springfield rifle (left me by the Yankees) and loaded her up. Well sir, I went back into the hole and when I seed the old she bear's eyes ar shinin', I let her have it right square pine blank atween 'em. That got her, and when I drug her out she weighed over 300 pounds an' the fat on her back was as thick as the length of a case knife!"

With such yarns as this the journey was lightened and our way made pleasant. They showed us the "Green Mountain Spring," a solid stream of water six inches through, and very cold. It comes just rushing and surging up from the mountain and forms the head of a small river. [Green Mountain lies just a bit west of Wiseman's View on Linville Mountain.]

Bynum's Bluff was our next stopping place. It is about one mile from Franklin's (boarding house). The view simply overtaxes my stock of adjectives. From the top of the bluff to the river below is almost perpendicularly half a mile. Down in front of us was lying the peaceful Linville valley—the river winding in and out like a band of silver. To the left were Table Rock and Hawks Bill, while in the distance rose peak over peak and range over range as far as eye could reach. The towering masses of rock on each side of the valley looked like grim fortresses guarding the calm and quiet below. This view is decidedly the finest I have seen in Western North Carolina. It is beautiful, it is grand.

Soon we arrived at Franklin's [Linville Falls Hotel, still standing] and changing our wet garments for dry ones (borrowed from our host) and sat by the fire listening to the patter of the rain. Our appetites were something astonishing. To say we felt like "chewing up fence rails" is to put it mildly. How two slender young men could "get outside" of so much ham, chicken biscuits innumerable, and three or four glasses of milk must always remain a problem to our host.

Next morning, bright and early, we walked to the Linville Falls. Formerly the fall was much higher, but the careless pour has worn the rock down considerably. After making several very pretty cascades and turns, the river, with one grand bound, throws itself about forty feet into a pool below—measureless in its depths. All around this basin are beetling masses of rock, rising from one to two hundred feet. As we saw them, the falls were simply beautiful, with something of the grand—giving one a faint hint of what Niagara might be. The river was up and just muddy enough to give the water a creamy tinge. As the big mass of water comes over in resistless power, the mist and water smoke rise around it as if trying to veil its beauty from the sight. To a day dreamer or one fond of the romantic the Falls are very suggestive. It requires only a small exertion of the imagination to once more people the valley with the redskin warrior and maiden. Again the Wataugas roam the forest and amid the wild roar of the cataract one easily fancies he hears the soft wooing of the brave Hi-co-co-lupta and his lovely Euola-loo. Our next trip is to the old Grandfather Mountain in whose bosom rest hundreds of red warriors of the Wataugas, slain in a battle near the summit. [Area folklore holds that the mysterious lights seen on nearby Brown Mountain are the spirits of Catawba and Cherokee warriors slain there.]

13

THE BALSAM GROVES OF THE GRANDFATHER MOUNTAIN

Shepherd M. Dugger, who titled himself "The Bard of Otterey" (or western North Carolina) is known today chiefly as the author of *The Balsam Groves of the Grandfather Mountain*, a romance published in 1892 in response to a contest held by the Linville Improvement Company for the best story set in the Grandfather Mountain area. Dugger didn't win first prize, but with the help of the company, his work was published and ran through four editions, the latest in 1934. Famous for the outlandish vocabulary of its author, the novel gives much accurate detail of mountain life in the 1830s, displays a remarkable ecological awareness and includes as appended material such data as a list of mountain elevations, extracts from the journal of French botanist Andre Michaux and a glossary of Cherokee words. The novel recounts the adventures of summer visitors to the Linville area: Miss Lydia Meaks, a schoolteacher from Raleigh, and "probably the fairest of North Carolina's daughters," and Mr. Charlie Clippersteel. Their romance blossoms into marriage, and Clippersteel insists that their "nuptials be performed at the great falls." The climax of the novel is the scenic wedding at the Falls with an attempted interruption by the villain of the tale, Leathershine, neatly foiled. Today, the National Park Service maintains a short trail to a waterfall and creek named for Dugger. It is at the Linville Falls Visitor Center on the Blue Ridge Parkway.

Next morning, when twilight still spread her dusky pinions over the land, and the morning star, hanging just above the eastern horizon, cast a pale glare on the saffron-gild from the sun, Clippersteel re-entered the tent where his precursor, having returned, was again wrapped in the restoring arms of Morpheus [ancient Greek god of sleep]. In his right hand, which rested on his brow, was the marriage document, while around one of his great toes, at the other extremity of his long person, was a bandage of green leaves tied on with a string of hickory bark and bloodied from a wound within. Seeing that all was well, he left the man for an hour to his peaceful slumbers, and then returned with a waiter heavy laden with hot coffee and wholesome food, and as he entered the tent Skipper arose, and, extending his hand, said:

"I got 'um, goody; her's yer licengers."

"And here," said Clippersteel, "is your money," passing him a handful of silver dollars. Skipper smiled behind his ears, and his short coat danced up and down to the roaring chuckle that inflated his ribs.

"Did a snake bite your toe?" inquired Clippersteel.

"No sar," replied Skipper, "I stumped the nail off'en it," and putting his hand in his pant's pocket, he drew out the great bloody toe armor, and handing it to Clippersteel said, "Thar it is. I'll give ye that to remember who brought yer licengers."

"Thank you, Skipper," was the reply, "It is a nice souvenir, and I shall ever keep it among my most valued treasures." Skipper thought he had never heard a toe-nail called a "Susandear," but, not doubting the authenticity of the word, he adopted it into his vocabulary, and ever afterwards applied the name to toe-nails that had been knocked off by accident.

The blue sky that adorned the wedding day was decked with a bright sun that had risen a few degrees above the horizon when the party filed through the gate, by Skipper's tent, and turned down the murmuring stream. Riding in front was the lone Mr. Skiles. Next in order was the bride and groom. Then came Colonel and Mrs. Palmer, followed by the two younger couples, while the rear was brought up by a boy riding a long-eared donkey and bearing on his arm a large basket of lunch.

Skipper, who had gone in advance, was so elated by his connection with the affair that he told every yeoman he met by the way what was going to take place by the falls; and these early settlers, whose amusements were few and far between, looking upon the outdoor-wedding as a public affair, dropped their hoes and ploughs in the fields, and, putting on their best garments, went toward the scene.

In consequence of the above, Mr. Skiles soon found an equestrian partner in the person of a Mr. Buchanan, who had quit the irksome monotone of his plough for the exhilarating pleasure of nuptial festivities.

Before the equestrians had reached the falls, Skipper, whom they had passed on the way, had gathered to his side a company of twenty persons or more, made up of both sexes, in about equal numbers. The women wore homespun dresses, which they had made for themselves, by carding, spinning and weaving the fabric of the sheep, and finally, cutting and fitting the fabric to their persons. Their head-gear consisted of plain calico bonnets, while their waists and bosoms were set about with fillets of red ribbon that flaunted to the gales of the woods.

Each man was armed with his long firelock rifle, which, when stood upon its breech, extended to the top of his head. These were carried as a means of killing the abundant deer and other game that frequently crossed the roads and paths.

In the party was a mustached man, middle-aged and handsome, by the name of Clark, who seemed to have descended from some professional family that had strayed into the far-off mountains and retrograded from their former learning and dignity.

Beside him was his daughter, Miss Ada, a blooming girl of sweet sixteen, whose form was cast in neat proportion's mould. Her queenly hands, tapering and fair as the lily, were gloved with a pair of red mits of her own knitting, which exposed the ends of the fingers and the first joints of the thumbs.

Her golden hair was like a shower of primrose petal falling, and her cheeks were finished with the artistic touches of Aurora's rosy hand. Her eyes were like the corolla leaves of the blue-veined violet, the nose was a posy to her face, and her pearly teeth sparkled with nectarine dew. "She was a flower born to blush unseen and waste its sweetness on the desert air."

In those days it was customary for a gentleman to propose his escort to a lady in the following manner. Walking up to her side, he said, "Do you love chicken?" If she answered "Yes," he then presented his arm with the words, "Have a wing," whereupon she put her arm through his. But if the answer was "No," he was refused, or, in the parlance of the times, she had "kicked" him. Such scenes usually occurred in large crowds that were going the distance of ten miles or more, to or from church, on the Sabbath day, and the fellow who got "kicked" was always greatly derided by most of those who witnessed the chagrin of his disappointment.

On the present occasion, when all were bound for the falls, a fellow, with the blood-red topknot of an imperial woodpecker in his hat-band, stepped up to the side of Miss Ada; but just as he would have propounded the poultry question her father gave him a disapproving glance, by which his heart failed him, and he passed on to the side of a chunky girl with a flaxen head and a frisky air, and, looking her in the face with a grin, he said: "Aggie, do you love chicken?"

"I don't love roosters," was the pert reply.

The answer being new and thoroughly original, the fellow was for a time completely dumbfounded for something to say, but finally he got his mouth off, and said, "Will you let one walk with you to the wed'en?"

"Yes, if he don't crow too loud," she replied.

A creature not too bright or good
For human nature's daily food;
For transient sorrow, simple wiles,
Praise, blame, love, kisses, tears and smiles.

The heterogeneous gathering was now on the west bank of the river, at the top of the cataract, where the stream passed transversely over a saddle of rock, and dropping off, at the lower skirt, fell the height of a tall tree into a pool of matchless depth and beauty. But since that time the ledge has broken down, so that the water leaps and cascades alternately through a curved and partly concealed groove, and finally terminates in a clear fall at the bottom.

The pool, however, which is about fifty yards wide and twice as long, with the corners slightly rounded, has lost none of its original beauty, unless it is in the diminished magnitude of the white breakers that ruffle its dark bosom. The long way of this beautiful lake is at right angles to the fall, and its outlet is through a narrow channel at the east end.

The party, having satiated their aesthetic vision from the top, now started for a landing at the bottom, and there never was a wilder way than theirs. The little track wound, and still winds, through and under laurel and ivy, around and over cliffs, and then turns down a slope of forty-five degrees, and runs as straight as a gun-barrel for the distance of fifty yards. This visible section of the path, canopied by the lapping boughs of the rhododendron and kalmia, is crossed by many rocks and tree-roots, which, having been divested of soil by clambering feet, look like the rounds of a long ladder leading down to the subterranean falls and glittering stalactites of a cave. At the foot of this shaded escalade is a narrow beach adjoining the rock over which the water pours; from this the way turning down the stream to the right passes up into and down through crevices, where the overhanging rocks bestow a symbol of purification by sprinkling the heads of the passersby with clean water. And indeed, it seems quite thoughtful in these stones to prepare the traveler at this point for death, because the next fifty yards of this path are the most dangerous that the writer has witnessed in all North Carolina. Here the south side of the pool is bounded by a perpendicular rock that walls an unknown depth of water, and then rises from ten to thirty feet above its surface; and we do not exaggerate in the least when we say that the track is on the very brink of this ledge, and in some places barely wide enough for the feet. The fears of the tourist are to some extent removed by the laurel hangings above and a fringe of light vegetation on the brow of the rock below, but the latter would not support the weight of a falling babe, and the former might be missed by the clutch of one who had lost his footing.

Our wedding party, now quadrupled by the country people, following this hazardous tract to where it spreads into a bench of rock about as wide as the floor of a bedroom and several times as long. If we imagine this seat occupied by a giant of suitable size, his calves will rest against the perpendicular wall of the pool and his feet will be washed by its breakers. Before him the white torrent flows down into the boiling pot, while immediately on the right of the foaming cataract rises a great ledge of stone, from whose summit a high diver might make a beautiful leap into the pool, a hundred feet below.

The back of our imaginary giant is supported by the smooth face of a cliff about thirty feet high, which breaks at the top into a succession of ivy-mantled crags that rise almost perpendicularly for several hundred feet, to where they are crowned with a grove of Carolina pine *(pica Caroliniana)*. While these crags are exceedingly beautiful in elevation, they are also equally picturesque in their longitudinal extension far down the stream, where the rocks rear their gray crests above their evergreen mantles, and, with their surroundings, blend into a scene as wild and varied as can be woven of the warp and woof of mystery and repose.

The country gentlemen, having leaned their rifles against the cliff, stood with their women folks, anxiously awaiting the expected event. In due time, the bride and groom, attended by Mumpower and Lotus on the right and Mabel and Bodenhamer on the left, were arranged for marriage.

Their backs were in the neighborhood of the guns, and their faces toward the great pouring column, whose white wings and boiling pedestal sent forth a breeze that set all the near flora and other equally moveable objects in motion—bush, weed and flower, as well as ribbons, tresses, whiskers and mustaches, and even the leaves of the minister's book were all dancing to the wind of the falls. As Mr. Skiles composed the fluttering pages beneath his thumbs, he drew so near and spoke so loud, in order to be heard above the roar of the waters, that his manner, elsewhere, would have been suitable only to those who were partially deaf. The charming bride, with dove-like eyes, looked steadily upon the minister; and, as he proceeded with the Episcopal service, there never was a bliss more wild and warm and boundless than that which thrilled her heart. "If any man," said the clergyman, "can show just cause why they may not lawfully be joined together, let him now speak, or forever hold his peace."

To the great surprise of all present, a sneering voice, on a different key from the thundering of the falls, was heard to say, "I object." This came from none other than Leathershine, who had resolved to avenge his defeat by vexing the occasion with this obnoxious objection, based, as we shall see, upon an odious falsehood; and, the better to accomplish his design, he had concealed himself in the green of the steeps, so as to appear at a time when the groom could not contravene his purpose nor do his violence.

"What is the ground of your objection?" inquired the minister.

"She is engaged to me," was the reply.

No one can describe the trembling pallor that seized the person of Lydia. With eyes full of overflowing fondness, she looked upon him she loved, as if to say, "I am innocent."

Her chin dropped upon the flowers that adorned her bosom; every nerve and muscle of her frame lost its energy, and she sank at the feet of the groom, not in the fashion of one who falls under the influence of excessive excitement, but like a pure woman borne down by the weight of a calumny perpetrated upon a warm life that no sin had ever tarnished.

The copious pool, so near the fainting bride, was yet so far that not a drop of its pellucid contents could be had with which to bathe her brow.

But the groom quickly produced from his pocket a little bottle of brandy, which he had carried, as a precaution, in case of accidents, and spreading a portion of its contents over her pallid face, the signs of restoration soon became apparent. The country folks had gathered round like the people of a city rushing to see what has happened, when those at disadvantage look over the shoulders of those in front to get a view of the within.

By this time Leathershine had run down the lake, and was ascending the heights at a point below, when Clippersteel, darting through the crowd, snatched a rifle from its leaning-place, and was aiming a shot that would have despatched the retreating coward, had not Mr. Clark grabbed the muzzle of the gun and borne it downward until he had gone out of sight.

A few minutes later the infamous dude mounted his horse, and, riding directly to Valle Crucis [near present-day Boone, North Carolina], packed his trunks and fled before Mr. Skiles had returned.

The tumult was now ended; the bride was able to sit upon a shawl which had been offered by a good mountain matron; and an hour later the marriage service was closed. [Thus ending the romance; ed.]

Note: The quotation "flower born to blush unseen" is from Thomas Gray's "Elegy Written in a Country Churchyard," lines 55–6. The quatrain is from William Wordsworth's "She Was a Phantom of Delight," lines 17–20.

Above: Linville Falls. In this shot made by Asheville photographer Ewart M. Ball around 1928, the Linville River pours over the Upper Falls and cascades partly unseen through a stone passageway to spill into the Plunge Basin. *Pack Library, Asheville, North Carolina.*

Opposite: Ewart M. Ball also captured the view downriver from the falls, including a dramatic "chimney" formation of rock. *Pack Library, Asheville, North Carolina.*

Table Rock from Wiseman's View, Full Moon, May, 2002 by Frances Hairfield, acrylic on canvas, 16" x 20". *Photographed by editor.*

View of the Chimneys and the Camel from Table Rock by D.R. Beeson in July 1914. *Archives of Appalachia, East Tennessee State University, Johnson City, Tennessee.*

Table Rock in morning mist, photographed by D.R. Beeson Sr. in July 1914. Beeson captured this view from the summit of Hawksbill Mountain. *Archives of Appalachia, East Tennessee State University.*

The Great Eyrie. Engraved illustration by Georges Roux for Jules Verne's *Master of the World* (1904). *From* Burke: The History of a North Carolina County, 1777–1920 *by Edward W. Pfeifer Jr.*

Above: Portrait of the Beeson party atop Table Rock in July 1914. Beeson (*second from left*) is taking the shot with the aid of his camera cord. *Archives of Appalachia, East Tennessee State University*.

Left: Devil's Cellar on the northwestern side of Table Rock. Beeson sited his friends to convey the scale of this cleft, which may be the rock fissure in the Great Eyrie described by Verne's Mr. Strock. *Archives of Appalachia, East Tennessee State University*.

Table Rock in its fall splendor, viewed from the south, October 1967. *Photograph by Christopher Blake.*

North Carolina Outward Bound Crew Anakiwa ascending Table Rock in October 1967. Visible is the obsolete Plymouth Goldline Rope, one half inch diameter, 150-foot length, used in early NCOBS courses. *Photograph by Christopher Blake.*

North Carolina Outward Bound Crew (Max, Tom, Gene and Chris) atop Table Rock in October 1967. Note the fire-spotter's shack, long since removed. *Picture from the editor's archive.*

John Lawrence rappelling in Devil's Cellar, Table Rock, October 1967. *Photograph by Christopher Blake.*

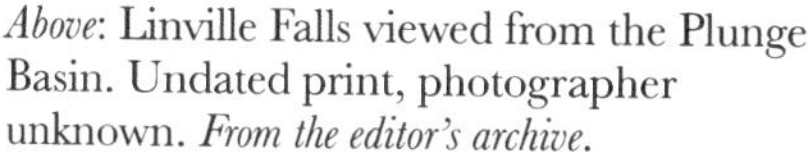

Above: Linville Falls viewed from the Plunge Basin. Undated print, photographer unknown. *From the editor's archive.*

Right, top: Local artist Peggy Hamlin painted this cheery view of the Falls as a roadside sign on the approach to the Linville Falls Community. It appears a mile north of the village on U.S. Highway 221 as one is heading southward. *Photograph by Christopher Blake.*

Right, middle: The editor as a Green Beret radio operator trainee cranking the handles on the ANG-RC-109 radio power generator, known as the "OD Monster." *Picture from the editor's archive.*

Right, bottom: Staff Sergeant Burtnett recording message traffic. Beside his logbook lies the case of crystals used to set the radio transmitting frequencies; in the foreground is the "OD Monster" power generator. *Photograph by Christopher Blake.*

The north, or top, end of the Gorge seems like a hanging garden, where woody growth crowds rock ledges or clings to the sheer walls. *Photograph by Christopher Blake.*

Linville Falls in snow. The Blue Ridge Parkway attraction holds a special appeal for visitors at off-season; in this image, the snowfall dims the view. *Photograph by Christopher Blake.*

"C-Team" member in communications shack at Fort Bragg, receiving the coded communiqués from Pisgah (Linville Gorge). *Photograph by Christopher Blake.*

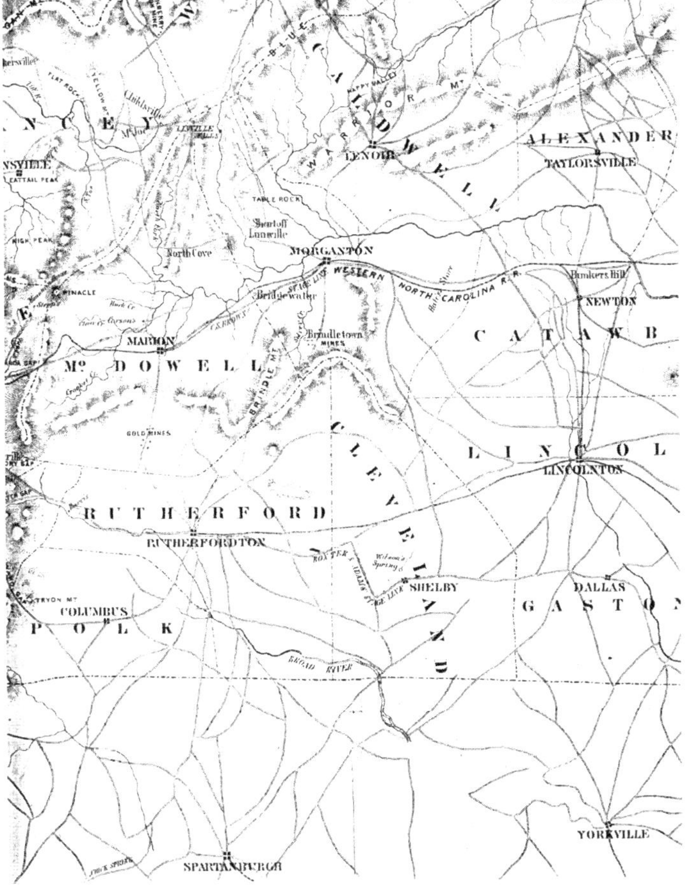

This detail from a map published in Henry Colton's *Mountain Scenery* (1859) includes Linville Falls, Table Rock and Shortoff. Former Childsville appears west of Linville Falls; the Western North Carolina Railroad ends at Morganton, with C.S. Brown's stage line conducting travelers farther west to Asheville. Bridgewater appears south of Morganton. *From* Mountain Scenery *(1859).*

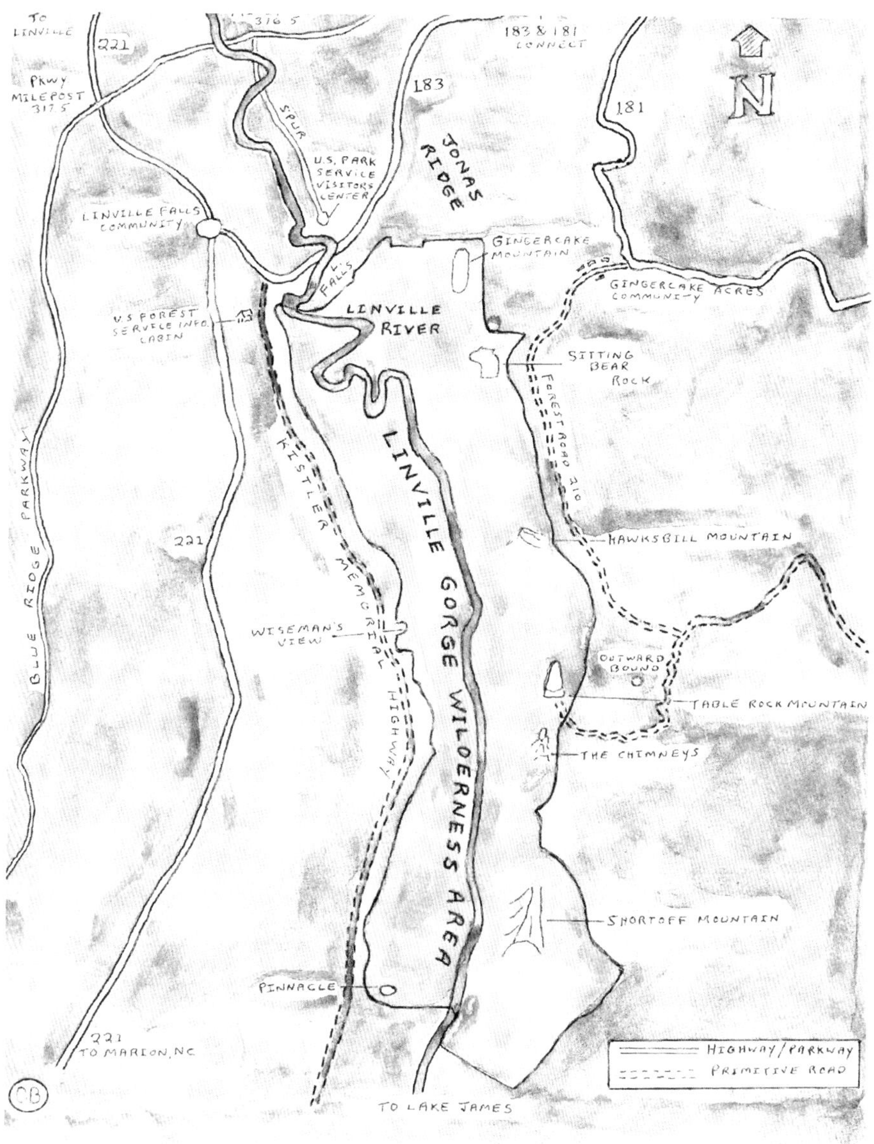

Above: This hand-drawn map by the editor includes major scenic features of the gorge as well as the government facilities for visitors: the National Park Services Visitor Center off the Blue Ridge Parkway and the U.S. Forest Services Information Cabin on the Kistler Memorial Highway. *Map by Christopher Blake.*

Opposite, top: The National Park Service's map of the Linville Falls trail system reveals how the U.S. Park Service and the U.S. Forest Service jointly manage the approaches to the falls. The USFS Visitor Center should more properly be named the Information Cabin, and Wiseman's View Road is the Kistler Memorial Highway. *Blue Ridge Parkway handout.*

Opposite, bottom: Sitting Bear Rock is silhouetted against Jonas Ridge in this view made by J. Alex Mull sometime in the 1970s. *Photograph from the editor's archive.*

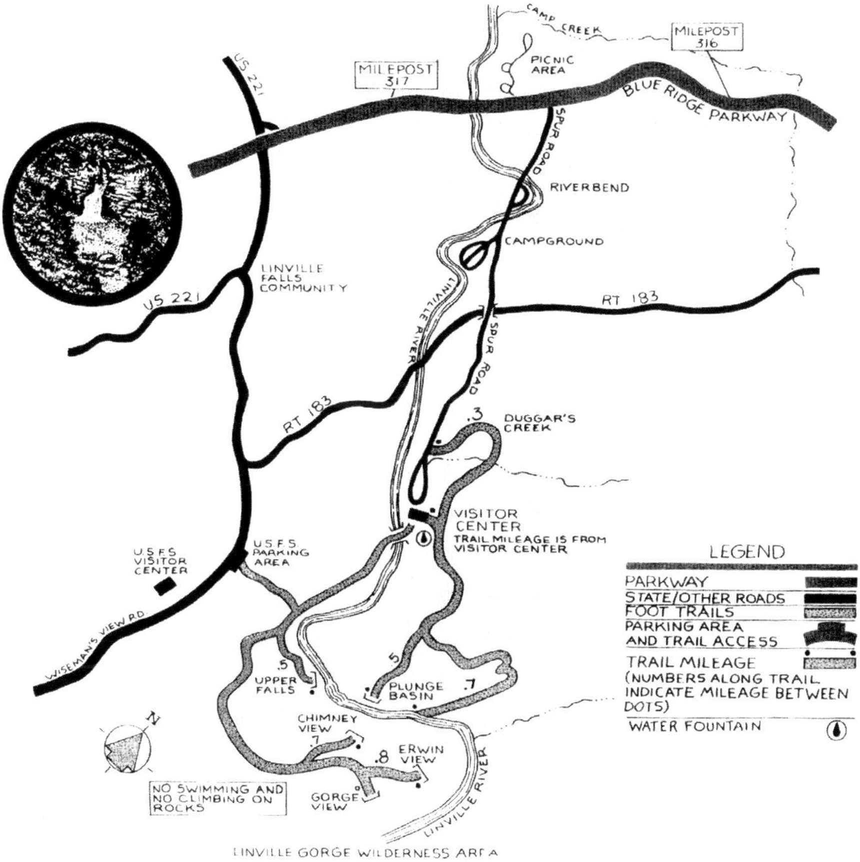

CAMP CREEK
MILEPOST 316
MILEPOST 317
PICNIC AREA
US 221
BLUE RIDGE PARKWAY
SPUR ROAD
RIVERBEND
CAMPGROUND
LINVILLE FALLS COMMUNITY
US 221
RT 183
LINVILLE RIVER
SPUR ROAD
RT 183
.3
DUGGAR'S CREEK
VISITOR CENTER
TRAIL MILEAGE IS FROM VISITOR CENTER
U.S.F.S. VISITOR CENTER
U.S.F.S. PARKING AREA
WISEMAN'S VIEW RD.
.5
UPPER FALLS
.5
PLUNGE BASIN
.7
CHIMNEY VIEW
.7
.8
ERWIN VIEW
GORGE VIEW
LINVILLE RIVER
N
NO SWIMMING AND NO CLIMBING ON ROCKS

LEGEND

PARKWAY
STATE/OTHER ROADS
FOOT TRAILS
PARKING AREA AND TRAIL ACCESS
TRAIL MILEAGE (NUMBERS ALONG TRAIL INDICATE MILEAGE BETWEEN DOTS)
WATER FOUNTAIN

LINVILLE GORGE WILDERNESS AREA

14

MASTER OF THE WORLD

Before the techno-villains of Ian Fleming—those legendary mad scientists such as Dr. No and Ernst Blofeld—there were the anti-heroes of Jules Verne. They were doomed solitaries, outcasts and men of genius far ahead of their times in the creation of marvels of advanced technology. Captain Robur (his name is Latin for "oak") may not be as well-known as Captain Nemo of the submarine *Nautilus*, but his visit to Table Rock Mountain in the astonishing first chapter of *Master of the World* (1903) has garlanded Linville Gorge with classic science-fiction laurels as a spectacular Verne setting. This novel, one of Verne's last, depicts a man determined to impose peace on earth by brute force via the military superiority of his paper flying ship, the *Albatross*.

Nearly sixty years after the book appeared, Hollywood tried to adapt it to the screen, casting the famed horror actor Vincent Price as Robur and Charles Bronson as the federal agent pursuing the captain. Unfortunately, the film names the locales as Morganton and Pleasant Gardens, Pennsylvania. Verne, however, is quite specific about his settings being in North Carolina. Verne relied on travel literature for *Master*, coming to America only once and seeing the Niagara Falls, where the fugitive Robur appears next. One is left puzzled, I think, wondering how those wild parakeets, leaping possums and banyan and palm trees of the third chapter could have been seen in the Linville Gorge of the early 1900s.

Chapter One

What Happened in the Mountains

If I speak of myself in this story, it is because I have been deeply involved in its startling events, events doubtless among the most extraordinary which this twentieth century will witness. Sometimes I even ask myself if all this has really happened, if its pictures dwell in truth in my memory, and not merely in my imagination. In my position as head inspector in the federal police department in Washington, urged on moreover by the desire, which has always been very strong in me, to investigate and understand everything which is mysterious, I naturally became much interested in these remarkable occurrences. And as I have been employed by the government in various important affairs and secret missions since I was a mere lad, it also happened very naturally that the head of my department placed in my charge this astonishing investigation, wherein I found myself wrestling with so many impenetrable mysteries.

In the remarkable passages of the recital, it is important that you should believe my word. For some of the facts I can bring no other testimony than my own. If you do not wish to believe me, so be it. I can scarce believe it all myself.

The strange occurrences began in the western part of our great American State of North Carolina. There, deep amid the Blue Ridge Mountains rises the crest called the Great Eyrie. Its huge rounded form is distinctly seen from the little town of Morganton on the Catawba River, and still more clearly as one approaches the mountains by way of the village of Pleasant Garden.

Why the name of Great Eyrie was originally given this mountain by the people of the surrounding region, I am not quite sure. It rises rocky, grim and inaccessible, and under certain atmospheric conditions has a peculiarly blue and distant effect. But the idea one would naturally get from the name is of a refuge for birds of prey, eagles, condors, vultures; the home of vast numbers of the feathered tribes, wheeling and screaming above peaks beyond the reach of man. Now, the Great Eyrie did not seem particularly attractive to birds; on the contrary, the people of the neighborhood began to remark that on some days when birds approached its summit they mounted still further, circled high above the crest, and then flew swiftly away, troubling the air with harsh cries.

Why then the name Great Eyrie? Perhaps the mount might better have been called a crater, for in the center of those steep and rounded walls there might well be a huge deep basin. Perhaps there might even lie within their circuit a mountain lake, such as exists in other parts of the Appalachian mountain system, a lagoon fed by the rain and the winter snows.

In brief was not this the site of an ancient volcano, one which had slept through ages, but whose inner fires might yet reawake? Might not the Great Eyrie reproduce in its neighborhood the violence of Mount Krakatoa or the terrible disaster of Mont Pelee? If there were indeed a central lake, was there not danger that its waters, penetrating the strata beneath, would be turned to steam by the volcanic fires and tear their way forth in a tremendous explosion, deluging the fair plains of Carolina with an eruption such as that of 1902 in Martinique?

Indeed, with regard to this last possibility there had been certain symptoms recently observed which might well be due to volcanic action. Smoke had floated above the mountain and once the country folk passing near had heard subterranean noises, unexplainable rumblings. A glow in the sky had crowned the height at night.

When the wind blew the smoky cloud eastward toward Pleasant Garden, a few cinders and ashes drifted down from it. And finally one stormy night pale flames, reflected from the clouds above the summit, cast upon the district below a sinister, warning light.

In presence of these strange phenomena, it is not astonishing that the people of the surrounding district became seriously disquieted. And to the disquiet was joined an imperious need of knowing the true condition of the mountain. The Carolina newspapers had flaring headlines, "The Mystery of Great Eyrie!" They asked if it was not dangerous to dwell in such a region. Their articles aroused curiosity and fear—curiosity among those who being in no danger themselves were interested in the disturbance merely as a strange phenomenon of nature, fear in those who were likely to be the victims if a catastrophe actually occurred. Those more immediately threatened were the citizens of Morganton, and even more the good folk of Pleasant Garden and the hamlets and farms yet closer to the mountain.

Assuredly it was regrettable that mountain climbers had not previously attempted to ascend to the summit of the Great Eyrie. The cliffs of rock which surrounded it had never been scaled. Perhaps they might offer no path by which even the most daring climber could penetrate to the interior. Yet, if a volcanic eruption menaced all the western region of the Carolinas, then a complete examination of the mountain was become absolutely necessary.

Now before the actual ascent of the crater, with its many serious difficulties, was attempted, there was one way which offered an opportunity of reconnoitering the interior, without clambering up the precipices. In the first days of September of that memorable year, a well-known aeronaut named Wilker came to Morganton with his balloon. By waiting for a breeze from the east, he could easily rise in his balloon and drift over the Great Eyrie. There from a safe height above he could search with a powerful glass into its deeps. Thus he would know if the mouth of a volcano really opened amid the mighty rocks. This was the principal question. If this were settled, it would be known if the surrounding country must fear an eruption at some period more or less distant.

The ascension was begun according to the programme suggested. The wind was fair and steady; the sky clear; the morning clouds were disappearing under the vigorous rays of the sun. If the interior of the Great Eyrie was not filled with smoke, the aeronaut would be able to search with his glass its entire extent. If the vapors were rising, he, no doubt, could detect their source.

The balloon rose at once to a height of fifteen hundred feet, and there rested almost motionless for a quarter of an hour. Evidently the east wind, which was brisk upon the surface of the earth, did not make itself felt at that height. Then, unlucky chance, the balloon was caught in an adverse current, and began to drift towards the east. Its distance from the mountain chain rapidly increased. Despite all the efforts of the aeronaut, the citizens of Morganton saw the balloon disappear on the wrong horizon. Later, they learned that it had landed in the neighborhood of Raleigh, the capital of North Carolina.

This attempt having failed, it was agreed that it should be tried again under better conditions. Indeed, fresh rumblings were heard from the mountain, accompanied by heavy clouds and wavering glimmerings of light at night. Folk began to realize that the Great Eyrie was a serious and perhaps imminent source of danger. Yes, the entire country lay under the threat of some seismic or volcanic disaster.

During the first days of April of that year, these more or less vague apprehensions turned to actual panic. The newspapers gave prompt echo to the public terror. The entire district between the mountains and Morganton was sure that an eruption was at hand.

The night of the fourth of April, the good folk of Pleasant Garden were awakened by a sudden uproar. They thought that the mountains were falling upon them. They rushed from their houses, ready for instant flight, fearing to see open before them some immense abyss, engulfing the farms and villages for miles around.

The night was very dark. A weight of heavy clouds pressed down upon the plain. Even had it been day the crest of the mountain would have been invisible.

In the midst of this impenetrable obscurity, there was no response to the cries which arose from every side. Frightened groups of men, women, and children groped their way along the black roads in wild confusion. From every quarter came the screaming voices: "It is an earthquake!" "It is an eruption!" "Whence comes it?" "From the Great Eyrie!"

Into Morganton spread the news that stones, lava, ashes, were raining down upon the country.

Shrewd citizens of the town, however, observed that if there were an eruption the noise would have continued and increased, the flames would have appeared above the crater; or at least their lurid reflections would have penetrated the clouds. Now, even these reflections were no longer seen. If there had been an earthquake, the terrified people saw that at least their houses had not crumbled beneath the shock. It was possible that the uproar had been caused by an avalanche, the fall of some mighty rock from the summit of the mountains.

An hour passed without other incident. A wind from the west sweeping over the long chain of the Blue Ridge, set the pines and hemlocks wailing on the higher slopes. There seemed no new cause for panic; and folk began to return to their houses. All, however, awaited impatiently the return of day.

Then suddenly, toward three o'clock in the morning, another alarm! Flames leaped up above the rocky wall of the Great Eyrie. Reflected from the clouds, they illuminated the atmosphere for a great distance. A crackling, as if of many burning fires was heard.

Had a fire spontaneously broken out? And to what cause was it due? Lightning could not have started the conflagration; for no thunder had been heard. True, there was plenty of material for fire; at this height the chain of the Blue Ridge is well wooded. But these flames were too sudden for any ordinary cause.

"An eruption!" "An eruption!"

The cry resounded from all sides. An eruption! The Great Eyrie was then indeed the crater of a volcano buried in the bowels of the mountains. And after so many years, so many ages even, had it reawakened? Added to the flames, was a rain of stones and ashes about to follow? Were the lavas going to pour down torrents of molten fire, destroying everything in their passage, annihilating the towns, the villages, the farms, all this beautiful world of meadows, fields, and forests, even as far as Pleasant Garden and Morganton?

This time the panic was overwhelming; nothing could stop it. Women carrying their infants, crazed with terror, rushed along the eastward roads. Men, deserting their homes, made hurried bundles of their most precious belongings and set free their livestock, cows, sheep, pigs, which fled in all directions. What disorder resulted from this agglomeration, human and animal, under darkest night, amid forests, threatened by the fires of the volcano, along the border of marches whose waters might be upheaved and overflow! With the earth itself threatening to disappear from under the feet of the fugitives! Would they be in time to save themselves, if a cascade of glowing lava came rolling down the slope of the mountain across their route?

Nevertheless, some of the chief and shrewder farm owners were not swept away in this mad flight, which they did their best to restrain. Venturing within a mile of the mountain, they saw that the glare of the flames was decreasing. In truth it hardly seemed that the region was immediately menaced by any further upheaval. No stones were being hurled into space; no torrent of lava was visible upon the slopes; no rumblings rose from the ground. There was no further manifestation of any seismic disturbance capable of overwhelming the land.

At length, the flight of the fugitives ceased at a distance where they seemed secure from all danger. Then a few ventured back toward the mountain. Some farms were reoccupied before the break of day.

By morning the crests of the Great Eyrie showed scarcely the least remnant of its cloud of smoke. The fires were certainly at an end; and if it were impossible to determine their cause, one might at least hope that they would not break out again.

It appeared possible that the Great Eyrie had not really been the theater of volcanic phenomena at all. There was no further evidence that the neighborhood was at the mercy either of eruptions or earthquakes.

Yet once more about five o'clock, from beneath the ridge of the mountain, where the shadows of night still lingered, a strange noise swept across the air, a sort of whirring, accompanied by the beating of mighty wings. And had it been a clear day, perhaps the farmers would have seen the passage of a mighty bird of prey, some monster of the skies, which having risen from the Great Eyrie sped away toward the east.

In chapter two, Mr. Strock is directed by the head of the federal police in Washington to inquire into the phenomenon of the Great Eyrie. In Morganton, Strock contacts the mayor, Elias Smith, who, like Strock, is filled with curiosity about the recent events at the Great Eyrie but who doubts volcanic activity is responsible for them. The two agree to set out the next morning, accompanied by two intrepid local guides familiar with Mount Mitchell and other nearby peaks. Moreover, a huge block having recently broken off from the side of the Great Eyrie, the men feel hopeful that a way has finally opened for its ascent.

Chapter Three

The Great Eyrie

The next day at dawn, Elias Smith and I left Morganton by a road which, winding along the left bank of the Catawba River, led to the village of Pleasant Garden. The guides accompanied us, Harry Horn, a man of thirty, and James Bruck, aged twenty-five. They were both natives of the region, and in constant demand among the tourists who climbed the peaks of the Blue Ridge and Cumberland Mountains.

A light wagon with two good horses was provided to carry us to the foot of the range. It contained provisions for two or three days beyond which our trip would surely not be protracted. Mr. Smith had shown himself a generous provider both in meats and liquors. As to water, the mountain springs would furnish it in abundance, increased by the heavy rains, frequent in that region in the springtime.

It is needless to add that the Mayor of Morganton in his role of hunter, had brought along his gun and his dog Nisko, who gamboled joyously about the wagon. Nisko, however, was to remain behind at the farm at Wildon, when we attempted our ascent. He could not possibly follow us up the Great Eyrie with its cliffs to scale and its crevasses to cross.

The day was beautiful, the fresh air in that climate is still cool of an April morning. A few fleecy clouds sped rapidly overhead, driven by a light breeze which swept across the long plains, from the distant Atlantic. The sun, peeping forth at intervals, illumined all the fresh young verdure of the countryside.

An entire world animated the woods through which we passed. From before our equipage fled squirrels, field-mice, parroquets [parakeets] of brilliant colors and deafening loquacity. Opossums passed in hurried leaps, bearing their young in their pouches. Myriads of birds were scattered amid the foliage of banyans, palms, and masses of rhododendrons, so luxuriant that their thickets were impenetrable.

We arrived that evening at Pleasant Garden, where we were comfortably located for the night with the mayor of the town, a friend of Mr. Smith. Pleasant Garden proved little more than a village; but its mayor gave us a warm and generous reception, and we supped pleasantly in his charming home, which stood beneath the shades of some giant beech-trees.

Naturally the conversation turned upon our attempt to explore the interior of the Great Eyrie. "You are right," said our host, "until we all know what is hidden within there, our people will remain uneasy."

"Has nothing new occurred," I asked, "since the last appearance of flames above the Great Eyrie?"

"Nothing, Mr. Strock. From Pleasant Garden we can see the entire crest of the mountain. Not a suspicious noise has come down to us. Not a spark has risen. If a legion of devils in hiding there, they must have finished their infernal cookery, and soared away to some other haunt."

"Devils," cried Mr. Smith. "Well, I hope they have not decamped without leaving some traces of their occupation, some parings of hoof, or horns or tails. We shall find them out."

On the morrow, the twenty-ninth of April, we started again at dawn. By the end of this second day, we expected to reach the farm of Wildon at the foot of the mountain. The country was much the same as before, except that our road led more steeply upward. Woods and marshes alternated, though the latter grew sparser, being drained by the sun as we approached the higher levels. The country was also less populous. There were only a few little hamlets, almost lost beneath the beech trees, a few lonely farms, abundantly watered by the many streams that rushed downward toward the Catawba River.

The smaller birds and beasts grew yet more numerous. "I am much tempted to take my gun," said Mr. Smith, "and to go off with Nisko. This will be the first time that I have passed here without trying my luck with the partridges and hares. The good beasts will not recognize me. But not only have we plenty of provisions, but we have a bigger chase on hand today. The chase of a mystery."

"And let us hope," added I, "we do not come back disappointed hunters."

In the afternoon the whole chain of the Blue Ridge stretched before us at a distance of only six miles. The mountain crests were sharply outlined against the clear sky. Well wooded at the base, they grew more bare and showed only stunted evergreens toward the summit. There the scraggly trees, grotesquely twisted, gave to the rocky heights a bleak and bizarre appearance. Here and there the ridge rose in sharp peaks. On our right the Black Dome [Mount Mitchell], nearly seven thousand feet high, reared its gigantic head, sparkling at times above the clouds.

"Have you ever climbed that dome, Mr. Smith?" I asked.

"No," answered he, "but I am told that it is a very difficult ascent. A few mountaineers have climbed it; but they report that it has no outlook commanding the crater of the Great Eyrie."

"That is so," said the guide, Harry Horn. "I have tried it myself."

"Perhaps," suggested I, "the weather was unfavorable."

"On the contrary, Mr. Strock, it was unusually clear. But the wall of the Great Eyrie on that side rose so high, it completely hid the interior."

"Forward," cried Mr. Smith. "I shall not be sorry to set foot where no person has ever stepped, or even looked, before."

Certainly on this day the Great Eyrie looked tranquil enough. As we gazed upon it, there rose from its heights neither smoke nor flame.

Toward five o'clock our expedition halted at the Wildon farm, where the tenants warmly welcomed their landlord. The farmer assured us that nothing notable had happened about the Great Eyrie for some time. We supped at a common table with all the people of the farm; and our sleep that night was sound and wholly untroubled by premonitions of the future.

On the morrow, before break of day, we set out for the ascent of the mountain. The height of the Great Eyrie scarce exceeds five thousand feet. A modest altitude, often surpassed in this section of the Alleghanies. As we were already more than three thousand feet above sea level, the fatigue of the ascent could not be great. A few hours would suffice to bring us to the crest of the crater. Of course, difficulties might present themselves, precipices to scale, clefts and breaks in the ridge might necessitate painful and even dangerous detours. This was the unknown, the spur to our attempt. As I said, our guides knew no more than we upon this point. What made me anxious was, of course, the common report that the Great Eyrie was wholly inaccessible. But this remained unproven. And then there was the new chance that a fallen block had left a breach in the rocky wall.

"At last," said Mr. Smith to me, after lighting the first pipe of the twenty or more he smoked each day, "we are well started. As to whether the ascent will take more or less time—"

"In any case, Mr. Smith," interrupted I, "you and I are fully resolved to pursue our quest until the end."

"Fully resolved, Mr. Strock."

"My chief has charged me to snatch the secret from this demon of the Great Eyrie."

"We will snatch it from him, willing or unwilling," vowed Mr. Smith, calling Heaven to witness. "Even if we have to search the very bowels of the mountain."

"As it may happen, then," said I, "that our excursion will be prolonged beyond today, it will be well to look to our provisions."

"Be easy, Mr. Strock; our guides have food for two days in their knapsacks, besides what we carry ourselves. Moreover, though I left my brave Nisko at the farm, I have my gun. Game will be plentiful in the woods and gorges of the lower park of the mountain, and perhaps at the top we shall find a fire to cook it, already lighted."

"Already lighted, Mr. Smith?"

"And why not, Mr. Strock? These flames! These superb flames, which have so terrified our country folk! Is their fire absolutely cold, is no spark to be found beneath their ashes? And then, if this is truly a crater, is the volcano so wholly extinct that we cannot find there a single ember? Bah! This would be but a poor volcano if it hasn't enough fire even to cook an egg or roast a potato. Come, I repeat, we shall see! We shall see!"

At that point of the investigation I had, I confess, no opinion formed. I had my orders to examine the Great Eyrie. If it proved harmless, I would announce it, and people would be reassured. But at heart, I must admit, I had the very natural desire of a man possessed by the demon of curiosity. I should be glad, both for my sake, and for the renown which would attach to my mission if the Great Eyrie proved the center of the most remarkable phenomena—of which I would discover the cause.

Our ascent began in this order. The two guides went in front to seek out the most practicable paths. Elias Smith and I followed more leisurely. We mounted by a narrow and not very steep gorge amid rocks and trees. A tiny stream trickled downward under our feet. During the rainy season or after a heavy shower, the water doubtless bounded from rock to rock in tumultuous cascades. But it evidently was fed only by the rain, for now we could scarcely trace its course. It could not be the outlet of any lake within the Great Eyrie.

After an hour of climbing, the slope became so steep that we had to turn, now to the right, now to the left; and out progress was much delayed. Soon the gorge became wholly impracticable; its cliff-like sides offered no sufficient foothold. We had to cling by branches, to crawl upon our knees. At this rate the top would not be reached before sundown.

"Faith!" cried Mr. Smith, stopping for breath, "I realize why the climbers of the Great Eyrie have been few, so few, that it has never been ascended within my knowledge."

"The fact is," I responded, "that it would be much toil for very little profit. And if we had not special reasons to persist in our attempt—"

"You never said a truer word," declared Harry Horn. My comrade and I have scaled the Black Dome several times, but we never met such obstacles as these."

"The difficulties seem almost impassable," added James Bruck.

The question now was to determine to which we should turn for a new route; to right, as to left, rose impenetrable masses of trees and bushes. In truth even the scaling of cliffs would have been more easy. Perhaps if we could get above this wooded slope we could advance with surer foot. Now, we could only go ahead blindly, and trust to the instinct of our two guides. James Bruck was especially useful. I believe that that gallant lad would have equaled a monkey in lightness and a wild goat in agility. Unfortunately, neither Elias Smith nor I was able to climb where he could.

However, when it is a matter of real need to me, I trust I shall never be backward, being resolute by nature and well-trained in bodily exercise. Where James Bruck went, I was determined to go also; though it might cost me some uncomfortable falls. But it was not the same with the first magistrate of Morganton, less young, less vigorous, larger, stouter, and less persistent than we others. Plainly he made effort not to retard our progress, but he panted like a seal, and soon I insisted on his stopping to rest.

In short, it was evident that the ascent of the Great Eyrie would require far more time than we had estimated. We had expected to reach the foot of the rocky wall before eleven o'clock, but we now saw that mid-day would still find us several hundred feet below it.

Toward ten o'clock, after repeated attempts to discover some more practicable route, after numberless turnings and returnings, one of the guides gave the signal to halt. We found ourselves at last on the upper border of the heavy wood. The trees, more thinly spaced, permitted us a glance upward to the base of the rocky wall which constituted the true Great Eyrie.

"Whew!" exclaimed Mr. Smith, leaning against a mighty pine tree, "a little respite, a little repose, and even a little repast would not go badly."

"We will rest an hour," said I.

"Yes; after working our lungs and our legs, we will make our stomachs work."

We were all agreed on this point. A rest would certainly freshen us. Our only cause for inquietude was now the appearance of the precipitous slope above us. We looked up toward one of those bare strips called in that region, slides. Amid this loose earth, these yielding stones, and these abrupt rocks there was no roadway.

Harry Horn said to his comrade, "It will not be easy."

"Perhaps impossible," responded Bruck.

Their comments caused me secret uneasiness. If I returned without even having scaled the mountain, my mission would be a complete failure, without speaking of the torture to my curiosity. And when I stood again before Mr. Ward, shamed and confused, I should cut but a sorry figure.

We opened our knapsacks and lunched moderately on bread and cold meat. Our repast finished in less than half an hour, Mr. Smith sprang up eager to push forward once more. James Bruck took the lead, and we had only to follow him as best we could.

We advanced slowly. Our guides did not attempt to conceal their doubt and hesitation. Soon Horn left us and went far ahead to spy out which road promised most chance of success.

Twenty minutes later he returned and led us onward toward the northwest. It was on this side that the Black Dome rose at a distance of three or four miles. Our path was still difficult and painful, amid the sliding stones, held in place only occasionally by wiry bushes. At length after a weary struggle, we gained some two hundred feet further upward and discovered ourselves facing a great gash, which broke the earth at this spot. Here and there were scattered roots recently uptorn, branches broken off, huge stones reduced to powder, as if an avalanche had rushed down this flank of the mountain.

"That must be the path taken by the huge block which broke away from the Great Eyrie," commented James Bruck.

"No doubt," answered Mr. Smith, "and I think we had better follow the road that it has made for us."

It was indeed this gash that Harry Horn had selected for our ascent. Our feet found lodgment in the firmer earth which had resisted the passage of the monster rock. Our task thus became much easier, and our progress was in a straight line upward, so that toward half past eleven we reached the upper border of the "slide."

Before us, less than a hundred feet away, but towering a hundred feet straight upwards in the air rose the rocky wall which formed the final crest, the last defense of the Great Eyrie.

From this side, the summit of the wall showed capriciously irregular, rising in rude towers and jagged needles. At one point the outline appeared to be an enormous eagle silhouetted against the sky, just ready to take flight. Upon this side, at least, the precipice was insurmountable.

"Rest a minute," said Mr. Smith, "and we will see if it is possible to make our way around the base of this cliff."

"At any rate, said Harry Horn, "the great block must have fallen from this part of the cliff; and it has left no breach for entering."

They were both right; we must seek entrance elsewhere. After a rest of ten minutes, we clambered up close to the foot of the wall and began to make a circuit of its base.

Assuredly the Great Eyrie now took on to my eyes an aspect absolutely fantastic. Its heights seemed peopled by dragons and huge monsters. If chimeras, griffins, and all the creations of mythology had appeared to guard it, I should have been scarcely surprised.

With great difficulty and not without danger we continued our tour of this circumvallation, where it seemed that nature had worked as man does, with careful regularity. Nowhere was there any break in the formation; nowhere a fault in the strata by which one might clamber up. Always this mighty wall, a hundred feet in height!

After an hour and a half of this laborious circuit, we regained our starting-place. I could not conceal my disappointment, and Mr. Smith was not less chagrined than I.

"A thousand devils," cried he, "we know no better than before what is inside this confounded Great Eyrie, nor even if it is a crater."

"Volcano or not," said I, "there are no suspicious noises now; neither smoke nor flame rises above it; nothing whatever threatens an eruption."

This was true. A profound silence reigned around us; and a perfectly clear sky shone overhead. We tasted the perfect calm of great altitudes.

It was worth noting that the circumference of the huge wall was about twelve or fifteen hundred feet. As to the space enclosed within, we could scarce reckon that without knowing the thickness of the encompassing wall. The surroundings were absolutely deserted. Probably not a living creature ever mounted to this height, except the few birds of prey which soared high above us.

Our watches showed three o'clock, and Mr. Smith cried in disgust, "What is the use of stopping here all day! We shall learn nothing more. We must make a start, Mr. Strock, if we want to get back to Pleasant Garden tonight."

I made no answer, and did not move from where I was seated; so he called again, "Come, Mr. Strock; you don't answer."

In truth, it cut me deeply to abandon our effort, to descend the slope without having achieved my mission. I felt an imperious need of persisting; my curiosity had redoubled. But what could I do? Could I tear open this unyielding earth? Overleap the mighty cliff? Throwing one last defiant glare at the Great Eyrie, I followed my companions.

The return was effected without great difficulty. We had only to slide down where we had so laboriously scrambled up. Before five o'clock we had descended the last slopes of the mountain, and the farmer of Wildon welcomed us to a much needed meal.

"Then you didn't get inside?" said he.

"No," responded Mr. Smith, "and I believe that the inside exists only in the imagination of our country folk."

At half past eight our carriage drew up before the house of the Mayor of Pleasant Garden, where we passed the night. While I strove vainly to sleep, I asked myself if I should not stop there in the village and organize a new ascent. But what better chance had it of succeeding than the first? The wisest course was, doubtless, to return to Washington and consult Mr. Ward.

So, the next day, having rewarded our two guides, I took leave of Mr. Smith at Morganton, and that same evening left by train for Washington.

15

THE CAROLINA MOUNTAINS

Margaret W. Morley (1858–1923) authored the popular travel book *The Carolina Mountains* (1913). Before making her home in Tryon, North Carolina, she had been a schoolteacher in the New York and Wisconsin school systems. Her book is a little gem of picturesque word painting that remains an unequaled if somewhat idyllic description of the scenic attractions of western North Carolina. Chapter 31 describes Linville Falls and the Gorge below them.

Linville Falls

One goes to Linville Falls to see the beautiful river at the point where it takes that leap into the gorge, forming the most noted cataract in the mountains. Linville, under the Grandfather Mountain, lies in a green bowl with tree-covered hills for its sides. Above the hotel, on the green edge of the bowl, look out cottages and summer houses, for Linville is a well-known resort. The river flows sparkling and dancing along one side of the bowl on its way to the falls ten or twelve miles south of here. The Linville is a delightful river, a clear trout stream from its birth-spring back of the Grandfather down to the falls and on through the ten-miles-long canyon below them, the canyon it has worn between Linville Mountain and wild Hawksbill and Tablerock.

The way to the Linville from Ledger [a small village south of the Mitchell County seat of Bakersville, North Carolina] is by a pleasant and varied route up the North Toe River, then over ridges, up the Plumtree Creek, across the Blue Ridge, past Crossnore under the Snake Den Mountain, and on through Kawana, where you will stop to visit the Highlands Nursery that has done so much to make the beautiful growths of these mountains known to the outside world. It began twenty-five years ago with half an acre of land as an experiment. Now it covers one hundred acres, and every year sends out many carloads of the beautiful things that grow here and which find their way, not only to distant parts of our own country, but all over Europe. This nursery owes its existence to Mr. S.T. Kelsey, of New York State, who came here from Kansas, and, with the energy and optimism of the North and West combined, tried to transform the mountains. But he came too soon; the hour of awakening had not struck; so when he laid out a whole town on the Highlands plateau after the Western fashion, the people looked on in amazement and Highlands remained untransformed, as remained the rest of the mountains at that time, excepting for the roads he projected. For Mr. Kelsey had yet greater genius for making roads than towns, and laid out the finest of those first made in the mountains, among them the beautiful Yonahlossee Road that crosses the southern slopes of the Grandfather Mountain, scarcely changing its grade for a distance of nearly twenty miles. It was also Mr. Kelsey who planned Linville with its hotels and its lake. But the best thing he did was making the gardens and taming the most decorative and beautiful of the wild growths, not only the royal rhododendrons, laurel, and azaleas, and the noble forest trees, but the silver-bell, the sourwood, the leucothoe, the yellow-root, the wild lilies and orchids, and a hundred other charming wild flowers, including *Shortia* [*glacifolia,* or Oconee-bells] that gave the botanists such long search, inducing them to tolerate the conditions of a man-made garden, and also to bloom yet more freely, if possible, there than in the wilderness. Although no longer alone in its work, the Highland Nursery was the first native enterprise to distribute the decorative plants of this region from the North Carolina Mountains, and from it the estate of Biltmore supplied its first needs.

It is an interesting fact that, long before the people of America had learned to appreciate the beautiful plants with which their country is so richly endowed, these were used and highly valued in European gardens, and English estates were beautified with our rhododendrons, laurels, and azaleas long before we had learned to value them as ornamental growths for cultivated grounds. It was Michaux, who, transported by the beauty of the wild flowers of the New World, took many of them home and introduced them to the people of Europe. It was he also who taught the mountain people the value of ginseng and how to prepare it for the Chinese market.

It is but a few pleasant miles from Kawana to Linville, along a road very much interfered with by little tributaries of the Linville River, among them the pretty Grandmother Creek. But if you want to go directly to the falls from Kawana, you turn towards the south instead of the north, and follow the road a few miles down the river to the Linville Falls settlement; this is about a mile from the falls to which a rough road leads, for the country about here is extremely wild; the woods are choked with dense growths of laurel and rhododendron, and the land is torn by ravines. For we are now on the outer side of the Blue Ridge adjoining the peculiarly wild foothill country, and whether the Linville River breaks through the wall of the Blue Ridge depends upon whether you consider the narrow Linville Mountain a part of the Blue Ridge or a part of the foothills, for it is over the upper ledge of the deep gorge that separates Linville Mountain from a high ridge of the foothills that the river makes its escape. But however geology may decide the matter, in appearance the Linville Mountain belongs to the Blue Ridge, and one always thinks of it as ending the mountain plateau at that point.

Across the clearing, at the end of the rough road that leads to the falls, stands a house on the very brink of the precipice [the white cottage overlooking the Upper Falls occupied by Frank Bicknell and his wife]. As you approach it, the thunder of the water grows louder: you have a sense of nearing some catastrophe in nature. At the brink the mountain stops short without the slightest preparatory slope, without a buttressing spur. It drops in an upright wall, along the face of which a path descends through the rhododendrons that have grown along a narrow ledge. Down the path you take your way. At a certain point in it you can step out on the top of a large rock and see the river raging between cleft walls directly below you. As you continue the steep descent beyond here, rhododendrons offer you long, curved arms to hold by, and lend you their roots to step on. Finally, you jump down to a broad stone floor, and before you in its bed of solid rock lies the large pool of the upper falls into which the river enters in two wide, low cascades that are separated from each other by tree-covered rocks.

The shining Linville steps down from the forest, through which it has sparkled and sung all the way from its source at the back of the Grandfather, to rest as it were in the beautiful pool and make ready for that great leap down the wall of the mountain. High walls clad with living green encircle the pool on whose calm surface are mirrored the trees and the sky. To the eye it is a scene of peace, but in the ears is the tumultuous beating of the waters. The outlet of the pool is a deep and narrow crack. It is as though the broad river-bed had suddenly been set up on edge. The water plunges with a roar into this winding channel, rages about the impediments there, and finally escapes through a cleft in the rock to leap over the wall of the mountain.

Across a wide stone floor one walks to the scene of commotion in the narrow channel, but it is impossible to get a view of the final plunge without gaining a point of vantage by a jump too dangerous to think of. It fills one with a sense of impending danger to stand shut in by the high walls and hear the strife between the water and the rocks; and if it is terrible at this safe season of the year, imagine it in the spring floods! Standing on the wide, dry pavement, you look up to see a drift-log caught in the bushes in the cliff-side high above your head. It is hard to realize it, yet you know the water put it there. It was at a time of high water that the upper rim of the lower wall gave way, forming a step, and considerably lowering the final leap, thus taking away something of its impressiveness.

Climbing up again to where the path branches, if you want to go to the foot of the fall, where you can get a near view of it, you turn aside here—and take the consequences. A stream of water trickles down the slippery path, which is half rock, half rhododendron roots. The limbs of the rhododendrons twist about you like enormous snakes. You step down where you can, but where the distance is too great you have to jump, that is, you jump if you dare, but it is not likely you will dare, knowing what is below. The alternative is to sit down and slide over the rocks covered with black and sticky mud. It is a breathless scramble and your arms ache from holding to the rhododendron cables. Finally, you reach the narrow ledge of rock that borders the deep pool into which the river drops. There it is, close to you, a high, white mass of foam and deafening you with its thunder. If the sun is shining you may see rainbows playing about it, and in any event you will get a wetting from the spray. A wall of rock rises above you and there is scarcely room to take a step, so close to your feet lies the deep water. There are big wise trout in this pool, the people say, but it takes a very wise angler to lure them out.

Getting back again is worse than getting down. Unfortunately, gravity prevents sliding up, and a sudden descent into Avernus seems quite fearfully imminent as you slip and struggle and cling to the rhododendrons. But before starting up you can if you like follow along the edge of the cliff, as far as your nerve lasts, for the path is over rhododendron roots that have fastened themselves into the face of the rock. How they got footing here is a mystery; but here they are, and in behind their contorted limbs you creep along like an ant, hoping with every step that the roots will not give way.

This path, that grows less as it goes on, is followed by ardent fishermen, who either go back if it gets too lonesome for them, or else keep on. For if you keep on long enough you can get down to the bottom of the gorge,—not so hastily as the description may seem to imply, though that too is possible,—and when you get down, it must almost be worth the effort, for you will find yourself in the famous Linville Gorge that for the next ten miles is seldom traveled by a human being, although it is the finest trout stream in the mountains. The river runs between walls that rise many hundreds of feet high, and in some places the gorge is so narrow that there is room only for the river, and he who ventures in much wade as best he can through the swift water as it dashes about and over the rocks and boulders. Those who have been in the gorge speak enthusiastically of its grandeur and beauty.

Ordinary humanity, however, views the falls from a point down the ravine, on top instead of at the bottom of the mountain wall. To get to this point you follow a path partly though scrubby undergrowth, partly through dark pine reaches that make soft walking, and where the edge of the abyss is hidden by impenetrable rhododendron jungles.

When you get to the open, rocky edge, you forget to look upstream to the falls, because of the wonderful blanket of trees that covers the opposite side of the narrow gorge. There is nothing like it; the walls seem made of foliage; the river far below runs through walls of living green, the crowns of superb forest trees that have managed to grow on what appears to be an upright cliff. You hardly see the stems, only the green crown of the hardwood trees blending their colors and their shapes with black interspersed shadows and interwoven with the dark-green of firs and the pale feathery effect of white pines, a marvelous tapestry wrought by the hand of nature.

The steepness of the walls makes this growth of large trees the more remarkable, and your heart aches to recall that this whole gorge, one of the wonders of the mountains, has been bought by a lumber company. [Packer and Harrison are mentioned as the gorge owners in a 1916 deed.] But looking at that tapestried wall falling sheer into the mountain torrent below, your sympathy takes a humorous leap to the side of the lumber company. Any tree they can get out of there they will have earned! "Float the logs downstream? Not down *that* stream, unless you want to collect wood pulp somewhere beyond the foothills," a man who knows the gorge assures you.

As you stand on the brink of the precipice you hear the confused thunder of the fall, that at this distance is a mere white ribbon hung from the end of the gorge. Its voice alone asserts its importance. And how insistent, how unbroken, how hard and tiresome it is, a stupid unchanging roar, and blended with it is an echo as unresonant and monotonous as itself. You find yourself listening for a change that never comes, except a loudening when the wind blows toward you.

Irritated by the monotonous sounds you go on and around a curve out of sight of the vociferous ribbon. You seat yourself on a bed of dry, crackling moss that sends out waves of fragrance every time you move. Here the murmur of the far-down river is full of modulations, the harsh sound of conflict has given place to gentler tones and the subdued roar of the fall itself now makes an agreeable accompaniment.

To the song of the river is here also added voices from the forest, a sighing from the pine trees overhead, gentle rustlings from the crisp shrubs, a staccato chirp from the grass, a trill from some bird in the air, the clapping of a woodpecker on a dead tree, the drumming of some unknown creature, the ticking of a borer in a dead log. There are drowsy notes in this orchestra of the summer, with which the mighty perfume of the earth seems gradually to blend, and the warmth of the sun to mingle and hold all together in its tenuous threads—and—and—the sun conquers and you are sound asleep on the fragrant mosses, although it is mid-afternoon and you have planned a walk down that long ridge where the huckleberries grow. Thanks, oh, sun!—there is something altogether lovely in falling thus asleep against one's judgment.

There are "chimneys" over the edge of the precipice, whose tops have been conquered by brave little fir trees, and mossy things and a few flowers. And the precipice, do you realize that you are hanging your feet over the edge of the mountains—that the wall across the river belongs to the same foothill formation?

What a sweet place is this edge of the high world! On a mountain top all things unite to smell sweet, and on none more than this. Crisp moss crackles whenever you move, hard-leaved, red-stemmed huckleberries crowd the crevices of the rocks, and *Dendrium buxophyllum*, whose thick carpet is seen to be made of tiny imitations of rhododendron bushes shares the crannies with other growths. But everywhere, and by far the choicest thing here, is a species of dwarf rhododendron with a charming architectural structure, the curving brown stems crowned with upward-pointing, curled little leaves, green above, the underside dusted with a rich brown bloom, the red-tinged veins and red petioles giving a red flush to the whole plant. Seed pods on these charming shrubs tell of bloom earlier in the season, and who would not be here then! It would be hard to imagine a wilder, sweeter place than this edge, overlooking the gorge. To be here fills you with contentment. You imagine you would like to stay with the rabbits the rest of the summer.

The long and narrow Linville Mountain that borders the gorge on the west is not very well known to outsiders, but the people tell you of wonderful minerals there, among them large quantities of flexible sandstone. The Linville Country is very wild, but nowhere does the galax more riotously abound, this region being one of the favorite collecting grounds for this charming little plant.

16

"A WALKING TRIP TO TABLE ROCK MOUNTAIN

JULY 3-6, 1914"

D.R. Beeson was born in 1881 in Uniontown, Pennsylvania. He worked as a draftsman for U.S. Steel in Gary, Pennsylvania, before coming to Johnson City, Tennessee, in 1912 to start his architectural practice. Having moved to the area, Beeson became an ardent hiker and mountaineer, taking numerous camping trips into the wilderness with his friend C. Hodge Mathes, an English professor at East Tennessee State Normal School. In the journal, Beeson refers to his friend as "The Deacon." Beeson made several photographic and narrative records of his outings between 1913 and 1920, trips into the Smokeys, Mount Mitchell, Grandfather Mountain and Roan Mountain. In July 1914, he tackled the gorge. For nineteen years beginning in 1921, he was a Boy Scouts troop leader. He died in Johnson City on January 17, 1983.

Saturday, 12:15 p.m., July 4, 1914.
West bank of Linville River, at foot of Table Rock Mountain, North Carolina.

All well,—and ten minutes yet before we start up on the way to the top of Jonas Ridge and with Table Rock as the objective point. The straight up part is about 1600 feet and the horizontal distance probably half a mile.

We averaged about an hour late getting away from Johnson City last night by the C.C. & O [Charleston, Cincinnati and Ohio Railroad] and reached Altapass [a Mitchell County, North Carolina rail community on the crest of the Blue Ridge chain] about the middle of the following week [*sic*]. The train stopped at Erwin [Tennessee] an hour and had work getting away from most all the stations from there to Spruce Pine [Mitchell County, North Carolina]. Mrs. McCormick had put me up a dandy lunch but the other three,—Hodge Mathes, Schoen, and Buford Mathes,—had to get along on six ham sandwitches from a lunch joint near the station.

Then about the time the train pulled out on its leisurely way, the Deacon discovered a little black boy with two ice cream cones left and stood on the back platform and hollered encouragement while the kid chased the train well out to Okalona and handed over the remains. Buford ate one and Schoen the other. Schoen announced that he didn't believe in eating a big lot of food and then starting out on a hard walk. It was well to put us wise to this or we certainly wouldn't have found out his true feelings in the matter.

Last night we slept on the train for about three hours and on some grass across from the Altapass station for about four more hours. Breakfast was very good to behold, especially the coffee, and we took a train for the South at a quarter after five, leaving the said train at the Linville Falls station [rather, the Ashford station, seven miles south of Linville Falls]. Here's where the walking started. The railroad trip down from Altapass was nice and clean as there were enough freight cars ahead of the coaches to make a smokeless ride.

This here is the wildest country I have ever seen and the Linville River gorge is far ahead of the Toe and Chucky [that is, Nolichucky] gorges so far as the scale of everything is concerned,—deeper, more rugged and lined with almost unbroken lines of cliffs on both sides. The depth where we crossed is about 1600 feet according to the government map.

Table Rock, so far as we can see so far, is in about the same class as Grandfather tho not nearly so high above sea level, being only 3909 compared with 5964. The view of the rock from across the gorge, however, is fully as imposing as any we had of Grandfather last fall and I think we saw it from about all angles. The wildness of the region we are in makes the trip the most satisfying I can imagine. The weather is, I'm sorry to say, hazy and nothing is visible except in the near and middle distances.

Johnson City, Tenn. July 6, 1914.
After the trip.

The Deacon and I being the only members of the quartet that indulged in the pleasure of a write up, we have been unable to get any opportunity for uninterrupted composition during the trip. So we have had to wait till it was all over.

After leaving the railroad at seven o'clock on the morning of the 4th, we proceeded by easy trails and gentle slopes up to the top of Linville Mountain, where, as Shakespeare says, we struck a snag. The Linville Gorge was decorated on our side with a fringe of rocks and precipices and we had been told that it was possible to get down to the river only at one place in seven miles. We all believe it. I had been setting the pace and picking out the trails but just at this stage we passed a young man who seemed scared or possibly drunk and whose directions Buford insisted so on following that I got sore and proceeded to get personal. It was the only discord of the trip and lasted but a short time. We lost an hour and at last reached the river through a sort of slot in the crags that proved to be "The Only Way." Buford and I made up without the kissing and everybody was in perfect accord when we stopped at the river for dinner about noon. But the worst was still to come yet, as Schoen expressed it, and the climb from the river up to the base of Table Rock was surely it. We were two hours and a quarter in making the half mile. Schoen, who had been talking about Lookout Mountain and the Adirondaks, grew silent except for a grunt here and there and explained, as soon as he got his voice back, that they were not mountains at all.

We all made a compact at the start not to talk any business en route. It worked well and was a big advantage to every one of us. Slush is about all a person should talk on such a trip; it keeps up a pleasant atmosphere of companionship and doesn't weaken the system like discussions of modern methods and egotistics.

There's no use to try to describe the beauty of the various forms of nature. Silence is the best means of description when magnificent, wonderful and sublime, all take to the trees. Schoen acknowledged that German went back on him the same way already.

The climb up from the river to the top of Jonas Ridge was the pull of the trip and I guess the other three must have had harder packs to manage than the stuff I carried, tho the weight at first was about the same and all the others grew less while my own remained the same from start to finish, owing to the fact that none of the photographic outfit nor the map case were eaten and the canteen was always refilled as soon as Buford or Schoen decided that the water supply was running low. The other packs all had some food stuff in them and we tried to lighten them at about the same rate and with all the speed possible. I must say tho, that I have seen much better eating than was done on this trip. The packs were about twenty pounds each at the start.

The more I write, the more I am convinced that my style is too much to the rambling order. A person would have a mean job finding any system or plan in the same vicinity. To begin again about supper time Saturday night, that meal passed off amicably and we had a fine location well sheltered from the rain that fell at intervals, they say, through the night. There were a couple of stakes driven into the ground on my side of the tent to keep me from rolling off the gorge into North Carolina. I guess several of us hated to leave the place the next morning.

This Jonas Ridge is not so much as far as altitude is concerned but it shows about the greatest collection of rough mountain formations I have ever seen. The Hawksbill, Table Rock, and Shortoff occur on top of the ridge within ten miles of distance and any one of them would make the ridge worth going to see. Then there is Linville Falls at the North end of the ten miles,—to some people, the most wonderful of the lot.

The early morning fog and cloud effects were beyond description and we stood on top of Table Rock for a half hour or so along about five o'clock in the morning, and about seven on the Hawksbill, watching the fleecy white clouds dodging through the gaps in Jonas Ridge and disappearing into thin air as soon as they got well out above the gorge.

The Table Rock from Hawksbill is sharp at the top and much like the McRae view of Grandfather while all the views from the C.C.&O. are flat on top and straight up at the ends making the rock appear unscalable. But neither from the side nor from the end does the prospect look so easy of ascent as it really is, for there is a good easy trail clear up to the top and down through the Devil's Kitchen [a defile or crevice on the rock's northwestern side] tho the latter is much worse than that to the top. The crop of heather [sand myrtle] on top is the most luxuriant I have ever seen. The rocks on top are well supplied with initials, in some cases very old. On many of the highest of these rocks and crags and cliffs, we found small bowls worn in the upper surface of the rock. [These craters are formed over eons by winds spinning stone in a natural pocket.] These basins fill with water during rains and were of great assistance to all of us in the way of water supply,—for drinking only. The rock formation seems to be most granite with numerous ledges of quartzite. It occurs in masses and very little stratified formation are to be seen till we reached Linville Falls, where there is some sandstone.

But to back to the scene of the start of my last digression,—the Hawksbill. The gorge of the Linville River is so rough and precipitous that it is said to be about a mile an hour job to travel up it, at the stream or along the top of Jonas Ridge. So we laid out a route up the valley to the east, about three miles back from the river and parallel with it. And just to show that good feeling still continued, we celebrated the start by getting lost twice in the first two miles,—once through my own blindness and once on general principles. However, it's just as well we did for Buford was not feeling well at all and after about five miles had to stop and stretch out on the ground. We let him take the time cure for an hour and after that much rest the whole party seemed better and the rest of the trip was not so hard. Buford said he felt guilty at delaying the proceedings but of course no person minded that a bit and we were all mighty glad to see him come round so well. And from that on, he was one of the strongest of the company.

We had planned to dine on the Linville River near the Falls but the various delays made it impossible, so we stopped about eleven in the morning for a light lunch (about the size of a ten course dinner) and dined at three beside a little stream near an old lumber camp. It was this meal chiefly that earned me the proud title of being the "Hollow Man" of the party. I ate too much to burden my memory with. The coffee was especially good, same as for the other meals, and we had apricots and sweet chocolate for dessert and a half hour to recover. Buford ate a pretty good meal and didn't seem to feel the recent unpleasantness at all.

The walk from there on was the easiest of the day, mostly down grade and partly along the top of Jonas Ridge at the northern end. The trees and undergrowth were too thick to see through, however, and we had to guess at the view.

Well, as I have probably said before, we dropped down into the valley and reached the river about seven o'clock with the idea that the Falls were about a half mile below. Of course the dusk was about on us, but I was anxious to see the place and perhaps get some sort of picture of it, and, the others being tired and preferring a rest, I set out alone for the Falls and found that the distance was two miles instead of a half of one. This made it out of the question to get a picture so I just explored the place for a few minutes and went back to camp. There are really two sets of falls but the lower one, a couple of hundred yards below the other, is the one that is generally referred to. It has a drop of about fifty feet and is far ahead of what the descriptions and photographs I had seen led me to look for. I am certainly glad to have seen it. At the lower fall the river flows through a slit in the side of the cliff and drops to an almost circular pool whose sides, except at the lower end, are perpendicular for a height of about a hundred and fifty feet. The only place to get down to the water at the pool is at the west side and is through a narrow break in the cliffs, down a path that is pretty hard to follow when you are new to it and night is about with you. There is a ledge of rock about five feet wide almost down to the water level where a person can walk around to a point almost in front of the falls. I got back up to terra firma with only one fall, and reached camp a little after dark.

No person wanted any more supper so we retired at once with the idea of a two o'clock start staring us in the face. Hodge tore down a couple of shocks of rye and we piled them flat on the ground with the heads together for a mattress and laid out the tents with the blankets inside, without any attempt at setting up the tents. It was the coldest night of the trip and we all slept well, what there was of it. When we got up the temperature was but very little above the absolute zero where all matter, they say, ceases to move. I secured my old regular job of making the coffee and straddled the fire while I made it, which was all that kept me from freezing solid. I think the whole crowd was feeling better than the day before and the repartee on the road to Pineola was not nearly so strong as it had been the previous afternoon. Schoen had his leggings on, front side in front, and found that they didn't hurt his feet nearly so much. Buford was as lively as a mountain goat and led the way at a good gait the whole nine miles. For my part, I enjoyed the luxury of bringing up the rear.

The road was good and the country not much to rave over so we made good time and had over half an hour to spare at Pineola before the train was due to leave. So we made a picture or two, bought a pound or so of milk chocolate and confiscated the back platform of the little parlor car by climbing over the fence onto the said platform before the car was opened.

Mathes and Mathes washed in the Linville River before boarding the train but the other two put it off. I was a little surprised at Schoen.

All in all, it was a very enjoyable trip and did us all a lot of good. The mileage was not so great but the effort exceeded that which a much longer ordinary walking trip would have required. The first day we measured 11 miles; the second, 22; and the morning of the third, 9. That was what the Deacon and Buford registered by their speedometers. That was, in all probability, excessive and I suppose 35 miles would have about covered the horizontal distance. My own mileage would be about ten miles greater than any of the others. I suppose the pedometers measured about two miles up the mountain to Table Rock on Saturday while the actual horizontal distance was about a half or three quarters.

Of course I want to make the trip to Mt. Mitchell and the Smokies, the former on account of the altitude and the latter because of the difficulty of the going, but after that I don't believe that altitude will have much effect when laying out a mountain walk. Table Rock is only 3909 feet in altitude but it seemed to me to show up better in all respects than Grandfather at 5964. And Buford, who had been on Mitchell recently, said that it had been very tame in comparison with this little trip of ours. There could be a great sermon founded on such a text but I don't feel qualified to go into the matter of what constitutes true greatness either in human nature or in the sort we went out to see. I suppose in any case we are attracted most by the unusual, the rugged and unyielding, and the picturesque,—the more attraction, the more these characteristics predominate.

This is all for the present.

17

VACATION DAYS IN THE SUMMITLANDS OF THE BLUE RIDGE AND CUMBERLAND MOUNTAINS

Western North Carolina travel and tourism leaped forward with the arrival of railroads. The Western North Carolina Railroad crested the Blue Ridge above Old Fort to reach Asheville in 1880; the ET&WNC, or "Tweetsie" joined Johnson City, Tennessee, with Newland and Linville, North Carolina. Promotional literature lavished praise on the Southern Highlands as summer havens. The Clinchfield (CC&O) opened passenger service in 1907, from which period comes the anonymous, undated *Vacation Days* illustrated brochure. Basing its adventures in Altapass, a small community on the Blue Ridge Parkway near Spruce Pine, the guide refers to the Crest of the Blue Ridge scenic highway begun in 1913 to join Marion, Virginia, with Tallulah Falls, Georgia. World War I stopped the project. The highway was completed past the Gorge from Altapass north to Pineola. Guilt for the perpetuation, if not the original creation, of the bogus myth of Table Rock as a Cherokee sacred altar rests squarely on this modest leaflet; further, its report of two-thousand-foot walls in the Gorge likewise calls for correction.

Altapass, North Carolina

The Gateway to the Summitlands

On the crest of the Blue Ridge, surrounded on every side by the tallest peaks of the Appalachian System, is Altapass, the gateway to the many picturesque mountain resorts which dot the landscape of western North Carolina and eastern Tennessee.

From Spartanburg, S.C., the Clinchfield Route heads directly for the center of the circle which contains the tallest peaks of the Blue Ridge, including Mount Mitchell, Clingman's [Dome], the Black and Green Mountains on the west; Pumpkin Patch, Roan and Yellow Mountains on the north; and Beech, Grandfather, Hawksbill, Table Rock (Attacoa) and Linville Mountain on the east.

After boring its way through eighteen tunnels, chiseling a path from the solid rock of the mountain and spanning deep ravines over trestles of steel, the road attains the Crest of the Blue Ridge at Altapass and accomplishes a feat in railway engineering which has made it famous throughout the world.

From the peep of rosy-fingered dawn until the last rays of the setting sun fade into darkness on the surrounding mountain peaks, the life of Altapass is aglow with interest and everchanging excitement. By mountain trail or bridle path, by coaching road or railway train, the Summitlands of the Appalachians disclose to the eye of the explorer the masterpieces of American scenery.

Linville Falls, six miles east of Altapass, is one of the most attractive show places in the mountains of North Carolina. It is reached over a portion of the Crest of the Blue Ridge Highway or by mountain trail or bridle path. Here the Linville River offers the finest trout fishing in the eastern section of the United States. Its beautiful cascades and wild canon attract sight-seers from all parts of the country.

From Linville Falls a good road leads to Linville, N.C., the popular summer resort at the foot of Grandfather Mountain.

Just beyond the Linville River lies Attacoa (Table Rock Mountain), the mystic altar of the Cherokee Indians, on whose summit human sacrifice is said to have been offered to the gods. Nearby is Hawksbill Mountain, one of the most noted and interesting peaks of the Appalachian System.

The Crest of the Blue Ridge Highway

Among the greatest scenic highways in the world is the superb automobile road, which is now being constructed along the crest of the Blue Ridge Mountains, crossing the Clinchfield Route at Altapass, N.C. A roadway of modern construction, twenty-four feet in width, perfectly surfaced, and with a maximum grade of only four and one-half percent, will soon connect with

Bristol to Washington Highway, on the north, with the Central and National Highways, on the south, and will open up to the motorist the Summitlands of the Appalachians, containing the tallest peaks east of the Rockies.

At Blowing Rock, N.C., the Crest of the Blue Ridge Highway connects with the Central Highway, which leads to Charlotte and Salisbury, N.C., where connections are made with the National Highway from New York to Atlanta.

From Blowing Rock to Linville, N.C. the route is over the celebrated Yonahlossee Road [present-day U.S. 221], which enjoys the distinction of being one of the first good mountain roads built in North Carolina. From Linville, the Crest of the Blue Ridge Highway is now being built to Altapass, from which point the survey lies through Little Switzerland, past Mount Mitchell, and thence via Asheville, Hendersonville and Tallulah Falls to Cornelia, Ga., where connection is again made with the National Highway.

On the north the Crest of the Blue Ridge Highway connects with the Bristol to Washington Highway, at Abingdon, Va., the route passing southward through Boone to Blowing Rock, N.C.

The section of the Highway around Altapass, N.C. is now completed for a distance of seven miles, and serves as a scenic road for horseback riding, driving and coaching, and also as an approach to Linville Falls, the little Niagara of the mountains.

Near Altapass, the Crest of the Blue Ridge Highway ascends to the summit of Humpback Mountain, where, at an elevation of over 4,000 feet, the view includes all of the noted peaks of the Blue Ridge and extends far beyond to the Piedmont on the south and the Cumberland Mountains on the north.

Linville Falls, North Carolina

The approach to Linville Falls, the little Niagara of the mountains, is through Altapass, the highest point on the Clinchfield Route, and thence over the completed portion of the Crest of the Blue Ridge Highway, past Jackson Knob and the northern end of Humpback Mountain, which overlooks the valley of the Linville River. From the present terminus of the Highway a mountain trail leads the way through brilliantly colored gardens of rhododendron, kalmia and azalea, which tempt the traveler to loiter in this floral fairyland.

Linville Falls may also be reached from Linville Falls Station [at Ashford], on the Clinchfield Route, by a six-miles ride up the picturesque canyon of the North Fork of the Catawba River. The route lies between Humpback and Linville Mountains and is most comfortably made on horseback, though the road is open to vehicles. Still another approach to this show place of the mountains is over a good mountain road from Linville, N.C. A road has also been opened from the Falls to Spruce Pine, N.C. a station on the Clinchfield Route north of Altapass.

By whatever route the traveler journeys, the way seems all too short, for the scenery in this section embraces the wildest and most spectacular features of the western North Carolina landscape, and after a delightful ride of three to four hours the neat and attractive cottages of Linville Falls come into view.

Linville Falls Park, with its hundreds of acres of virgin forest, is in the very heart of the Southern Appalachian Forest Reserve, and it has been the special care of its owners to preserve the region undisturbed in all its pristine beauty and native wildness. No sound of the lumberman's axe or shrill call of the locomotive is allowed to disturb the restful solitude of this beautiful mountain retreat. Its only appeal and invitation is to the botanist, the angler, the huntsman, and to those who, weary of the fretful turmoil of the strenuous life, long for a haven of rest and recuperation "far from the madding crowd's ignoble strife." To the true lover of Nature, no spot in all the world has greater charms

The Falls and Canon of Linville River

"No gorges in eastern America can equal in depth and wildness those carved across the Blue Ridge by the Linville River." These are the sober words taken from the report of Secretary James Wilson, which was submitted to Congress with the enthusiastic endorsement of President Roosevelt, in connection with the proposed Southern Appalachian Forest Reserve.

The following report by Messrs. H.A. Pressey and E.W. Meyers, hydrographers of the United States Geological Survey, will give the reader an unbiased description of this natural wonder: "The falls proper, which are located about three miles below the Mitchell-Burke County line, have a perpendicular plunge of forty feet, and the cascades above are about fifty feet in height, this fall of ninety feet occurring in a linear distance of about one hundred feet. For a distance of about ten miles below the falls the river flows in a series of cascades through a narrow gorge, the sides of which are from five hundred to nearly two thousand feet high, the walls being cut down through the eroded Linville quartzites into the granite below. In the first six miles below the falls the descent averages two hundred and eight feet to the mile, and the total descent from the head of the falls to the lower end of the gorge, a distance of about ten miles, is eighteen hundred feet, as determined by a line of levels. Along the upper six or seven miles of this distance the bottom of the gorge is scarcely wider than the stream. The total fall of the stream, from its source in Linville Gap to its mouth, is about three thousand and thirty feet in a distance of about thirty-six and one-half miles."

Fishing and Hunting

The Clinchfield Route has opened to the sportsman the latest great fishing and hunting ground in the eastern section of the United States. Shut in by impassible mountain ranges, this region had for centuries been accessible only by difficult mountain trails, whose asperities repelled all but a few of the hardiest and most adventurous sportsmen. Its virgin forests and wild canons have remained for centuries the native breeding place of the choicest game and fish.

From its source near the summit of Grandfather Mountain to its confluence with the Catawba, three thousand and thirty feet below, the Linville River affords thirty-six and one-half miles of the finest trout fishing to be found in all the country. Rainbow trout, black bass and mountain trout find an undisturbed breeding place in the unfathomable canon below Linville Falls, where precipitous walls, rising five hundred to two thousand feet, have created a natural and undisturbed hatchery extending a distance of nearly ten miles. The waters of Linville River are also protected against poaching and are systematically restocked with game fish by agents of the companies which own the property.

NOTE: At the time of the appearance of this booklet, the Falls property was owned and managed by the Hossfeld family; local Turner Vance served as the fish and game warden. Former Agriculture Department farming expert Frank Bicknell and his wife, Jessie, lived in a small white cottage overlooking the Upper Falls. Bicknell's photographs illustrate part of the CC&O guide. The line of verse is from Thomas Gray's 1750 "Elegy Written in a Country Churchyard"; lines 73–76 run: "Far from the madding crowd's ignoble strife, / Their sober wishes never learn'd to stray; / Along the cool sequester'd vale of life / They kept the noiseless tenor of their way."

18

THE HISTORY OF LINVILLE FALLS

Part of the charm of this simple narrative is the jerk it gives the reader in moving from Genesis to the Fourth of July 1898 in its opening lines. Artie Green Laws grew up in the Falls community, the daughter of a country doctor. As a journalist, she owned and operated the *Avery Advocate*. Laws's account of daily life in the Linville Falls area at the turn of the last century gives some valuable glimpses into mountain living long ago, though she bungles in her account of the Linville Massacre.

In the beginning, Linville Falls was a vast wilderness with only the cascades for attraction. It was inhabited by numerous animals, birds, and reptiles. On the fourth of July, 1898, Louis, Hamp, and Azor Barrier and Dock Franklin reportedly killed 58 rattlesnakes with rocks and sticks, 47 on Saturday and 11 on Sunday.

Linville River got its name from two brothers by the name of Linville from down state, who settled near the town that is now called Linville, which is located near the head of the river. The Indians scalped one of the men and killed him. He was buried near the town of Linville. The other escaped and reached home.

One of the earliest settlers here was Levi Franklin, a descendant of Benjamin Franklin's brother, John. He lived near Linville Falls and became the ancestor of the offspring of the pioneer settlers who possessed the old historic courage of their forefathers. They wrestled with the wilderness in order to carry out their dreams of life. They were composed of both political parties, Democrats and Republicans. Jefferson Hyams and Stokes Penland, Democrats, and Wash Hyams, a Republican, succeeded in having a post office established. The most difficult part about it was selecting a short name. They finally decided on "Linville Falls." The post office was established in 1899, thus opening the region for occupation and development by others. Since the village was situated on the corner of three counties, the post office was built on the Burke side. At that time the three counties were Mitchell, Burke, and McDowell. Since Avery County was inaugurated [in 1911] the village is situated in Avery, Burke and McDowell.

Following is a bit of information obtained from the records of the post office department in the National Archives, which shows that a post office was established at Linville Falls, Burke County, North Carolina, on June 20, 1899. The Linville Falls Post Office has had nine postmasters since its establishment. The names of the postmasters who served at this office and their dates of appointment through May 12, 1972 are: Jefferson C. Hyams, June 20, 1899; Thomas S. McKinney, April 2, 1902; M. Columbus Biggerstaff, June 20, 1903; Jennie Clark, February 8, 1907; Clara Penland (Miss), March 6, 1908; Jackson M. Franklin, January 3, 1925; Eula Penland (Miss), February 1, 1940; Gurney Franklin, May 1, 1957; Albert D. Franklin, Sr., May 12, 1972 Ms. Leandra Slate succeeded Albert D. Franklin Sr. as postmaster, then Ms. Cathy Miller served as postmistress, followed by Ms. Debbie Winebarger. In interim periods, Ms. Debbie Franklin has served as officer in charge as have gifted sculptor Mr. Chuck Robertson and well-informed Falls local Mr. Bill Faulkner, all at the charming little river-stone post office near village center.

In the days before the hardtop roads were on the scene in this neck of the woods, the postmasters and postmistresses faced the howling wind and trod though the deep snow afoot, sometimes taking a narrow, beaten path through the woods; sometimes, while clad in their woolens and longies, they boldly ventured forth in the chill of the open range in order to pay respect to the duties of Uncle Sam. Since the past 28 years or so Old Glory flies atop a new stone building here. Rom Franklin and son, Claude, built the rock post office, having hauled the rocks from near the Linville Caverns.

The people of Linville Falls had their mail come to Altamont, which was called Trout prior to 1899, when the name was changed from Trout to Altamont. The first post office in Linville Falls was established in the home of Jefferson C. Hyams. The building is now owned by Mrs. C.R. Williams, a resident also of St. Augustine, Florida. [The structure, known later as the

Fant house, burned down around 2014 from an electrical short. A log cabin home now occupies the former site. Across Highway 183, beside the old historical Penland, later Linville Falls Hotel, stands a rough timber-sided shed, the community's first real post office.] T. Earl Franklin's grandfather was usually the mail carrier then. He made one trip each week and brought mail for the whole community by horseback. When Uncle Sam was revising the postal routes in 1957, the outgoing postmistress, Miss Eula Penland, begged the inspector to leave this office at Linville Falls and not put the people here on a route from Newland [Avery County seat]. He promised to do so and respected her wish.

Following is a list of the early mail carriers in the area: Theodore Franklin had a contract to carry the mail from Morganton to Altamont, it being the first route in 1890. During this term he lodged in the home of Henry Wiseman at Altamont every other night. His son, Paul, carried the mail on this same route. James Franklin had the contract to carry the mail from Montezuma to Linville Falls. The mail came to Montezuma on a narrow-gauge railroad from Johnson City, Tennessee [the East Tennessee and Western Carolina Railroad, known popularly as "Tweetsie"]. That route was eventually changed from Montezuma to Pineola. The mail carriers had no certain way to go and went by different trails. Henry Franklin carried the mail also. Robert (Bob) Franklin drove a surrey and carried tourists to and from Linville Falls and other places. James Franklin carried the mail to and from Ashford over the Winding Stairs Road [near-present day Highway 221, running south from Linville Falls four miles to the Linville Caverns and North Cove]. He had little individual mail bags strung over his arm and hung them on their respective posts because there were no mailboxes. Potter Brown and George Wadkins paid for their mail to be delivered. Potter Brown paid fifty cents each month, and Mr. Wadkins paid one dollar.

Occasionally, a mail carrier was the recipient of a little joke, such as the one time Henry Franklin was passing by a house on the first day of April. He spied a letter lying in the middle of the road. Apparently he presumed he had lost it the previous day. He got off his horse and picked it up, and seeing that the letter was addressed to him, he opened it and read, "April Fool."

The first Sunday school in the community was held in a vacant log house in the late '90s. This log house has since been torn down. In 1900 a one-room school-house was built, which served for both school and church, thus paving the way for education and religion. Will Wiseman, a Baptist minister, was one of the very first to serve in the old schoolhouse. Afterward, Rev. Clapp, a Presbyterian, served. Then Rev. Delph, a Methodist, served. A few years later the building was enlarged a little and Rev. C. McCoy Franklin, a Presbyterian, preached some there.

The village is situated on the corner of three counties. Therefore, some folks blazed a trail through the woods and walked through three counties in order to obtain an education and to listen to a minister pour out his soul.

As time rolled by, McCoy Franklin came down from the Crossnore Chapel and started the ball rolling to raise funds toward the building of a much needed church. In order to the get project started, folks from all around donated money and some signed up to do so many days of work to aid in the construction of the building. F.W. Bicknell operated a saw mill at the time [upstream from the falls] and furnished lumber at cost for the project. He allowed all who would to donate time and labor of sawing material for the church. A group of five men, F.W. Bicknell, J.M. Franklin, Bob Franklin, Rom Franklin, and McCoy Franklin got together and started work on it. The building was completed in 1919.

The property for the church was donated by Henry Lewis Smith, President of Davidson College. The articles of incorporation and the by-laws were formed and passed in 1920. The first board of directors were Mrs. Stella Dellinger, Miss Eula Penland, Mrs. Lottie Burleson, J.M. Franklin, R.C. Franklin, and F.W. Bicknell. Plans were completed, building site selected, and work on the site began in 1920. Arthur Dellinger furnished the tree bark for it.

The church was destroyed by fire in 1961 and the present church was built in its place. In August, 1971, the mortgage for the new church was paid in full and Rev. C. McCoy Franklin, fifty years after building the first church, dedicated the present building. The church is now nondenominational. People of various denominations attend services here and worship together. Also, ministers from various denominations serve in the Linville Falls Community Church. [Until 2013, Dr. Lawrence Bond of Appalachian State University in Boone, North Carolina, held services in the Falls church. Fluent in Latin, Greek and Hebrew, Dr. Bond is best known academically for his study of the late medieval Italian mystic Nicholas of Cusa and was head of the Cusanus Society. To churchgoers, his words and example will long last in memory, and a new meeting hall wing has been added to the distinctive red church in his name. Just north of village center on U.S. 221 lies the lawn of Bond Park with its grand abstract iron sculpture known as *Pirouette,* created by Falls iron artist Bill Brown. Today (2016) services are conducted by a former Vietnam War chaplain, Kenny Hartman.]

Once our Sunday school had a picnic on a nice green grassy spot above the waterfall. That was a great day of excitement, for things happened to make us both laugh and cry. Dinner was placed on white linen tablecloths, which were spread end to end on the grass. That was the old-time way of having a picnic, as there were no tables and benches like we have in these modern times. It was spoken of as "dinner on the ground." There were no push button water fountains to drink from, no paper cups [a reference to facilities installed at the Falls visitor center by the National Park Service]. We searched for an open spring and drank from cupped-up laurel leaves. When dinner was over the crowd took a stroll around the bluff, sightseeing. This was during the day of hobble skirts. One woman in the crowd wore one and for that reason could not cross over the rail fence. Not wanting to be left alone, she sat on the fence, turned around, held both feet up and rolled over it [i.e., exposing her "bloomers"]. Imagine the laughter that broke out. Immediately after this, a small boy got into a bees' nest and was badly stung. This was when the crying was done.

Later in the day, we went down on the big rocks at the water's edge and took pictures. There, we spied a boat. A couple of men entered it and collected a group of children for a joy ride between the upper and the lower waterfalls. When they were well out toward the middle of the river, the boat sprang a leak. Water was entering it so fast that the man who was chaperoning the children had to work hard and fast dipping out the water with an old bucket which happened to be in the boat. During this episode the mothers who were looking on let out screams loud and shrill.

The beautiful cascades have been the scene of many happy days. When in our youth, my sister and I gathered slick chips from the water's edge, below the lower falls. We wrote dates on them and kept them for souvenirs.

Another episode of interest was when a wedding was performed on the hill in the open air where the bride and groom could see the waterfall. They stood by a thicket of blooming rhododendron which served as a perfect setting for the occasion. The groom wanted to marry at Niagara Falls, but since he was in service he could not get away from the base long enough, so they came to Linville Falls for the wedding. Their mothers came from Missouri to be present for the occasion. Dr. Gordon performed the ceremony.

Another interesting wedding took place under a big oak tree which stood at the corner of the three counties. They were supposed to be married in Mitchell County at that time and they didn't know just where to stand. Miss Clara Penland placed them in the proper place. The groom was Brack Wiseman and the bride was Miss Lily Knoblett. Brack had to run away from his mother to get married. He lost the license on the way and had to go back to look for it. Rom Franklin's little boy found it. The preacher, Uncle Billie Mace, forgot his glasses and performed the ceremony from memory.

The church and school were closely woven. Prior to the building of the schoolhouse in 1900, school was held for one term in John Wiseman's store and was taught by Miss Willimena Penland. She was the sister of Stokes Penland, who operated the famous Penland House [later, Linville Falls Hotel, still standing on Highway 183 across from the site of the former Hyams House].

Following is an incomplete list of teachers covering a span of 25 years, upon which time, approximately 1925, the school was consolidated with Crossnore School under the guidance of Mrs. Mary M. Sloop [see *Miracle in the Hills* by Mary T. Martin Sloop, MD, and Legette Blythe, 1953]: Miss Willimena Penland, Miss Florence Peck, Stokes Penland, Jefferson Hyams, Sam McKinney, Miss Lucy Laxton, Miss Mary Gillam, Miss Ulalia McClelland, Miss Mary Ann Justice, Miss Lila Stroman, Miss Mary Francis Angel, Miss Dovie McKinney, Earl Sick, Miss Alice Fox, Miss Libby Clontz, Claude Franklin, Mrs. Jessie V. Bicknell, Miss Louise Brown, Miss Beatrice McKinney, Miss Mary Ann Miller, Miss Lois Cromwell, Miss Lula Murray, and Mrs. F. Green. Mrs. Green taught subscription schools.

The first free school consisted of children from three counties, once Burke, Mitchell, and McDowell. Those from Burke County paid more money per pupil than the others, and when they became aroused about something the Burke children would throw it up to the others that they were paying more money.

How well I remember when my mother, Mrs. F. Green, taught school at Linville Falls. During a heavy snow she wore her ankle-length waterproof skirt and walked ahead of us in order to make a path through the knee-deep snow for us to follow.

There was a little girl in the neighborhood by the name of Belle. Being the youngest child in a large family, she received a pet name, "Bellie." Every member of her family always called her "Little Bellie." Little Bellie's sister and brother were in the habit of walking home from school with us in the afternoon and partaking of our after-school lunch. They refused to eat with us in the kitchen. They took their portions out behind the house where they could watch the wiggletails in the barrel of rainwater under the corner eaves while they ate.

The village has had thirty-two storekeepers in the past. Jeff Hyams was the first one. Prior to that, folks had to walk to Altamont, a distance of three miles, for their commodities. They crossed the [Linville] river on foot-logs or forded it. Sam McKinney and John Wiseman were the next to put up a store. In 1923, R.D. (Bob) Franklin put a store in where the Texaco station is now and had a restaurant in the side road. [The gas station has become once again a store and eatery with the opening of Linville Falls General and Hunt Brothers Pizza in 2015 by Martha Piercy.] Claude Franklin put up a building next to Bob's place and kept a restaurant.

Theodore Franklin built the first boarding house and later sold it to Stokes Penland. It has remained the Penland House [until becoming the Linville Falls Hotel]. At that time the occupants carried their water from a spring down at the foot of a hill. Later Mr. Penland dug a well near the house, which served as a reservoir after they got electric power established. [The well practically adjoins the hotel foundations; from the second story, with its eight rooms and outdoor balcony, a bucket rope runs through a trapdoor in the floor to the well for the upstairs guests' convenience.] They paid thirteen to fifteen dollars a year for Delco lights. Later, they paid five hundred dollars to get a light system installed. They had the first telephone in the village as well as the first radio. People came from miles around just to hear the radio. Mr. and Mrs. Jackson owned the first television set, which was given to them for a present. [Delco-Lights was an electrical power system for rural areas introduced by Charles Kettering in 1916 and produced at his factory in Dayton, Ohio.]

Later, other well-known boarding houses were built and operated. Henry and Robert (Bob) Franklin, brothers, kept boarders for forty-eight years. They were both famous for serving "Ham, a specialty." Bob Franklin is the only surviving male pioneer at this time (1975). Miss Clara Penland is the only lady pioneer left.

At one time, Ken Franklin operated a small cannery by the roadside in the village and canned food for the residents.

In the latter part of the 1880, the Ritter Lumber Company of Pineola constructed a railroad from Pineola to near the cascades of Linville Falls and erected a band mill lumber plant. After the lumber company had finished using the line, the Niagara Power and Light Company bought up a lot of the land in anticipation of putting in a power dam. It never did, however. [In fact, the preliminary foundation work for a hydroelectric plant at the falls was swept away in the great flood of 1916.]

The Franklins were the first permanent settlers here. John and Samuel Franklin exercised their rights to the Revolutionary War veterans' land grants in the Linville Falls area, which accounted for their emigration here.

David Franklin built several log cabins on his farm. He hewed and shaped the twenty-inch-wide logs from white pine, using a broad axe with a foot-wide blade. One of these particular log cabins still exists. It is the summer home of Mrs. Pauline Spoffard of Florida. The cabin was disassembled and moved to its present location by James P. Dodge, Sr. and Rom Franklin. [A Franklin cabin still exists, dovetail joints, outhouse, shutters and all, just north of the village center on Highway 221, off the triangular Bond Park with the iron abstract *Pirouette* sculpture.]

One of the first old log houses is where Samuel Franklin lived. Samuel was a grand-nephew of Benjamin Franklin and was the great-grandfather of the Rev. William Colbert (Uncle Bob) Franklin at Altamont.

Another of the early houses is where Major and Mrs. Harwell Davis lived until they recently sold it to Mr. and Mrs. Hayden Roberts, who occupied it during the summer months. It was first owned by Rich Carpenter. The house was moved from its original site to its present location and remodeled. Captain Newman lived in it and had a fireplace built. R.D. (Bob) Franklin hauled rocks from the highway in a Model-T truck for building the chimney. Incidentally, Captain Newman used to show old silent moving pictures in the schoolhouse.

The Ezra Mace log house has also been remodeled. Mr. and Mrs. J.L. Maness now own and occupy it. Unfortunately, a number of other log houses have passed into oblivion.

The Albert J. (Uncle Bert) Franklin house has been removed and remodeled. Uncle Bert was one of the pioneers. His grandson, Albert D. Franklin, Sr., owns this house now. [This grand old white frame, two-story home sits on a rise overlooking U.S. 221 and upon its picturesque Christmas tree farm and stone huts in a perfectly "alpine" evergreen setting, in this "Shrubbery Capitol of the World."]

The first house for summer residents was built in 1911 by Jake Haltiwanger from Greenwood, South Carolina. The following year, James Dodge built a summer house and several others followed later.

In 1910, Dr. F. Green moved in and served the people far and wide. He was the only medical doctor Linville Falls ever had. He was a good and faithful physician in the horse-and-buggy days. And his policy was: "Let the knife be the last chance."

The village children lived a happy-go-lucky life. They lived next to nature and as a result were quite healthy. They participated in various games out in the open air and these gave them plenty of spunk. The parents held to the old idea that "it took just so much dirt to make kids healthy." It seemed to work in those days, for they made mud pies, jumped into deep beds of fallen leaves that completely covered them up, turned summersaults, skinned cats, jumped ropes, made sand dunes, waded the river, threw snowballs, and otherwise did just about everything that could be thought of, even to riding bareback on a horse. One little eight-year-old girl rode a runaway horse. He ran at least half a mile, jumped a rail fence into the barnyard, and went into his stall in the barn without stopping. The little girl stayed on his till the very last.

The older set of young folks had different resources for pleasure. Some of the young men indulged in cockfighting and bet fifty cents on the winning rooster. They had various ways of having fun, but they all went to church on Sunday.

Those are by-gone days. It is all different now. More buildings and places of business have entered the scene. New stores, restaurants, motels, gift shops and many fine homes have blossomed. There are campgrounds, picnic grounds, and everything that goes into the making of up-to-date living [save for cell phone reception and high-speed Internet].

One nice development worthy of special mention is "Chestnut Heights," a cozy nick [niche?] in the woods with a number of cottages for rent. It is owned by Dr. Charles Stockard. [In 1923, Dr. Stockard and Albert D. Franklin incorporated the Chestnut Heights residential community, which went bust in the Depression of 1929. Franklin had advanced the land and the doctor the startup capital for the venture. Hundreds of lots were laid out and never built on. For years, Stockard rented little red gingerbread cabins along Laurel Lane off 221. In 2013, six acres of this wild ravine were purchased by Ms. Dorothy Watson of Atlanta, Georgia, to be set aside as a National Wildlife Foundation Certified Wildlife Refuge. Chill, clear spring water in Chestnut Heights Park joins with nearby creek systems to form the north fork of the Catawba River, snaking down beside 221 to the Linville Caverns and the blind fish.]

THE WINDING STAIRS. Come with me, dear reader, and let us take a return trip to the past over the Winding Stairs [near present-day U.S. 221, the climb from the English Farm in the Carolina Piedmont to the crest of the Blue Ridge in Linville Falls].

The Winding Stairs was the first route between Linville Falls and Ashford, North Carolina, and in order to get the grade, about half this road zigzagged back and forth down the mountain; its shape resembling a stairway, it got the name "Winding Stairs." A bold stream of water constantly flowed over the stony roadbed almost the full length of the winding part [north fork of the Catawba River]. The Linville Falls depot on the C.C.&O. Railroad was at the lower end of the route, while the post office at the same place was named Ashford, North Carolina. In the early days, tourists coming to see the cascades at Linville Falls got off at the station, expecting to see a wonderful site then and there because of the name of the depot. When they discovered that what they were looking for was seven miles further up on the mountain, it caused so much confusion and disappointment that the name of the depot was changed from Linville Falls to Ashford, the same as that of the post office.

In those days the United States mail was transported back and forth over this route in a hack drawn by two horses. The same vehicle was used to carry passengers to and from the depot. Sometimes, during rough weather, the mail got through only once a week, and sometimes, on rare occasions, only once a month because of so much ice and snow along the way. At times it was carried on horseback. Such a time was called two-shirt weather. Mail carriers had a rough life in those days. I recall a time in the early teens when I saw a man enter the post at another post office with the mail on horseback. It was a cold, snowy, blustery time and he had taken a drink of whisky to "keep warm," as he thought. Instead of keeping warm he had keeled over on the horse's back, was unconscious and nearly frozen. The wise and faithful horse automatically carried him to his regular stopping place in front of the post office. This happened on a different pioneer trail.

If the Winding Stairs could talk, I am sure it could unfold many interesting stories of the past. Once, somewhere along the way, there was a tiny shack that acquired the name, "Buckeye Hotel," probably because of its Tom Thumb size. Travelers tarried here to rest, not in the shack, but on the spot. Further down the road was a place where two people camped. It was reported that a couple of writers lodged at this place and wrote a book. There was also a spot along the way called "Lovers Lane."

In days of yore, young men sometimes walked down the road, across the creek, to visit fair maidens once a week. It was told of one handsome gentleman that while visiting in the home of his girlfriend, her mother asked him: "Did your mother raise any poultry this year?" He replied, "I think she planted some, but the chickens scratched it up."

When I was a young girl I traveled this interesting road to the depot to catch a train for Morganton to visit with some friends. I have a vivid memory of some things that occurred on the way down (and it really was down much of the way). I recall smelling sweet-scented wild flowers while passing through the wilderness of this terrain, and just as I was drawing a deep breath and feeling so light and gay, I got a whiff of odor from a different source. It was an entirely different kind of perfume carried by the wayward wind. There were various kinds of bushytails in the forest. Some were nice and allowed us to pass through their domain unnoticed. I learned that creatures in the wild have different kinds of dispositions—the same as human beings do. Some are kind and gentle and tend to their own business, while others seem to enjoy hurting those of a different nature. When we sum it all up, we come to the conclusion that it takes both, good and bad, to make the world go round. After all, human beings possess a kind of animal nature within, and when this is allowed to dominate we can become as cruel as the untamed beasts of the wilderness.

When we got away from the rank smell that hung in the air and could once again inhale pure, clear air and enjoy seeing the pretty birds flitting from branch to branch, we bade adieu to the Winding Stairs and entered open range at the head of North Cove, where we saw tree-fringed homesteads and huge farms with livestock grazing. At one point we saw a long whiskered billy goat standing with his front feet propped upon a stump while chewing his cud. It brought back haunted memories of days gone by because he resembled old Grandad chewing his homespun in the shade of an old apple tree. Someone remarked, "Does that billy goat give milk?"

All this happened many years ago. Now the old Winding Stairs has disappeared and we have in its stead a modern hard-top highway, bypassing the old pioneer trail and being traveled by all kinds of vehicles. Since the great change took place, many tourists come from afar to see the cascades and other attractions. On the way up the mountain from Ashford, on Highway 221, they can stop by the wayside and visit the famous Linville Caverns.

Let us take a brief pause and concentrate on another attraction, "Wiseman's View." This is a lookout point from Old Highway 105 [the Kistler Memorial Highway, part of North Carolina Scenic Byway 49] on Linville Mountain, which has been turned into a government [U.S. Forest Service] project for the benefit of the tourists who come to view the spectacular scenery of the Linville Gorge. From here one can look directly across the gorge to see Table Rock and Hawksbill [on one's left], and also the mysterious Brown Mountain Lights, which caused much controversy and speculation a few years ago. From here, one can stand at one of several rock balconies and gaze with awe and wonderment down over the rugged cliffs into the deep chasm and behold the breathtaking scenery that Old Mother Nature has wrought. This is a regular campsite for boy scouts and many other groups of people with varying branches of interest. Many thrilling adventures have been experienced in this great mountain terrain where sunshine and shadows meet.

Another attraction not far from Wiseman's View is a ridge named Dogback Ridge. There is a marsh beside the trail where there is no water flowing yet where reeds such as cattails can be found growing. [Springs, creeks and even ponds on the gorge rim run low or dry up in drought weather.]

Gone are the days of those old pioneer trails. And along with them some old customs have gone too. Customs such as old-fashioned neighborly get-togethers for the purpose of house raisings, log rollings, husking bees, apple peelings, molasses boilings, quilting parties and the like—but hospitality still flourishes in another way. Customs change with the times. The great change here came with the modern highways and when automobiles came on the scene.

Much enthusiasm flourishes among the many tourists who visit this place to see the mountains high and the valleys low. Some have purchased land at Linville Falls and have built homes and have settled down to stay. Some of these new inhabitants hail from as far south as Florida and as far north as Canada. I joined the rank and now I own a beautiful little nest here.

We have just been down over the Winding Stairs and back up over Highway 221. Now I hasten me home to my own retreat. It is a place, by the way, where two brooks meet. I named it "Twin-Brooks." Here, I relax at sundown and watch the jolly fellow take his last peek through my window for the day, leaving a brilliant halo in his wake over the horizon while the shadows lengthen. Then I look out my front window, across the lawn at my fish pond where the hungry bass leap. I look again to my left at the handy picnic area where I often go for a drink of cold well water, after which I settle down for the night, give thanks to the Maker and begin day-dreaming while I listen to the hoot owls and other night creatures. A whippoorwill wakens me in the morning and it is the beginning of a new day.

J. Alex Mull made this atmospheric study of Hawksbill Mountain from Wiseman's View. The tree in the foreground is the Table Mountain Pine, a fire-adapted species that needs intense heat for its cones to unfold. *From the editor's archive.*

J. Alex Mull offers a closer view of the Sitting Bear with a woman standing at its base, lending a sense of scale to the rock. *Photograph from the editor's archive.*

Table Rock is famous for the different faces it presents to viewers around it. This undated, anonymous picture includes the Table Mountain Pine for effect. *Photograph from the editor's archive.*

George Masa, early activist for the Smokey Mountains National Park and the Appalachian Trail, was an Asheville photographer who visited the Gorge sometime in the 1940s to take this view of Hawksbill (*left*) and Table Rock (*right*). Friends recalled his penchant for drawing sprigs of foliage into the frame to enhance his views. *Photo courtesy of Pack Library, Asheville, North Carolina.*

To the right of the Hawksbill crest in this George Masa view, the long, level ridge of Brown Mountain appears, source of the fabled and mysterious lights that still intrigue investigators. *Photo courtesy of Pack Library, Asheville, North Carolina.*

Douglas C-47 D "Skytrain." The twin-engine C-47 D is similar to the one that crashed into Gingercake Mountain on a foggy afternoon on May 15, 1943. *U.S. Air Force Museum.*

View of Table Rock from Wiseman's View. George Masa catches a trio of hikers on the Gorge's western rim, including in this shot the Table Mountain Pine. *Photo courtesy of Pack Library, Asheville, North Carolina.*

Bo Franklin squats with his bear dogs to the right in this undated picture supplied by LeRoy Rose of Jonas Ridge. The other hunters are members of the Barrier family. *Photo courtesy of LeRoy Rose.*

A National Park Service photographer captured this view of the Falls from the edge of the Plunge Basin around the time the Blue Ridge Parkway acquired the scenic attraction in 1953. *From the editor's archive.*

Left: In this National Park Service view captured around 1951, the Linville gathers force as it narrows, prior to its ninety-foot plunge through the two stages of the falls. *From the editor's archive.*

Below: *The Life of a Hunter, or A Tight Fix*, an 1861 Currier & Ives print, depicts a woods encounter remarkably similar to J. Alex Mull's account of "Dan the Bear Man." *From the editor's archive.*

Outward Bound Anakiwa Crew poses with instructor Dick Erickson (*far right*) on a drizzly day. On a lanyard, each crew member carries a compass, a whistle and a steel container for wooden strike-anywhere matches. *Photo courtesy of the North Carolina Outward Bound School, Asheville, North Carolina.*

"Let's drift south over Linville Gorge." Hugh Morton took this aerial view of the gorge in July 1955. On the right runs Jonas Ridge with its geologic features, Shortoff, Table Rock and Hawksbill. Also shown is Gingercake Mountain. In the distance lies Grandfather Mountain. *From the High Morton Collection of the Wilson Library at the University of North Carolina at Chapel Hill.*

Cato lounging north of Conley Cove. Brad Sanzenbacher's image of Dr. Cato Holler at ease on the Linville shows how eons of water flow has sculpted the riverbed into fantastic shapes. *Photo courtesy of Brad Sanzenbacher.*

The Hollifield Farm in snow with the Gorge's twin sentinels on the horizon. This is a National Park Service view taken from Avery County. *Courtesy of Blue Ridge Parkway archives, Asheville, North Carolina.*

The Grandfather Ranger District's fire-spotter tower greeted hikers at the summit of Table Rock until the structure was removed in the 1970s. *From the district headquarters office in Nebo, NC.*

TRAILS
ERWINS VIEW CHIMNEY &
GRAND VIEW OF FALLS AND GORGE
GRAND VIEW
ERWINS VIEW
CHIMNEY VIEW

Hugh Morton had his pilot buzz the Sitting Bear Rock for this unusual view of the stacked rocks in the northeastern area of the wilderness. *From the Hugh Morton Collection, Wilson Library, at the University of North Carolina at Chapel Hill.*

Above: Gateway to the Falls as a commercial attraction owned by the Hossfeld family; a National Park Service photographer took this shot around 1951, when the Falls were added to the Blue Ridge Parkway. *From the Blue Ridge Parkway archives, Asheville, North Carolina.*

Opposite, top: Rustic hand-carved signs directed tourists along the Falls's commercial attraction in the 1950s, before parkway acquisition. *From the Blue Ridge Parkway archives, Asheville, North Carolina.*

Opposite, bottom: Wiseman's View faces the gap between Hawksbill and Table Rock; to the right of the seated viewer, the North Carolina Wall and Shortoff Mountain dominate the Jonas Ridge on Linville's eastern side. *Undated Park Service photograph from the Blue Ridge Parkway archives, Asheville, North Carolina.*

The U.S. Forest Service captured this aerial view of Table Rock with sections of Lake James visible in the distance. *From the Grandfather Ranger District office in Nebo, North Carolina.*

This U.S. Forest Service aerial shot from mid-gorge captures the bluffs of Shortoff high above Lake James. *From the Grandfather Ranger District office in Nebo, North Carolina.*

D.R. Beeson Sr. made this early morning gorge view south from Table Rock as mist shrouded the Chimneys and Camel, the NC Wall and Shortoff. *Photo courtesy of the Archives of Appalachia, East Tennessee State University, Johnson City, Tennessee.*

James A. Goforth's detailed study of the beak of Hawksbill fills the foreground as the profile of Grandfather Mountain defines the horizon. *From the Archives of Appalachia Collection at East Tennessee State University, Johnson City, North Carolina.*

Above: Bayard Wooten made numerous studies of rural life in the Appalachians but turned her lens here on Table Rock with the inevitable Table Mountain Pine balancing her composition. *Photograph courtesy of the North Carolina Collection, Wilson Library, University of North Carolina at Chapel Hill.*

Left: Brad Sanzenbacher of Greensboro, North Carolina, caught Gorge legend Bob Underwood ensconced in a colossal river stone. Active in the wilderness since the mid-1960s, Underwood designed and cut the original Rockjock Trail. *Photo courtesy of Brad Sanzenbacher.*

A U.S. Forest Service crew in the 1960s lays out the original Table Rock summit trail, which has since been rerouted. Note the metal helmets. *Photo courtesy of the Grandfather Ranger District office in Nebo, North Carolina.*

19

"LINVILLE GORGE LEGENDS"

Maude Minish Sutton was a Caldwell County woman who made records of the tales and customs of the mountain folk, publishing them in various North Carolina newspapers in the mid-1920s. Her informant for the Gorge legends was Stokes Penland, proprietor of the Penland Hotel, located east of Linville Falls village center on Highway 183.

A great many real estate transfers have been made in Western North Carolina in the last two years [1924–25]. Developments, divisions, and subdivisions have been the order of the day. Some fortunes have been made, others have been lost, and thrilling stories are told of the land boom. None of these recent transactions, however, has the interest that the early deals in real estate made near the Linville Gorge have. The stories of these transfers were told to a party of campers on a hilltop near the gorge one evening. The storyteller was an old man who had lived within hearing of the Linville Falls, where the river enters the gorge, for 65 years. He was steeped in the lore of this land of romance. He knew the mountains in all their changing moods, yet never took them for granted. He knew the folk of the hills, loved and understood them, and drew shrewd conclusions about life information obtained from his keen observation of his neighbors.

The first of these stories belongs to the period just after the Revolution, when Indians, frontiersmen, and wild animals struggle for possession of the two beautiful valleys of the Linville and Toe Rivers.

"They wa'n't much money to change hands in these here deals," began our storyteller, "thar's things that's wuth more than money though. Men have allus been willing to give more fur live [*sic*] and family pride than they have fur money. Then money didn't have much value to the folks up in here back in them days. They couldn't buy nothin' with it. A deer skin went a dang sight furder in a trade than money. You had to go down the Windin' Stair trail, or 'cross Jonas Ridge, to git where you could buy anything with your money, and you could set right down and make your deerskin into leggings or even shoes. Why a good wife was wuth enough more to a man then than a farm was."

"Has that time passed?" I asked, "has not a good wife still some value?"

"Women ain't wuth nigh as much to a man as they onct was," replied our storyteller, who hunted, fished, and yarned to the tourists, while his capable wife earned the family living.

"They used to weave cloth, tan leather, tend the craps [*sic*] and do purt nigh anything. I don't know whether the woman I'm a-tellin' you about was much account or not; but she must to 'a' been a powerful purty thing. My grandsir told me that his paw said she was by far the purtiest woman he ever saw, when he was a young man, and she was way 'a' past 50 then. She was big folks down the country, too."

"Begin at the first and tell us all about her," we begged, and the old man told us this tale of two Revolutionary War heroes.

"You know that purty little valley where Potter Brown's house is?" he asked.

The valley in question is the prettiest home site on the Linville River. It is a glen that bisects two mountains, which shelter it from the cold winter winds that sweep up the river. A clear rocky creek runs through its center. It has a grove of beautiful big trees and is covered with a dense carpet of grass. The sides of the bordering mountains with their heavy growth of laurel, rhododendron, azalea, and dogwood are a riot of color in the spring and fall. Trilliums, tiger lilies, lady's slippers, violets, and every other variety of flowers grow in wild profusion in the cove at the head of the creek; while the charming home that is in the valley now is the scene of the most gracious hospitality imaginable.

"Well, that there little valley and the river bottoms below it make up the first farm ever taken up by a white man on this side of the Blue Ridge."

I have made very little effort to verify the old man's story. I prefer to believe it, but cannot vouch for its truth. There are skeptics who doubt there ever was a

Face that launched a thousand ships
And burnt the topless towers of Ilium.

But there is no doubt that woman's beauty has ever been a great force, in legend at least.

A young man who had followed John Sevier down from the Watauga settlements in east Tennessee to King's Mountain and acquitted himself there with distinction, was making a leisurely trip homewards. He left his comrades at the Old Fields of Toe, where Newland now is, and turned down the Linville River by Crossnore. When he came to the little stream which bears his name, "Bill White Creek," he camped for the night. The stream was alive with rainbow trout [more likely, the native brook trout]. He caught some and cooked them over his campfire. The beauty and fertility of the little valley attracted the hardy frontiersman, and he decided that he had discovered a home. The utter loneliness of the place did not seem a drawback to him, for he had spent his life on the frontier. He staked out a farm of manorial dimensions, and, after a few month's stay there, he went to the nearest authorities to establish his claim to the land. Our storyteller was a bit vague as to the exact persons from whom young White obtained his grant for the land, but he was perfectly sure that the grant was issued by the Sovereign State of North Carolina and sealed with her Great Seal.

When the pioneer returned with this precious parchment he found his rude shelter inhabited by two interesting invaders. A pair of lovers from below the mountains, fleeing from the wrath of the woman's husband, had taken possession of his pine pole cabin.

"They was right young, and they was big folks down the country," our narrator assured us. "They ain't no doubt about that. The rode two blooded hosses and led two others. The ones they led carried enough goods on their backs to set the couple up in fine style fur the backwoods in them days. The woman had some trinkets, too. I've seed a neck chain and a breast pin that was her'n. I hain't a-tellin' where I seed 'em, fur this here tale ain't quite old enough to be history; it's sorter scandal yit. You know the big difference between a grand rascal and a great hero is time."

The newcomers seemed a Godsend to Bill White. The man had followed McDowell down to King's Mountain, and the erstwhile comrades set to work clearing the land and carving a home out of the virgin wilderness. A woman was also an asset on the frontier, as our host had told us, and he let his keen imagination loose on the daily life of this North Carolina Helen.

"She must to 'a' had plenty to do, carin' fur two hard workin' men. Cookin' over a fire with a mite few skillets and cook pots, nothin' to cook but wild fruits and game; stretchin' out the few clothes they had brought, by patchin'; and plannin' how they'd make out when them was gone. It was a long, hard trip down to the settlement for supplies, and her man was afraid to go. Her husband and brothers would 'a' shot him on sight, so Bill had to make all the trips out fur supplies; and he had to play Mr. Shut-Mouth when he was down there. One time when he came back he brought her a present. It was a pair of store shoes. They'd been a-livin' up here five years then, and the poor things had been a-wearin' deerskin moccasins on her purty little feet. She was some proud of them shoes. That gift was the startin' point for trouble. You can't put two men and one woman, or for that matter, two women and one man, in a cove of the Blue Ridge, year in and year out, without the commencin' of one of those double-barreled love affairs. Tain't human natur. Bill was crazy in love with the woman, and she was with him. It was a hard place for the young folks. The young men had worked together till they was purt' nigh like brothers. But, for that matter, blood brothers has fought over a woman a-many of a time. This woman had run away from one man, and was ready to leave another, but she had had her 'nough of sneakin'. Her blood and raisin' had been again that all the time. They wasn't nuthin' low about Bill White, nuther. He couldn't bear to stab his friend in the back. Things stayed at this pass for a while, and then the sweethearts made up their minds to face the music and tell the other feller. They went at it with fear and tremblin', but he didn't seem to care much.

"'Looky here, Bill,' he says. 'I hain't the man to try to hold no woman ag'in her will. This here runnin' off has hurt my chances in life a right smart. Ef'n you git the gal and I leave here, whar'll I go and what'll I do? I can't go home without gittin' a bullet hole through me. I've give five years o' hard work to this place, but hit's in your name. The land is raley as much mine as hit is yours. How'll you trade?'

"Bill got that thar grant out and looked it over. He looked at his fine farm, then at the woman. He says:

'I'll transfer my title clear to you fur the woman.'

"That's the way the deal stood. Bill wrote out a transfer on the back o' the grant and rode 50 miles to get a witness to his signature. He headed the transfer 'Quit Claim Deed.'

"Then Bill and the woman got on two hosses and with nothin' but bare hands rode over to the Watauga settlements. Word come to them after a while that her husband was dead, so they married, and some of the finest folk over in thar is their descendants."

The other land transfer he told us of is a tragic story, a tale of youth and hot blood, and of calculating old age who traded on these qualities. This is the way the story sounded to me. The old philosopher of the hills had a kindlier viewpoint. His observation of life extended over a longer period than mine; it had been more extensive and it was abundantly seasoned with the milk of human kindness. As he told us the story, he made us see the characters and their reaction to the events in the light of his own seasoned, mellow wisdom.

"It's been a good while back," he began, "but there's a few folks a-livin' who remember some of the persons mixed up in this here land deal. So it's more scandal than history yit. Time'll come when these here tales I'm a-tellin' you won't be jest common talk; they'll be historical romances. This here trade was more like a war. Have you ever thought how much blood had been shed over land ownership? Hain't it a quare thing that when a thousand boys die over the border line between two countries, it's honorable war and they're heroes; when a dozen men kill each other over the boundary between two farms, it's a mountain feud, and books are wrote about it; but when a man dies, like the one in this tale, it's a murder?

"The fight proper wasn't ova the land. Fact is, nobody ever knowed exactly what it was over. A long time ago all the land on Toe River down to the Mitchell line belonged to a family of old-time aristocrats who lived down at the foot of the mountains. They hardly ever saw their big plantations up here, and what land was tilled at all was tilled by squatters, poor folk who took up a farm and build 'em a big house and made a scant livin' off'en the land. They never paid no rent and nobody never bothered them. The owners was free handed and free hearted like all old-time big folks. They didn't need the land, couldn't use it in fact, so they never begrudged these potlicker white folks their livin's. Some of these squatters was pretty rough. They lived powerful hard, and you know when folks live hard, they're mighty apt to act hard.

"In one of these little log cabins with a dirt floor there lived a family of girls, three of 'em, and I hate to try to tell you how purty they said them girls was. Strappin', black-eyed, red-cheeked mountain girls; they could sing and dance all night and do a man's work all the next day.

"Well, as the talk goes, they wasn't none too good. Have you eva noticed that the women in old tales are generally not exactly what they ort to be?"

With this shrewd observation upon the heroines of legend, our old storyteller plunged into his story.

There were two boys of very different race [*sic*] and training who had formed a close friendship. One, whom our storyteller called Willie, was the spoiled son of the owner of the vast estate he had told us of. The other, Walter, was the son of a mountain family who lived further down the Toe River.

"Walter's folks wasn't exactly poor folks and they was very fur from trash," said our historian. "In fact, they was a bunch of the proudest family this side the Ridge, and they was good livers fur them days. Of course they didn't have a host of blacks, and they didn't live like Willie's folks did.

"Like the most of the young blood of them days, and these too, fur that matter, these boys was wild. They did love likker and they would take a dram. When Willie wasn't down at Chapel Hill a-going to school, he was up here a-fishin' and huntin' with Walter. They was like David and Jonathan in the Bible. The tale goes that Willie had begged Walter to go down the country to college with him, but Walter pinted out how much more satisfaction was to be had ramblin' over the mountains with a dog and a gun. Willie was covetous of him for bein' so free.

"One Christmas Willie rode up to see Walter. Leastways, that was the word he give out to his home folks. They couldn't understand how he could give up the dances and big Christmas parties at home. Truth was, the summer before he had went right plumb hog wild over one o' them black-eyed gals in the pine-pole cabin up on his paw's plantation. His father was suspicious a little. He didn't like the trip nary a bit. He sent Willie's slave along with him. This slave was a fine old black man who had took care of the boy most all his life; he was as proud of his white folks and thought jest as much of the fine old name as his old marster did.

"Walter was a good deal leveler headed than Willie. He talked purty strong agin their goin' up to see the gals at this time. He knowed that they'd be a crowd of hillbillies takin' Christmas around thar, that they'd be drunk and jist nacherly honin' fur a disturbance. They wasn't any reason in Willie though. He was in love, he was twenty year old, and he'd brought the gal a Christmas present. I've seed that present many a time. It was a pair of cameo ear bobbies, brown stone, with a woman's head cut on 'em. Walter done all he could to break up the trip, but they wa'n't no use. Willie bantered him into goin' by sayin' he'd go by hisself ef'n Walter backed out.

"Christmas eve night they went over there. Uncle Sam, the body slave, went along. That was as brave a thing as he could have done since he wasn't any too popular with sober potlicker whites, and a drunken hillbilly wouldn't mind killing a negro, no more'n he would a hawg. Uncle Sam knowed this, and he'd promised his old marster to look after that boy and he done it.

"Well, the boys got purty good an' tight before they left Walter's. They was drinkin' good likker there. Before it had time to die in 'em, they loaded up on white lightnin' from up the creek. That mixture turned 'em both crazy as loons. They got to fightin', and the fust thing anybody knowed Willie had stabbed his friend to death and stompted his face in the dirt floor of that cabin. The old slave got the drunk boy out, somehow, and put him on his hoss and they rode a path 'cross the dividin' ridge and hit the Jonas Ridge trail fur home. Willie was plumb sobered up when he got thar. Him and the old slave together got the old gentleman told. It was the hardest lick the proud old feller ever got. The first time a stain had ever been on his fine name and this one a blood stain. His boy standing there in the old man's law office, like any criminal, confessin' to the murder of his best friend.

"The old man thought it all over.

"'I'll go up thar and see what I can do,' he says. 'Justice has got to be done, so far as it can be. You are my son, but you'll pay whatever is required.'

"Willie tuk it without a word. The old man left him a prisoner at home, with Uncle Sam ordered to look after him, and he got on his horse and rode up the ridge to Walter's home. I've thought about that trip a good deal. It was right smart of an undertakin' fur a man to ride up the mountains on an errand like that. He was in more danger than he'd ever been on the battlefield and he knowed it. He'd spent most of his life clos't enough to the mountains to know that in trouble of this kind 'one o' the name is good as the same' and that Walter's family would look on shootin' him as doin' plain justice.

"He got to the house purty soon after the buryin'. He found Walter's father settin' thar cleanin' up his old rifle and lookin' as hard as a rock. I reckin' his heart must to a-sunk in him. They say that he was the best hand pleadin' before a jury of any man in the state, and it must to a-been so. He never pled before when the prisoner at the bar was his own boy and the jury and judge a dead boy's father though.

"Accordin' to the way o' thinkin' then, a death like Walter's called fur more deaths. Nary one of them old men thought much about the state law. One of 'em was a good lawyer, but as far as he himself was concerned he was like Saint Paul: he lived above the law. So did the other old man. Nary one of them ever thought about lowdown things much less done one."

"But you just said Walter's father was cleaning his gun!" we said. "Did he not mean to kill Willie?"

"He sho' did," was the laconic reply. "Back in them days fusses was ginerally settled that way. The families involved tended to their own quarrels. It's a purty good way too. It beats these here jury trials the papers make so much of today. Sickens me to read how everything is drug out and aired before the world. It's a heap harder on the dead man than to let his murderer go.

"Nobody ever knowed what them two old men said in that trial. It lasted several hours, and they seemed to part respectin' each other, but, for the first time in the old lawyer's life, he rode away from a man's house without bein' asked to stay all night. It was the first time, too, that anybody ever rode out of that yard without bein' asked to break bread. Blood's thicker than water though, and they couldn't be no good feelin' there.

"Willie never did come back on this side. I ain't sure what become of him. About a month after the old man left, old Sam come back up here bringin' a deed to a monstrous tract of that mountain land. It was one o' these her 'fur value received and other considerations' deeds I reckin."

"Well, I am surely disappointed in that man!" exclaimed one of the listeners. "Accepting land in payment for his son's life."

"Yes, hit's likely you'd feel like that. Common sense and good judgment is powerful scarce articles," was the old man's scathing reply. "Ef'n a thousand boys had died over the ownership of that land, like as not you'd a been one of the first to praise the great statesman who started the fightin'. When one old man has the sense and judgment to see that takin' the land is the best thing he can do, under the hard circumstances, you condemn him."

"Your analogy is rather far-fetched, isn't it?" said the rebuked tourist.

"No, it hain't. Look at the thing calmly. Would shootin' one boy have brought back the other? Could the livin' boy have been drug through the dirt and mire of a criminal court without showin' the dead boy up too? Both of 'em was drunk, both of 'em was where they had no business to be. It was a happen-so which one of them got killed first. Willie could a-prived [*sic*] self-defense or insanity, ary one or both. Walter was the old man's look-to fur his old age. Would revenge a-fed and clothed him? The land done that. Willie had good sense when he was sober and it's likely this sobered him for life. Killin' his friend was plenty of punishment fur him. He carried the mark of Cain in his heart the rest of his life.

"Purt' nigh as much land changed hands in that deal as some of them little states in Europe 'ave been killin' men over fur a hundred years," continued the old man thoughtfully. "Depends on how many dies whether it's war er murder, don't it?"

Note: The quotation about Helen of Troy is from Christopher's Marlow's tragic play *Doctor Faustus*, scene xvii.

20

"BEA HENSLEY HAMMERS AN IRON CHINQUAPIN LEAF ON HIS ANVIL NEAR SPRUCE PINE AND COGITATES ON THE NATURE OF TWO BEAUTY SPOTS"

Jonathan Williams (1929–2008), Black Mountain College poet, essayist, photographer and publisher (Jargon Press), was a master of the found poem in the American idiom, mainly the mountain dialect he found in western North Carolina. Bea Hensley (1919–2013), Mitchell County blacksmith and National Heritage Fellowship Award winner, made art in iron at his forge in Spruce Pine. Punctatum is the Carolina rhododendron. The tulip tree is the yellow poplar (*Liriodendron tulipifera L.*), whose yellowy-green flower resembles the tulip.

in the Linville Gorge I
know this place

now it's a rock wall
you look up
it's covered in punktatum all
the way to Heaven

that's a
sight

•

up on Smoky
you ease up at daybust
and see the first
light in the tops of the tulip trees

now boys that just naturally
grinds and polishes
the soul
makes it
normal
again

I mean it's really
pretty!

21

LINVILLE GORGE IN THE 1950s

Feature articles on the Linville Gorge in the middle part of the twentieth century continued to equate a wilderness hike with a perilous trek into the unknown. Chester Davis's headline screams, "We Came Out Alive!" The anonymously published first article came from the April 23, 1955 issue of the *State* and records a feat "worth putting in the history books." It is followed by Davis's two articles from 1955 and 1959, appearing in the *Winston-Salem Journal and Sentinel.*

LINVILLE FALLS

This may be the year you'll decide to explore a pocket of the mountain country recently discovered by thousands of tourists. An impetus to discovery has been given by improvement of the Linville Falls area with easier access to it.

John. D. Rockefeller, Jr. donated the site of the falls and surrounding acreage to the government, and it is one of the high spots of a trip along the [Blue Ridge] Parkway. It may be reached also via N.C. 183 and U.S. 221. Here the river rushes over a 12-foot shelf of rock. Just below this, the water drops 90 feet over boulders into a large, clear pool.

At this point begins famous Linville Gorge, a deep gash walled in on one side by the Linville Mountain, on the other by Jonas Ridge and adjacent peaks. The gorge continues to Shortoff Mountain, a sheer precipice which is one of the odd sights of this area. Here the water slides on into Lake James.

The gorge has been declared a wild area, but a hiker's trail is being developed up its length—a distance of about 15 miles. Only the most hardy should try the entire trip.

One of the best views of the gorge is from Wiseman's View, reached via N.C. 105 from the town of Linville Falls. Good place for pictures, too, since from here you see the unusual formations of Table Rock, Hawksbill and Shortoff.

About the Gorge

You hear all kinds of stories about Linville Gorge—rattlesnakes, wildcats, bear, etc. One myth is the belief that only a few people have traversed the length of the gorge from the falls to Lake James.

T. Earl Franklin, judge of Burke County Criminal Court, says this is not true. At one time he operated the falls as a scenic attraction, and kept fairly good tab on the people who made the trip and he said that they totaled "a good number."

However, the trip was and still is tough, and takes a good man in training to do it. Judge Franklin says he started through once wearing a pair of army shoes with brand-new soles, and when he finished the soles both had holes through them and he couldn't walk for a week. He says he wouldn't try to go through now without training for a couple of months. You have to wade the river much of the way, because the canyon walls close right down on you.

Incidentally, Judge Franklin's great-grandfather, a nephew of Benjamin Franklin, once owned the falls and sold or traded the whole thing for a new suit of clothes.

Here's a feat worth putting in the history books. Have you ever been to Wiseman's View and looked down into the gorge from that precipice? Well, about 20 years ago Dr. Carl Mott of Asheville was in the gorge with R.C. Franklin of Linville Falls. They fished and camped for four days and one midnight Dr. Mott had an attack of acute appendicitis. Franklin hoisted him on his back and "carried" him out of the gorge to N.C. 105 right near Wiseman's View. The gorge is around 1,000 feet deep at this point, and the damnest "steep" deep you can imagine.

In the Mountains of North Carolina:...The Linville Gorge Country—Wildest and Grandest in the East

It was a rare day...a one-in-a-million day for the North Carolina mountains.

Up on the flanks of the Grandfather the air was crisp and its sparkle was not smudged by distance or by the haze which gives our great ranges, the Blue Ridge and the Smokies, their names.

High over the mountain, at 10,000 feet or so, a small plane wheeled in raven-like flight, now and then dipping its wings in an early morning salute to the sun-tipped peaks of the Grandfather.

Each time the wigs dipped, Hugh Morton's camera clicked, and Hugh added another shot—one more among thousands—to his collection.

To Hugh Morton the Grandfather is more than a majestic run of rock ridges and trailing timbered slopes. His toll road up the mountain and his mile-high swinging bridge are bread and butter to Hugh.

Capturing the mountain's moods on film is part of Hugh's work as a promoter of "Carolina's No. 1 Scenic Attraction." But there is more to it than that.

The mountain fascinates Hugh Morton and he lives in an endless race with light and shadow, always trying to put on film what the Grandfather is at all times and in all seasons.

He had gone aloft this particular morning to snap some air shots of the Grandfather reaching high to capture the first earth blossoms of the rising sun.

"We were well up over the Grandfather—at 10,500 feet or thereabouts," Hugh said later, "when I realized I could make out the smoke over Charlotte. I've been up over the mountain in a plane a number of times but I've never seen the air quite that clear. There just wasn't any haze."

That morning Hugh took a number of shots of the peaks of the Grandfather. Then he turned to the pilot and suggested, "Let's drift south over Linville Gorge and see what we can pick up there."

The picture on this page—one of the most remarkable shots ever made in the hazed runs of the Southern mountains—was the result of that flight.

Vertical Wilderness

The area in the picture is perhaps the roughest and grandest in all the mountains in Eastern America. It's formed by two spurs that fall away to the South of the Blue Ridge's main chain.

Jonas Ridge—with the cliffs of Shortoff, the jagged peaks Table Rock and Hawks Bill and the curious Sitting Bear Rock of Gingerbread [Gingercake] Mountain—forms the eastern bastion of Linville Gorge.

The softly created Linville Mountains pitch off in steep cliffs to wall the gorge on the west.

Between the two spurs the Linville River churns and twists around rock ledges and vast boulders on its roaring, white and green race to Lake James.

From the Linville Falls on down to Lake James—a distance of perhaps 20 miles—lies a rock-ridged, timber-quilted wilderness.

The gorge is easily accessible along its edges. In its core, however, it remains as untamed as it was at time's beginning. There are a few trails. That's all. And that is all there is to be because this land, now a part of the Pisgah Forest, has been set aside as a wilderness area.

The Linville country is not really well known to many North Carolinians, though it has more to offer more people than most of our mountain sections.

Weekend travelers will find the gorge cut precisely to fit their purposes.

How to Get There

You can, for example, leave Winston-Salem on Saturday morning (or afternoon, if you like) and drive to Morganton, a distance of about 100 miles [on U.S. Highway 70, in a pre–Interstate system era]. At Morganton you take State Highway 181 and travel up to the Blue Ridge Parkway on the flanks of Jonas Ridge.

If you like, you can stop along the way to visit Table Rock and Hawk's Bill.

There is an unpaved [now paved] road into a picnic area at the foot of Table Rock. From there you can follow a good foot trail up to the look-out tower on the top of Table Rock. It's a half hour hike.

Another unpaved—and rough—road leads into the base of Hawksbill. There's a trail up that mountain, too. It's a trail to delight the kids and one that makes the older folks aware of just how short they are in the wind.

But if you are primarily interested in a search for scenery, you probably would do just as well to bypass the Table Rock and Hawk's Bill trails. The views from both places are impressive and well worth seeing, but the overlooks along Jonas Ridge are not as breath-taking as those located across the gorge on the Linville Ridge.

Perhaps the best of all the overlooks is Wiseman's View. You reach it by continuing up Jonas Ridge to the Parkway and then traveling south to the village of Linville Falls. There you take to the left and follow Route 105 down the Linville Ridge to the overlook.

From Wiseman's View—and from other overlooks along the Linville Ridge—the gorge seems deeper, steeper and narrower. You sense the rugged character of this land that seems so softly carpeted in the sweeping green of heavy timber.

After visiting Wiseman's View, you would do best to turn back the way you come and visit the place where the Linville River plunges into the gorge. The falls are located on 105 just beyond the village.

The National Park Service, aided by Rockefeller money, has taken over the falls. There are foot trails—all of them easy walking and relatively short—through the area.

At the upper falls you see the Linville River swirl down a 12-foot ledge and then plunge in narrow green force through the gap that drops it 90 feet into the great pool below. From the Erwin and Chimney Lookout overlooks you get a full view of the Linville Falls.

After visiting the falls, you have the choice of returning home the way you came or turning back on the Parkway and visiting Grandfather Mountain, Blowing Rock and, if time permits, Boone with its "Horn in the West." That route, while it sounds long, won't run you much over 150 miles all the way back to Winston-Salem.

But remember this; the real thrills of the Linville wilderness area are reserved for those who travel beyond the reach of an automobile. The real character of that country is reserved for the hiker and the fishermen.

There are several trails that pitch down off Linville Ridge into the gorge.

The first of these—the Pine Gap Trail—takes off the ridge about two and one half miles below the falls. Going down that trail—and it is the gentlest of the lot [Bynum's Bluffs Trail, the next one southward, is much gentler than Pine Gap Trail]—is an experience in which walking gives way to a slipping, falling stumble. It's not really dangerous but it's hand-grabbing steep and no place for bones rendered brittle by age.

Once in the gorge, you can turn upstream and make your way slowly along the river towards the falls. There is a trail of sorts along the rock ledges and boulders that punctuate the stream bed. [Davis's upriver walk crosses the boundary dividing the U.S. Forest Service's wilderness area in the south from the National Park Service's Linville Falls Recreation Area in the north.]

The river wanders through a world set apart…a world where white water roars and echoes beneath cliffs hung in laurel and rhododendron…a world of extremes—the glare of white sun on naked rock and the green gloom of hemlock rooted in fern.

The muted growl of the water deepens as you wander up the staircase of the cascading river and come on the falls.

Seen from above, the Linville Falls are impressive. Seen from the floor of the gorge, those falls are majestic: a great gout of white water thundering down the face of a steep-walled rock amphitheater into the circular green pool below.

At the falls there is a trail—perhaps goat path is a better description—that staggers up to the lip of the gorge and to the tidy walks so carefully laid by the Park Service.

The trail is little more than a hand-hold-and-pray affair. But boys (teen-agers on up to optimistic middle-agers) and girls (of surprisingly varied ages) make it without difficulty.

For Fishermen

The truly tough trails—and the trails that tap the best of the Linville River fishing—lie farther down the Ridge. They lead into the wildlife refuge that is jointly managed by the state and federal governments.

The fishing (brown trout and small mouth bass) is generally good in the refuge. The prospects for overnight camping (you tote your bedding, food and whatever else you may need) are as fine as you will find anywhere in the mountains.

Still, trembling legs and rasping breath are quickly forgotten. And for no more investment than that you can visit a land where time is measured in the inches cut in bed rock by a river.

One Hike to Remember: We Braved the Gorge and Came Out Alive!

So you want to take a hike up the Linville Gorge from Lake James to Linville Falls?

Well, I can understand that. Up to a month or so ago I wanted to make that trip too. Since then I have made it. And, friend, what a bend that walk put in my point of view!

When Russell Brantley, Wake Forest College's director of publicity, first suggested such a jaunt, it struck me as a notably sensible notion. Russell's other recruits—Mark Reece, dean of students at Wake Forest, Irvin Grigg, Wake Forest photographer, and Jack Stark, a National Park Service Ranger—felt much the same way.

All of us had been in the gorge at least one time. Jack and I had fished the upper stretches and Irvin and Russ had gone down into the canyon just to get the feel of the place. From what we had seen—and that, as it turned out, was misleadingly little—we *knew* we could make the trip without difficulty.

Self-appointed "experts" on the area assured us that it was no more than 15 miles from Lake James to the Falls. Covering that distance should take no more than two and a half days and still leave time for fishing along the way. We laid our *harum scarum* plans on that basis.

At 11 a.m. on Sunday, June 7, the five of us shrugged on our backpacks, each pack weighing 30 to 35 pounds, and started up the dirt road which begins at high water on Lake James and wanders for five miles or so through Beech Bottoms to the foot of Shortoff Mountain.

An Auspicious Beginning

Despite the strain of the packs on neck and back muscles unaccustomed to loads much heavier than a hat, it was a pleasant walk. The road, suitable only for a Jeep, followed the river bank right to the base of Shortoff where, looking up stream, the two ridges—the Linville Ridge on the left and the Jonas Ridge on the right—pinch together to form the gorge.

These two ridges, rarely more than a mile air-line from crest to crest, rise in a great, rock-cliffed V above the white and green runs of the Linville River itself. The long and regular contour of the Linville Ridge—broken here and there by cap-stone cliffs which provide overlooks such as that at Wiseman's View—is quite different from jagged upheavals of Hawksbill (4,030 feet) and Table Rock (3,918 feet) which characterizes the Jonas Ridge. Both ridges, however, pitch down into the gorge at angles understandable only to goats.

In the V that lies between the two ridges—a canyon which at places, is more than 2,000 feet deep and which spurs at right angles off the main chain of the Blue Ridge—there is a 7,400-acre Wildlife Area administered by the National Forest Service and, near the falls, another 535 acres which belong to the National Park Service. This is the Linville Gorge Wilderness, one of the truly unspoiled sections of Eastern America. Because it is rugged beyond belief, it never has been logged. It is a place of rock and water and virgin timber which is visited quite often but rarely traveled for any distance.

The casual visitors, following trails that drop down from the two ridges into the gorge, make the long walk out of curiosity or, perhaps, to fish. They see a portion—rarely more than that—of the gorge that lies directly above and below the trails they travel.

The Linville Gorge, of course, has been walked from one end to the other. But that has not occurred as often as off-hand reports might lead you to believe. S.T. Henry, editor of the *Tri-County News* in Spruce Pine and a man who has made a close study this area, reports, for example:

> *So difficult and foreboding is the floor of the gorge that there is authentic record of very few men ever having traversed the gorge from its mouth to the vicinity of Linville Falls.*

This, however, our simple-minded little party did not know when we so confidently turned the shoulder of Shortoff Mountain that Sunday afternoon and made our way to a small tent camp where paratroopers and marines are schooled in the fine art—an art which includes catching and eating local snakes—of wilderness survival. The trail, such as it was, played out at this point. The soldiers we met at the camp—each one of them horrified that anyone would undertake a backpack hike except under threat of a general court martial, could tell us little or nothing of what lay ahead,

Then Came the Awakening

As a matter of fact, there was little enough to report that first afternoon. The mouth of the gorge is relatively easy to travel. In fact, we made such good time that, in the manner of greenies, we figured we had best slow down the pace else risk completing the trip a full day ahead of our allotted schedule. That afternoon we pitched camp early in what had once been a stream-side meadow and now was abandoned to the forest. That night it was steaks, with a warming dram of bourbon to sharpen the appetite. From there on out, however, it was dehydrated food and water and with only the water holding up in good supply. It was, with one or two exceptions, the last decent camp site we saw, too.

By noon on the second day we were well into the gorge and were awakened to the fact that our breezy little stroll was not going at all according to plan.

It was plain, for example, that those who spoke so glibly of the 15 miles from the lake to the falls were of an air-line route. By the river route—and that's the only route we had to follow—the innumerable goose-necks made it at least twice and, perhaps, three times that distance. My own guess is that, in terms of actual walking, the true distance is nearer 45 than 30 miles. I say this because, along with the twists in the stream itself, you climb and scramble at least two feet straight up and down for every one foot of progress you make.

By Monday night, our second night on the trail, we had reached an area where there was nothing flat excepting, perhaps, the occasional pools of the stream itself. Decent camp sites were all but nonexistent. Because the day had been rough, we spent that evening assuring ourselves that the worst was now behind and that by Tuesday night, right on schedule, we would reach the Falls.

Actually—as we learned in the early light of Tuesday—we had just reached the tough going. Both the upper and the lower ends of the Linville Gorge are relatively—and the word must be accepted with extreme caution—gentle to cross. The middle section, which includes the greater share of the total mileage, presents a seemingly endless series of baffling problems.

Time after time we came to places where cliffs on both sides pitched at right angles down to the stream. These rock walled water gates had no easy solution.

Sometimes we went into the timber—most of it really little more than rhododendron "hells" and laurel "slicks"—and, working painfully up and around the rocks, found our way back to the river above the cliffs. On the smaller cliffs this maneuver served nicely but there was one instance, when the cliff ran back from the stream and up the ridge, where we spent three hours getting back to the stream. When we finally made it, we discovered that we were less than 250 yards upriver from our starting point.

Some Precarious Passages

At other places we found rock ledges, some only two feet or so wide, across the face of the cliffs and were able to move by that precarious route. Snailing a backpack across these ledges, some of them rising a hundred feet or so above the river, is a spine-rattling experience. It is also an experience which teaches you the great value of a goodly length of stout rope.

The third solution was to work along the most promising side of the stream—a sometimes difficult trick because the river was swollen by heavy rains—and by fingering along the rock face of the cliff, wade up the pool. Invariably this mean floundering and paddling from one handhold to another.

There were no easy answers to these rock water gates. And all day Tuesday we came upon one after another. In places they were no more than a quarter of a mile or so apart. You covered the distance between them by scrambling over, under, and around a hell's litter of house-sized boulders. In so doing, we discovered that boulder jumping in wet boots is only a shade more desirable a sport than Russian roulette.

By Tuesday afternoon it was apparent that we had no chance of reaching the Falls before dark. There was no alternative but to spend a third night in the gorge and, by starting early, make another try for the Falls on Wednesday. Fortunately, we had food enough to carry us through this unexpected fourth day.

That day, although we were well past Wiseman's View on the left and the Table Rock and the Hawksbill on the right and, therefore, in the Upper Gorge, was a repetition of the day before. If anything—and this, perhaps, can be attributed to the fact that we were bone tired—the rock gates, with their cliff walls and gouts of white and swirling water, seemed more frequent and more difficult to pass.

Too Weary to Worry

At this stage we even ceased to become excited about snakes. On the trip we saw many snakes and the list included three big copperheads.

Our experience on this score tends to support the old woodsman's belief that when men are walking single file in snake country it's the second man that generally gets hit. In all three encounters with copperheads, the first man stepped within inches of the snake without seeing him. Fortunately, the second man didn't make the same mistake. At least one of the three, frightened as the first man stepped by, was coiled and waiting the next visitor.

On both Tuesday and Wednesday, we spent a good deal of time crawling across rock ledges located back in the timber and hundreds of feet above the river in our efforts to get past stream-side cliffs. These ledges, according to what we had been told, are favored places for rattlesnakes. However, we neither saw nor heard a rattler in the four days. In part, that may have been due to the fact that before crossing these places we were careful to make noise enough to warn any snakes of our approach.

I don't believe that the Linville Gorge is plagued with more snakes than you will find in any other really isolated and rocky section of the mountains. But, prior to this trip I had encountered just one copperhead in 15 years of ramming around such areas. On this trip I saw three. This would [break in text] even for a day's fishing, should carry a snake-bite kit in his pocket.

By mid-morning on Wednesday, however, we had ceased worrying about snakes, poison ivy (it grows in enormous patches among the river rocks) or much of anything else except how many more leaden steps it was to those elusive falls.

That's when we came on the two fishermen, the first human beings we had seen since leaving the Army survival camp four days before. Unlike so many of our voluntary advisors on this junket, the older of the two fishermen knew the gorge like the palm of his hand. He told us we were six to eight miles (river distance) from the Falls and that some of the roughest sections lay ahead. He said there was no chance of our reaching the Falls by night.

We were still cocky enough to disbelieve him. Fortunately, however, we did have sense enough to listen carefully to his instructions on how we could get out of the gorge if, by mid-afternoon, we were convinced the Falls were beyond our reach.

The Linville Gorge is curious in the fact that none of the trails which dip into this canyon from either of the two ridges can be spotted by a party traveling along the river's bed. You must know where the trails are to reach them and, even then, you don't come on the trails until you have climbed up into the timber well above the reach of the flood-driven scramble of boulders and logjams which litter the floor of the gorge itself.

A Side Stream Leads Out

For that reason, our fisherman friend did not attempt to tell us where we could find one of the well-used trails. Instead, he told us of a stream which poured down from the Linville Ridge some two-and-a-half miles upstream. "You walk up that stream-bed," he said. "There's a trace of a trail which was cut some years back to bring out the body of a drowned boy. You stick to that stream bed and you'll finally hit the Linville Gorge Trail. That's the best of all the trails entering the Gorge and it will lead you to Highway 105 that runs down the crest of the ridge from the village of Linville Falls."

We left the fishermen at 11:30 a.m., still confident we could reach the Falls by dusk. Four hours later, after climbing, floundering and paddling around cliffs that would baffle a goat, we came to the stream—Babel Tower Falls—that tumbled down the Linville Ridge in a white rush.

At this point we recognized that there was no possibility of reaching the Falls by night. Since we were completely out of food there was no choice—not that we seriously considered an alternative—but to start up this creek bed and hope that we hit the trail above.

For two hours we fought our way up the mossy rocks of Babel Tower Falls, scrambling for eight minutes and then gasping for three. (Or was it vice versa?) At the very end—at the place where the creek bed played out on the precipitous hillside and out legs played out completely—we hit the graded and maintained Linville Gorge Trail. By 6:30 on Wednesday evening—24 hours later than we planned and still five miles or so (river distance) short of Linville Falls—we were on Highway 105 and out of the gorge.

Since then—and with increasing optimism as time has worn away the sharper edges of our memories—we have asked ourselves, "Would you make the trip again?"

The answer—and it becomes more positive as pleasant memories replaced aching muscles—is "Yes, but…"

Yes, but on a schedule which allowed time to take it easy and, perhaps, to fish some of the lovely pools we passed along the way. This is an unbelievable beautiful area but it can not be fought if it is to be enjoyed.

Yes, but I would so schedule the trip to assure making it when the water was low. We hit the gorge when the Linville was running high. That fact compelled us to climb high and fight brush where, at a lower stage, the river could be waded without difficulty.

The Pleasant Remembrances

Yes, but on a second try I'd spend more time with natives who really know the area and nail down, as far as is possible, some of the tricks they use in by-passing the truly tough spots.

But there are things I would not change, too. Our party of five, although raised on a catch-as-catch-can basis (Russ recruited three Wake Forest men and two strangers) could not have geared together with less friction. Even when the going was the roughest, and fatigue had muscles and nerves quivering like harp strings, there were no sour notes. Bellyaching? Sure. But there was a laugh—most often a wry laugh—even then.

With that sort of fellowship this challenge of rock and water and wilderness has a savor to it that somehow is deeply satisfying to a city man. And, in seeking a source for such satisfaction, you need look no farther than the tangled and rock-ribbed wildness of North Carolina's magnificent Linville Gorge.

Having said all this I will, in the manner of the polite Alphonse, close by adding, "After you, Gaston!"

22

OUTWARD BOUND JOURNAL, OR, "HOW I SKIPPED SCHOOL FOR 26 DAYS"

I am puzzled at my temerity in releasing this account of a spoiled, self-absorbed male teenager, but such was the raw material for a fine character-building experience, and I was typical in that regard at the North Carolina Outward Bound School in 1967. Let me spell out the circumstances of the adventure. In the fall of 1967, Lee's Jewel Box, a jeweler's chain with a store in Asheville, awarded me a scholarship to attend the fourth Outward Bound course at the school based under Table Rock Mountain. Lee H. Edwards High School, now Asheville High School, released me from classes for the month. My mother outfitted me in khaki and denim and wool from the local army-navy surplus stores, and I was off on a Greyhound bus to "the wildest area east of the Rockies." During the course, our Anakiwa Crew dropped to four members; the others were Max, a young Jewel Box salesman; Gene, a Winston-Salem policeman; and Lusk, like me, a high school student. Our instructors were John Lawrence and Dick Erickson. Readers unfamiliar with Outward Bound's mission may want to turn first to my write-up for the high school paper on pages 182–83.

October 6, 1967

Arrived at the Asheville bus station at noon on October 6, 1967. Went through Black Mountain and Old Fort. At 2:00 I reached Morganton. Walked from the bus station to the Morganton Recreation Center. It is a beautiful building with flowing architecture. Has pool, tennis court, gym, and various other rooms. Played billiards and met other boys. A truck arrived with our boots; I got a size 10-D. At six o' clock we were picked up by a truck. We rode for half of an hour. We were then dropped at the bottom of Table Rock Mountain. Very impressive. Walk a mile with our luggage [an exaggeration] and were shown to our tents. Placed in Anakiwa group with eleven other boys. The other two groups are Moray and Kephart. [Anakiwa from an Australian Outward Bound school; Moray from the English Sea School; and Kephart, named for outdoors author and proponent of a Smoky Mountains National Park, Horace Kephart]. Go to dinner in Phillips Building and then were taught 24-hour clock time. We were introduced to Mr. Hollandsworth [director] and signed a pledge not to smoke. Go to bed.

"TENTS"

The tents were green wall tents elevated one foot above the ground on wooden platforms. Each tent housed 6 men. The lighting was one kerosene lantern. We slept on plastic ticks in [down] sleeping bags. We had footlockers in which to keep our clothes. There were two large canvas flies covering the tent for added protection. There were 2 tents for the Anakiwa group.

"WASH-HOUSE"

The washhouse was an open building 2 feet up from the ground. We washed in deep metal tubs. The lighting was two lanterns. Mirrors appeared in the structure.

"LATRINES"

"Disgusting!" [Actually clean and hygienic slop buckets with disinfectants under a wooden frame, to be freshened at course's end.]

OCTOBER 7, 1967

Wake up at 0600. Called outside and run a mile. We end up by taking a cold shower. [This is the "Run-and Dip" daily wake-up exercise: a jog from school down to Forest Road 210, then back up to stand under a frigid stream of spring water for the count of five.] The air is surprisingly warm. Get dressed. Eat breakfast. Straighten cabin [tent] and return to Phillips building. Return to cabin for inspection. Go to infirmary for inspection for checkup [by Nurse Shirey]. Go down to Phillips bldg. and receive climbing gear. Return to tent. Interviewed by Mr. Lawrence [Anakiwa crew leader, ex–Royal Marine, boxer, violinist and experienced climber]. Lunch at Phillips building. Go to tent. Called to Phillips building for rock climbing. Mr. Erickson and Mr. Lawrence teach us knots and how to climb. Scale 40-foot cliff in the rain. Use bowline knot. Use helmets and carabiners. Slipped a few times. Dinner. After dinner go on hike up Tablerock Mountain. Return and go to bed.

"I SHALL NOT QUITE"

OCTOBER 8, 1967

Wake up at 0600. Raining. Go on run and dip. Eat in swim trunks. Ten (10) boys quit. Dress and clean tent. Trouble with Lusk. Return to Phillips building for talk. Go to classes. Build fire. Do map-reading. Outside Mr. Lawrence tries to talk Bill out of quitting. Bill has already given away all of his clothes. I got a shirt. They expect me to keep a log but I can't find time to keep it. Haven't had a decent shower in three days. Smell like dog. Blisters all over feet. Wound on hand slowly healing. Erickson shows us rattlesnake skins. Very entertaining. Over 100,000 people have gone through O.B. In rock climbing the head man uses pitons and carabiners. Hikes are called expeditions.

We are going on an expedition tomorrow. Sounds tough. Mr. Lawrence is just back from S. Pole. Mr. Dick Erickson was a smoke-jumper and in *Lassie, Red Skies over Montana,* and Walt Disney [movies]. We are not very far from Lake James. A photographer takes three pictures of us at class. I have only had time to take one. We are on duty watch and are promised warm showers. Cleanliness at last. Go outside and study snakebite first-aid. Methods of carrying people were done next. Return to Phillips bldg. to prepare for dinner. Clean up cabin. Go to woods for woodcraft. Return to Phillips building for map-reading. Prepare for an expedition. Large groups of colored boys leave. Eat dinner. Cook catches me with two desserts. No seconds or dessert for a week.

OCTOBER 9, 1967

Wake up at 0600. Go on run and dip. Prepare for expedition. Start on expedition. Go to *Bad Mod.* [Devil's Cellar, the chasm on the northwestern side of Table Rock? I seem to recall this was a designation of Swedish climbing instructor Mr. Knute Smith.] Climb down into gorge. I have to lead the expedition up Hawksbill Mountain [a map-and-compass exercise off the regular trail]. Air was real thin. Ate lunch. Climbed down mountain and made camp later on. Set up tent [strung up a sheet of plastic] and had a lousy dinner. Go to bed. Starts raining and I get soaked.

October 10, 1967

Bellowed at to wake up. Can't start a fire in the rain. Mr. Lawrence cuts woods with a KUKRI [a heavy, machete-like knife with an angled blade, used by the Gurkhas, Nepalese soldiers in the British or Indian armies] and starts a fire. Fix packs and start hiking. At lunch time 5 boys quit and go back to camp. Mr. Lawrence is glad that I don't quit [on the forest road, he fixed me with his eye, "Blake, do YOU want to quit?" I said, "Yes." "Well then, ARE you going to quit?" "No!"]. After a tiresome hike we reach campsite. Eat and bed down. Starts raining. In one hour I find 1" of water in sleeping bag. No sleep that night. Everything gets soaked. [Of course, we'd camped on a slope where the path doubled as a rain gully.]

October 11, 1967

Third day of expedition. The 4 of us eat and get started. Return up trail. Climb Table Rock. Point out places on map. Can see Lake James and Mount Mitchell. Go down to parking lot and eat lunch. Climb chimney rocks. See course of future expeditions. Finally return to camp. Get a very inspiring letter from Mrs. Long [a friend of my mother who provided much encouragement and the loan of a 35-millimeter camera with color slide film]. Write to her and mom. Go to infirmary. Eat dinner. Return to tent and set out clothes and equipment to dry. Turn in.

October 12, 1967

Go on run and dip by ourselves. Get dressed and eat breakfast. Go to rocks and learn to rappel by Mr. Knute Smith. Climb up rock #2, lane 1. Very hard, took coaxing. Returned and ate lunch. Go to Fire Fighting. Learn the techniques. Put out fire. All of us work very good. On way back see the ropes course. Looks as frightening as I don't know what. Go to circuit course and 1) do step up; 2) stretch; 3) weight lift, and others etc. Run tackle exercise and tie with two other groups. Return to Phillips bldg. and sort out clothes of boys who have left. (Now have 16 out of 32). As I write diary now a boy quits. Terrible. I can take it. Got to dinner. Get program on Ecology after dinner.

October 13, 1967

SOLO

Wake up at 0600 and go on run and dip. Get dressed and go to breakfast. Had a talk with Mr. Lawrence on the solo. Wrote a letter home. Prepared for solo. Got picture taken. Inspection. Pack for solo. After lunch at 1:30 we leave. Skies clear up. Good hiking. After reaching the point designated by Mr. Lawrence we waited for 3/4 of an hour. Then he drove up in the white truck and gave us each a chicken. He carried his pack and a violin. He led us each to our solo area and I quickly prepared my site [this was an area about thirty feet wide in a rhododendron clearing beside a stream, to which I was restricted for four days.] While I was working he sneaked up on me. Shows how inattentive I can get. Write in diary. Check up on Gertrude [named for the goose that accompanies the explorers in the 1959 film *Journey to the Center of the Earth*]. Turn in. During night I am scared because my whistle chain is lost. Am lying upon it. Good Night.

October 14, 1967

Wake up at all times in the morning, arise at between 0900 and 1000. Looks like Gertrude is gone. Get dressed. Cross bridge. See Gertrude loose on out-of-bounds. Lay chase, gave up. Write in diary. Still haven't ate or lit a fire. Having fun. Hard expedition (60 miles) to Grandfather Mountain when I get back. Very lonely. I want some food but can't find any. No sign of life. Loneliness is getting to me. Feel terrible. Lit fire—gave me something to do. Will play around with map. Am building crummy leaf fire when I hear emergency whistle blow. Pick up stave and dash up creek. On road see Mr. Hollandsworth and Mr. Smith. Told to wait on road. In about 10 minutes they emerge from brush with Mr. Lawrence. Go back to campsite. On the way see Max. Work on the fire. Hunt for firewood. Feel better. Mr. Lawrence catches me by surprise again while I whittle. [Lawrence: "Blake, if I'd been an Indian you'd be dead."] We hunt for Gertrude. I can't find her. We go to bed. [Mr. Erickson called me down for letting my chicken escape, saying that it was careless cruelty and that's she'd starve to death if not first being eaten by a bear.]

October 15, 1967

Wake up. Very weak from hunger. Feel very dizzy. Get dressed. Try to start a fire. On the last match get a blaze going. Use up all of my wood. So what. Cross bridge and write in log. Come back and build up fire. Lie down and dream of food. Whittle some. Let fire burn out. Throw ashes and rock in stream. Talk to myself. Cross stream and write poetry. Not much but it is what I think. Hunger is starting to obsess me. Must have food. Feel sick. Hope Mr. Lawrence visits me. Try not to lose sense of humor. Very important. My clothes and I smell terrible. Haven't washed. Mr. Erickson drops by at 2:00 [1400]. Warns me of gunshots from hunters. Says the others aren't eating either. Will pick me up at 12:00 tomorrow. Go to bed. [We were also warned against eating any parts of the rhododendron or laurel as these are very poisonous.]

October 16, 1967

Sleep late. Wake up. Think about home. Very weak and dizzy. Need food. Get dressed. Pack sleeping bag, ground sheet, and poncho. Am yelling about my state of affairs when Mr. Erickson tells me to go on out to the road [F.R. 210]. We start walking to the truck. Max is the only one who has eaten his chicken. All of us are very weak. Gene ate some minnows. I don't know what Lusk ate [he later admitting to having a candy stash]. Nearly passed out on the way back. Finally reached school. Hot showers. Prepare dining room for Moray and Anakiwa groups for food. Eat dinner [wolfed down dinner and promptly threw most of it up]. Go back to bed. Sleep. Get some candy from shop.

October 17, 1967

Wake up at 0530. First out on run and dip. Cold shower feels good. Clean up tent. Prepare Phillips building for breakfast. Eat breakfast. Feel better. Get ready for rocks. Get in truck and go to the Chimneys. Climb rocks. I am the only one to rappel. Ride back. Walk a mile. Eat lunch. Orienteering and circuit course next. Stomach feels OK. Spend a long time on orienteering course. Talk with Mr. Lawrence. Take many pictures. Eat dinner. Return to Phillips building for a first aid course from Mr. Lawrence. After the first aid course we check out food for the next expedition and return to tents & pack. Go to bed.

October 18, 1967

Wake up at 0600. Go on run and dip. We are on duty. Eat breakfast and clean up. Prepare for expedition. Go get in school truck and we go by the [Jonas Ridge] post office. On the way to Grandfather it rains. Stop at gatehouse. Windy. Hike up to caves. [These were the Black Rock Caves, long ago closed to the public because of their endangered Virginia big-eared bat population. Mr. Lawrence pointed out the hibernating bats on the walls as we crept in by flashlight.] Cut firewood. [I recall everyone gathering dry leaves for mattress beds and how I was called down for lounging about with my hands in my pockets watching the others gather wood.] Very cold. Eat dinner. See bats. Bed down for the night. During the night we used up all the firewood. Cave very cold, windy, and wet.

October 19, 1967
Wake up and pack. Go cave exploring. Mr. Lawrence lets us find our way back out in the dark. Finally we find the way out. Put on packs and start hiking. Hike a very long time. I lead us up the mountain. Stop for lunch then hike on. Reach water place. Take pictures. Very cold. Snowing. We reach Calloway Peak [elevation 5,964 feet]. Can't start a fire. 18 degrees. Eat peanut butter sandwiches. Crawl into plastic shelter. Freeze to sleep. Can't move my hands very well. [Next morning was crisp and dazzling, with the stunted trees and our plastic tarp frozen stiff in the rime ice, formed by freezing mists on the exposed peak.]

October 20, 1967
Wake up. Finally get a good fire going. Sun is out. No wind. Eat good. Hash, grits, bread, and cream [a half pint of evaporated milk]. Fix packs. Walk down mountain. Eat lunch on highway 221 and are finally picked up and driven back to school. Clean up. Get letters from the Longs and Grandmother. Flash-bulb works. Take a picture. Go get a warm shower. Prepare for dinner. Eat dinner and it's good. Clean up, then we get a talk about how we did on the expedition from Mr. Lawrence. Return and go to bed.

October 21, 1967
Wake up at 0600. Max hurts. He doesn't go on run & dip. We do. Dress and go on duty. I am duty student. Kephart is the only crew in beside us. Return to tent and prepare for rocks. Climb to base of Tablerock and eat lunch. Mr. Smith and I lead. (P.S. Earlier on we had rock instruction. They dropped a 150-pound sandbag 6 feet and we had to stop it). Climb 150 feet on rocks. Coil ropes and prepare to descend. I am last. On last 30 feet I hang in mid air. Run all the way back. Prepare to eat dinner. We are the only ones in. Photographs for sale. Return to tent. Climb in bed and write in diary and write a postcard. Go to sleep.

October 22, 1967
Wake up at 0700. Go on run and dip. Water has mud in it. Return to tent and clean up. Only four of us at breakfast; cook fixes our food the way we want it. Clean up building. Go to solo area and fix a flat tire. Hunters look for dogs. Eat lunch. Go to ropes. Do very good. Get in truck and go to Tablerock. Finish taking 40 pictures. We take inventory on fire-fighting tools, take warm showers, and eat dinner. Mr. Phillips visits us. Mr. Erickson's wife returns. Lusk is duty officer. Clean up. Return to tents. Write diary & letters. Retire.

October 23, 1967

Wake up at 0600. Go on run and dip. Max is duty student. We have a good small breakfast and clean up for inspection. I get camera and gear and get in Mr. Erickson's ruck. Go to Tablerock. Lead climb to the top. About 100 feet high. Take many pictures. Eat two sandwiches and apple for lunch. Set up belay and belay everyone down [i.e., seated and secured to a tree, I played out the Plymouth Goldline nylon safety rope attached to the climber's harness, ready to break his fall as he descended]. As I come down Lusk takes two pictures of me. Coil ropes and run back to school. Clean up and eat dinner. Sweep and wash dishes. At 7:30 [1930] we talk about the purpose of the expeditions, the school, and the solos. Return to tent and turn in.

October 24, 1967

Wake up at 0600. Go on run and dip. Dress and eat breakfast. After breakfast we drag gasoline tank rubber liner down to the dip pool. Leslie White, Max, and I enter the box and drain out mud and water. Very cold. Catch several salamanders, crawfish, and frogs. [This box was a timber frame the size of a small motel swimming pool. After cleaning it out, we heaved the heavy mass of black rubber inside and began trimming it to fit as a liner. The pool was to replace the current run and dip practice of standing under a pipe of running stream water. Now there was to be a literal dip, though the project was uncompleted by course end.] Climb in truck and taken to road to shoot a movie. Took several bus shots [of students arriving under the towering Table Rock]. Went to Linville Falls and took several more shots. Met many tourists. They used the same camera as *I Spy* [a popular television show of the 1960s with Robert Culp and Bill Cosby]. Returned to camp. Cleaned up and wrote in diary. [The film was *Solo* (1969), twenty-five minutes, written and directed by Martin Hill and filmed and edited by Harry Joyner. In off-session times, NCOBS instructors and their wives fanned out across the southeastern United States promoting the North Carolina school to Scout troops, high school assemblies, Kiwanis and Rotary groups and other promising venues, running this film as part of the program.]

October 25, 1967

Wake up at 0600. Go on run and dip. It is pouring down rain. Get dressed and eat breakfast. Go and try to free a car stuck in the mud. Find some blasting caps. Finally free Mr. Mashburn's car. Go to dip pool. Finish cleaning and spend the rest of the afternoon cutting & putting the rubber tank into the pool. Eat dinner—have spaghetti. Return to tents and get the boys' notebooks. Store opens. I get another nice letter from the Longs. Store opens and I get some kandy. Go to the Phillips building and take notes on the next expedition.

FINAL EXPEDITION DETAILS

At Hawksbill there will be a pile of rocks in which we will place our name, information, and T.O.A. in a tin can. The junction is in the saddle in between Sitting Bear and Hawksbill. There will be another pile of stones and a tin can. A stone wall is on the ridge [and lies there still]. Meet instructors on east side of river going north, just before the bend. On the left is the Babel Tower Trail. Trail will be made obvious by red crepe paper. Don't go past the river bend. Tough country. Then south down to the Conley Cove Trail signpost down below Tablerock. Last trail signpost in the gorge for a long way. Leave another note at the signpost. The sign is the second one with only Conley Cove on it, nothing else. Go south down to the Pinchin Trail. There will be more crepe paper and instructions. On flat part of Cambric [Trail] we will meet the instructors. They will put us on the Pinchin Trail and from there we go to the Pinnacle. There are two instructors there. We will go to the chimney near the river. Leave a note at the chimney at the bottom of the Gorge. Turn north to the Pinchin Trail area up the side of the Gorge. More instructors who will see us across the river. Go north aside of the creek bed to Conley Cove. Go to sign which says Linville Gorge Wilderness Area. Leave a note there. The notes are very important.

"RULES OF EXPEDITION"

1. Follow 6 foot rule [don't climb anything over six feet high with pack on].
2. Never leave packs.
3. Never get split up.
4. Don't travel at night.
5. Eat & sleep well.

When reporting an accident tell WHO, WHAT, WHEN, WHERE, WHY, HOW.

Most important is WHERE.

At Babel Tower, at bottom of Pinchin flat, and at the Pinnacle, permanent instructors will be positioned [there for the duration of the expedition].

On the final day, after we have gone through the last checkpoint, the instructors will remain at their positions 2 hours before returning to the school.

Then the school is our last safety checkpoint.

October 26, 1967

Wake up at 0600. Go on run and dip. Prepare for the final expedition [in which all three crews are out in the gorge]. Start at 9:15 [0915] from school. Reach Little Tablerock at 10:00. It took 45 minutes. Good weather. We stick together, no outbursts or arguments. We're 1 hour behind schedule due to complications at school. Meet Erickson and [Peter] Sheehan at Tablerock parking lot. On schedule with no delays. Go up Shortoff Trail. It's the wrong way; turn back. 12:00. Return to Linville Gorge Wilderness Area sign at 12:10. Eat lunch. Left a note. Leave at 12:50. Bushwhack in a S.W. direction. At 2:30 [1430] we rest and check the map. At 3:15 [1515] we reach the Linville Gorge river. Rest for 10 minutes. Walk along river. Find Erickson and Sheehan building a bridge. We help. Mr. Erickson falls in. Then Woodrow falls in. The rest of us cross safely. [I recall the agile black student Woodrow slipping under the current, then bobbing up immediately by the buoyancy of his backpack. We pulled him out with our hiking sticks. He and Erickson hurried to change clothes, for it was cold.] We left them [the instructors] at 5:00 [1700]. Walk along the river. Reach a good campsite and get a good fire started. We used the remains of a good lean-to. Nice fire started and all of us eat very well. We turned in at 9:30 [2130]. We all slept in the one lean to.

October 27, 1967

Woke up at 5:30. Good fire. Everything goes without delay. Breakfast. At 8:40 we leave. Reach the broken chimney at 9:00. Brief break. Leave note. Start up old Murray Trail [?]. Reach the [Kistler] Memorial Highway. Go down it. Meet Lawrence and Mashburn. Reach the checkpoint on the Pinnacle at 11:00. Leave note. Walk along the Memorial Highway for 2 miles. Go down the Pinchin Trail. Eat lunch at the bottom. At 2:15 [1415] we started back up it and reached the top again. Everybody does OK. Reached the bottom of the Conley Cove Trail at 6:00 [1800], 35 minutes ahead of schedule. Leave a note. Set up a tent. Eat a good meal. Great fire. Turn in early.

October 28, 1967

Wake up at 5:30. Got a fire started. Eat a very filling breakfast. Break tent. Leave at 8:45. Reach Day and Jack Shirey. Wade across the river and go up the hill the wrong way. Steep cliffs. Turn back. Eat lunch at the bottom. Travel down river and come to the Sitting Bear Trail. Go up it to the top. Pitch camp at 6:30 [1830]. Leave a note. Turn in very early after a light meal. Sleep good.

October 29, 1967

Wake up at 8:00. Pack and move out. Go to Hawksbill. From Hawksbill go down the dirt road [Forest Road 210]. Meet Lawrence and Mashburn in the Volvo. Reach camp at 10:45. Told to clean up our expedition gear. Murray came in last night. Everyone is OK. Eat lunch. Fix the dip pool. Go to the zip cable [this must have been one of the first zip lines in the state]. I am the last to go down it. It is a lot of fun. I go to the infirmary to get my blister looked at and also get cold medicine. Eat dinner. Afterwards we have a vesper service and I see Mr. Hollandsworth. Go to tent. Do duty. Go to store. Get candy. P.S. Got letter from mom. Bought 3 photographs. Turn in.

October 30, 1967

Wake up at 0600. Go on run and dip. Go do duty at Phillips building and eat breakfast. Do duty afterwards. Go and get our expedition gear checked by Mr. Lawrence and Hollandsworth. Get ready for 6-mile marathon. Start on it. Fall coming down Tablerock. Come in last (17th). [The route of the marathon went from the school down to F.R. 210. Turning right on the road, we ran to 210-B, which ascends to the Table Rock parking lot. The racers climbed Table Rock to the Mountains-to-Sea Trail, taking this to the Spence Ridge Trailhead on F.R. 210. From here, we rounded back to the school.] Go to see nurse [scraped palm] and go to tent for a rest. Got dressed and went to the morning reading steps. [On most mornings, when the crews were at school, we would assemble for readings at a small clearing with log benches. Mr. Lawrence read us excerpts from a book called *Diretissima*, the account of an ill-fated Italian climbing team's failure at a direct ascent of the North Wall of the Eiger Mountain in the Bernese Oberland of Switzerland.] Go to the 14 foot wall first [for the end of course competitions]. Mr. Lawrence is made a crew member [since Anakiwa had fewer members than the other crews]. Max goes up first, then me, then Gene, Tom [Lusk], Mr. Lawrence, and Max. Next we went to the 7 foot log and did it in the same order. We messed up on the beams and ties. On the rocks, Lusk went first; he fell. I made it up. Gene went up. *He* fell. Mr. Lawrence made it up. Max fell. Lusk fell again. I made it up though. Gene then made it. As Max was coming up the 1/2 hour whistle blew. We then had a tug o' war. Our team lost. Eat dinner. Hang around Phillips building. Go to bed.

My time on the marathon was 6 miles in 75 minutes, 14 seconds.

OCTOBER 31, 1967

Wake up at 0600. It is raining. We all go on the run and dip except Lusk. Eat breakfast. Do latrine duty. Clean up. Pack up expedition gear and take it back to the Phillips building. I have all of my stuff and there are no charges. Write down my impressions of school after an interview with Mr. Lawrence. Also wrote a letter to Mr. Baker thanking him [for my scholarship]. I am all packed and ready to go. Took two more flash pictures.

NOVEMBER 1, 1967

Wake up very late. We all listen to Leon's radio thanks to Mrs. Long's batteries. Get dressed. Just made it to breakfast on time. Do duty and clean up tent for inspection. Go to morning reading. Mr. Shirey gives it. Then go get duffel bag and get on the truck with the others. Say farewell to Mr. Lawrence and Erickson. Go to Morganton Recreation Center and from there to the bus terminal. Get call from mom. Catch the bus and go to Asheville. It rains. Meet mom at the depot. Back at home.

"FINIS"

23

"OUTWARD BOUND—EXPLORE YOUR CAPABILITIES"

Upon returning to high school at Lee Edwards, I wrote up an account of my experience at Outward Bound for the school newspaper, *Sky High*, trying to convey my sense of the school's mission and history, together with its daily practice as it unfolded in the wilderness in 1967.

Located in the Linville Gorge Wilderness at the base of Tablerock Mountain, twenty miles from Morganton, North Carolina, is the North Carolina Outward Bound School. The school is designed to show young men [soon the school became coed], regardless of race, color, or religion, between 16 and 23, what they are capable of by placing them in difficult and unusual situations where they must think and work together.

Outward Bound was started during World War II in an effort to call a halt to the large number of British sailors in the North Atlantic who lost their will to survive in the open lifeboats after their convoys had been torpedoed. After the war ended, Outward Bound schools quickly grew in Africa, Germany, England, New Zealand, and the United States.

There are five Outward Bound schools in the United States. These are located in Colorado, Minnesota, the Northwest, off the coast of Maine, and in North Carolina. The North Carolina school at Tablerock is only four months old but is getting off to a good start. Students live in tents but eat in a large wooden structure called the Phillips building. The staff is headed by James "Pop" Hollandsworth, and two of the instructors are from the English Outward Bound school.

The course which I attended lasted from October 5 to November 1. New arrivals were placed into one of three crews. Each member of the crew worked closely with the other members, for sometimes our lives depended upon each other. During the course we made three "expeditions." On these we hiked, stressing compass and map work most of the day, and then made camp for the night. One of the most trying and difficult things we undertook was the Solo. A crew was taken to a particular area and its members placed separately in a limited area from which he could not move. We were left for three days and nights with only a sleeping bag, a plastic sheet, a canteen, a knife, our pack and ten matches to do what we wanted. Once or twice a day we were cheered on by an instructor [who swore us to a vow of secrecy about the chickens; hence Gertrude's absence from this account]. Sleeping was the best way to pass the time.

Each of the American Outward Bound schools stresses one particular skill. The Colorado school stresses [alpine] hiking, the Maine school boating, and the North Carolina school rock climbing. It was while on the rocks that we worked together best. We were told that while clinging to the face of a rock much of our character was revealed. It does not stress making all its students expert rock climbers or campers. It does, however, teach young men just what they are capable of and helps to coordinate their minds with their bodies to achieve what they never thought possible.

[The first Outward Bound school in the United States was the Colorado school, which opened on the western slopes of the Rocky Mountains, near the old quarry town of Marble, Colorado, in 1962 to teach alpine and mountaineering and skiing. The Hurricane Island School opened in 1964 in Camden, Maine, with a seafaring program. Another mountaineering school opened in 1965 in Eugene, Oregon, the Northwest, or Pacific Northwest School. Minnesota's Boundary Waters School, in the Superior National Forest near Ely, bases watercraft courses on Lake Superior. Fifth came the North Carolina school under Table Rock in the summer of 1967, specializing in rock climbing, rescue, firefighting and general woodcraft and orientation.]

Clothing and Equipment List for NC-3 and NC-4

1 heavy wool sweater
1 windbreaker or ski parka (if you have one)
1 rough jacket (denim satisfactory)
1 hat or cap (sun, wind, rain protection)
1 wool shirt (or heavy flannel)
3 cotton (or flannel) long-sleeved shirts
1 pair wool (or heavy whipcord) trousers (*Not* tight fitting)
3 pair cotton trousers (*Not* tight fitting. NO JEANS)
1 pair mountain boots (SEE BOOT ORDER FORM FOR MORE INFORMATION)
1 pair durable comfortable shoes
2 pair sneakers (grip soles best)
1 pair gym shorts (*Not* tight-fitting)
1 pair swim trunks (quick drying)
1 belt (Army web type best)
1 suit long underwear (light wool or heavy cotton, *NOT* thermal)
5 T-shirts (or undershirts)
5 undershorts
1 pair pajamas (flannel best)
3 pair heavy wool socks
4 pair sweat socks (heavy cotton)
6 handkerchiefs
2 bandanas (large)
3 bath towels
1 toilet kit (non-electric razor, razor blades, shaving soap, toothbrush, toothpaste, soap)
2 pair work gloves (leather palms if possible)
1 flashlight (2 cell with batteries)
1 pocket knife (sheath knife not suitable)

All items should be clearly marked with dri-mark pen or labels. Duffel bags should be tagged with your home address.

Storage space at the school is extremely limited. It is preferred that the above items be packed in an Army-type duffel bag rather than luggage.

Do not wear good clothes en route to the school from Morganton. Wear rubber-soled shoes. Your travel clothes may be stored at the school.

Solo

1. Introduction

Solo is not meant to be an ordeal. Properly handled it can be one of the most significant experiences of your life. Improperly handled, it can be extremely uncomfortable. Everything depends on your approach to the solo, and on your preparation for it, the energy and imagination, and above all the common sense you bring to adapting to life in the natural world.

There is ample food which you will be taught to recognize and use. We hope you will use your equipment, your training, your forethought, patience and versatility to get a deeper understanding of yourself and come to appreciate the intricate world of weather, of trees and mountains, insects and plants, birds and fish upon which we all depend and which will be yours for three days.

Plan out what you would do if you had to spend a week by yourself. Remember that you are alone, that your primary obligation is to return as well as you went off. Therefore, some activities which are possible with companions should be avoided without them. This is not cowardice but common sense and recognition of the obligation incumbent on everyone to cause no difficulty for others to help those in trouble. Do not become a casualty. There is enough to do in learning the geography and vegetation of your area and in working out the simplest and most efficient living scheme for yourself to keep you busy the whole time you are out.

Patience and versatility are basic for any sensible life in the woods. You must accept the fact that you live in an environment which, unlike a city or town, is not designed for you if you make urban demands on it. However, if you observe what it is and has to offer and adapt your life to its circumstances intelligently, you can live comfortably for an indefinite length of time. You must discover what is possible in terms of the terrain and the simplest and most efficient pattern of life it permits. There is no virtue in being uncomfortable because you did not take the trouble to find out how to be comfortable. Once you accept the wilderness for what it is, you can begin to find your place in it. Then it is full of resources which you can use.

Your powers of observation are probably the most necessary safety aid that exists. Every bit of lore you can acquire for reading the inter-related signs of weather, drainage, vegetation, the position of land marks, the behavior of animals may be of use. You will find much to think about and three days may seem even too short.

2. *Solo Equipment*

1. Pack
2. Sleeping bag (optional)
3. Shelter sheet or poncho
4. [deleted]
5. Water bottle
6. #10 can
7. Salt
8. 10 matches or flint
9. Knife
10. Whistle
11. Journal and pencil
12. First aid kit
13. Prayer book—Bible (optional)
14. Copy of "SOLO" instructions

YOU MAY NOT TAKE ANYTHING ELSE

1. SIGNALS

In case of genuine distress, blow your whistle in a group of 6 short blasts at [1] minute intervals.

11. SHELTERS

Pick the best possible site; make an adequate shelter and leave no evidence of it when you come in. Get plenty of rest.

111. FIRE

Build only the fire you need. Be extremely careful with fire. In gathering fuel, remember you may get only one chance to get a fire started.

IV. SANITATION

Camp in the wilderness spirit. Don't pollute or litter the environment. Dig a latrine and use it. Leave your area as clean and wild as you found it.

24

GREEN BERET RADIO EXERCISE IN THE PISGAH GORGE, JUNE 1969

Less than two years after completing the Outward Bound course at Table Rock, I was back in the wilderness pushing bush and scrambling, this time with the U.S. Army Special Forces, known popularly as the Green Berets. This field exercise was the culminating test or proving ground for radio operator training with the Special Forces Training Brigade, Company B, at Fort Bragg, North Carolina. After airborne jump-school at Fort Benning, Georgia, in January 1969, I began Green Beret training with the S.F.'s own version of boot camp—for the S.F. worked in an unconventional, or guerrilla warfare, style. Then followed radio training—with a one-week Fort Bragg field exercise, capped off by the Gorge exercise, always referred to as the "Pisgah Exercise" because of its location in this national forest. An endnote details the radio operators' duties and their equipment.

By this time in our training, we'd all attained proficiently in Morse code transmission and reception and in a three-component cryptograph system called DIANA, which used alphabetical keys and cipher books to encode messages.

It was June of 1969, and a small convoy of 2-1/2-ton olive-drab diesel trucks (called "Deuce-and-a-halfs") chugged up into North Carolina's Blue Ridge, hauling trainees to the Gingercake Acres Community on Jonas Ridge. Other training exercises sometimes dropped parachutists into

Pineola to the north, but this ride was literally door-to-door, from the fort to the gritty, white clay of Table Rock Road on the eastern side of the wild gorge. We piled out and, weaponless, shouldered packs.

From a clipboard, the sarge read the names, ranks, and serial numbers of the green troops, formed them into groups, each with a destination to reach that sunset, then chased them off like mutts, as it seemed. As we shuffled into the cool, moist air of the shady Forest Service road, adjusting the radio weight in our rucksacks or "ALICE" packs, it began to dawn on us that this two-week exercise was going to be every much a bit a test of endurance and stamina skills as it was of our radio skills. And I felt right away that we'd be observed and graded for our ability to cooperate, as at Outward Bound, as a small well-knit team.

We had all just come from a week's field exercise in sandy, pine-wooded Fort Bragg, where we built poncho shelter "hooches" next to the chain link fence perimeter of the base NCO's Club, i.e. for Noncommissioned Officers', or sergeants and their dependents. We worked on our encrypting codes, the frequencies and their crystals, and the construction of field antennae in the infernal heat of a pine tree clump within earshot of the swinging '60s sounds of the families recreating at the club. To this day, I remember the smack of the diving boards, shrieks of girlish laughter mingled with whiffs of Coppertone and the bursts of the beer cans being opened. And through this drifted the golden tones of Mr. Tom Jones performing "My Delilah" and "What's New Pussycat?" on jukebox .45s in unceasing repetition once the pool opened in the heat of the morning. The subliminal jukebox phased into our voice radio transmissions on the Vietnam era backpack, AN PRC 25, with its black handset as we spoke in clipped army signal alpha-numeric sequences: "Roger Kilo Lima; I copy your ten-niner last transmission. Over."

Five days of this, dug-in on the dunes outside the oasis, wore on our nerves, until, one baking afternoon, another radio trainee and I low crawled through the piny brush to the fence to watch the bathing bikini beauties, some swan diving from the clapping board high over shimmering aquamarine waters, others, the young moms and wives, oiling their pampered brown bodies on dazzling aluminum deck chairs and in the pools of shade under umbrellas festive bands of color. We gazed as Tom broke into perhaps his most famous chorus: "Lady! Whoa…whoa… whoa….She's a Lady." This commendation seemed good to both of us, saying that all was right here, and that it was time to be brave men and move onwards to The Pisgah. Back of my mind the place felt strangely fantastic, a 007 flashy James Bond–land, the Riviera.

The goal of the two-week exercise was quite simple. Once the teams had split up to move off to their different destinations as ordered by the instructor-sergeant, our common task was to transmit coded Morse Code messages to Fort Bragg, over two-hundred miles away, constantly, once an hour, every hour, throughout the 24-hour day. We were to be graded on the number of clear messages getting through as received by a "C" Team monitoring us. Our support for rations and black antenna wire came from the "B" Team quartered then upstairs at Franklin's Linville Falls Restaurant [now Famous Louise's]. Here we were again using the AN PRC-25 backpack radio to maintain 24-hour voice communication. Routinely, without warning, the sergeants would appear at a camp with orders to move out to new locations, typically across the gorge and up and down one side. We never moved at night.

Radio equipment took up most of our load, including the many spare batteries, plus the canteens of water in the rucksack's sturdy back pockets. As guerrilla warfare radio gear, what we carried was durable and compact, designed to withstand a 30-foot drop from an airplane. The AN/GRC-109 radio with its tiny key for code tapping was powered by a 22-pound electric hand-cranked generator with a folding stool, fondly known as the "OD Monster. The receiver ran off a long, flat dry cell battery and its frequencies or "channels" could be tuned with a dial. The transmitting frequencies were coordinated with day and hour, and the receivers at Bragg were likewise waiting on the same wavelength at a certain pre-set time for our several groups' thirty-some communications efforts. Rations, earphones, antenna wire, hefty dry cell flashlights, and spare socks made up the rest of our equipage. We each carried our own Beat Frequency Oscillator, a small device whose dial measured the strength or weakness of our transmission signals as we bounced them off the ionosphere.

Now, as it turned out, our Cherokee team leader, Staff Sergeant Burtnett was called away to his Oklahoma reservation because of grave sickness at home. That left our team short-staffed and made up, like Anakiwa at Outward Bound, of only four members. Larger teams were carrying the same amount of gear as we, so the sergeants sometimes let us get settled easily in position for three days or so. There was another young Cherokee Green Beret on the team who bragged that he could build a light-free shelter with our group poncho issue. And so he did, as the lax schedule permitted, a perfectly darkened cube with a twig frame.

We saw little signs of hikers or visitors and none at all of Outward Bound. Two memorable exceptions stand out, however. One was "Airborne Annie" and the other the friendly little black bear cub. "Airborne Annie" was a young McDowell County woman from Marion who would drive up to Linville Gorge in a blue Buick with a rebel flag plate in front. We'd heard about her back at radio school. She had, it seemed, a fondness for Special Forces and liked coming up to see us. Some of the other men put a veiled sexual motive behind her visits, but I tried to grasp her brand of girl-patriotism. She once drove me to a spring head to fill the team's canteens and asked me about the bad reputation she had amongst some of the men. "They're just talking to impress each other," I said, "and don't mean any harm by it." But plainly she was miffed by their talk and what it insinuated.

The last time I saw Annie, my friends and I had graduated radio school and were preparing for the famed Green Beret exercise known as Robin Sage, with its counterinsurgency missions inside the fictitious country of Pineland. A group of us commandeered a jeep and she followed us out to a derelict airstrip in her Buick. That day I'd brought along my collection of Gorge photos to show her and left the batch in her car, never to see them again. I recall the pictures of the little cub that visited our camp. He just emerged from the shrubbery one day into the clearing off Forest Road 210 where we had set up camp. The others were busy getting a message down to Fort Bragg, so I followed the bear around snapping shots as he poked into our lean-to, snuffed among our packs, and finally posed for me sitting on his haunches on a rock slurping out the contents of a C Ration can of spaghetti. "Leave him be, Blake" growled Sergeant Burtnett, "his mother's probably nearby." In less than a minute or two the cub had retreated into the thick brush. This camp, I believe, could not have been too far from my Outward Bound Solo site. One of the sergeants was interested to hear I'd been at Outward Bound and questioned me about what they did in the area.

Certain other vivid memories of the experience have persisted over the years. Lying in the poncho lean-to in the middle of a cool night with the soft rustle of the Linville River far below, I'd don the head-set and sweep the radio receiver oven an array of short wave signals, stations in London and Johannesburg, Havana and Paris, surfing the ionosphere for music while passing time before the next Morse contact with Bragg. The cacophony of foreign tongues crackling with static and the industrial drone of teletype waves combined with snatches of pop songs and the furor of mighty orchestras suggested to me a frenetic even maniacal energy which contrasted acutely with the serenity of the darkened Gorge around me.

There was one evening when some of the other outlying teams began making animal sounds, covertly they thought, over the voice radio. Furry mammal chirps and squeaks seemed a funny distraction to us until abruptly a voice of authority seemed to break out of Old Testament clouds to squelch the goofing-off with threats of speedy dismissal and return to the fort.

One cool gloomy wet dusk the sergeants emerged into our camp carrying the High Speed Burst Transmitter device, an experience described in Marci Spencer's *Pisgah National Forest*. We took turns punching in field messages that had already been encoded and the little CIA gizmo fired them off with a discreet little buzz, next to impossible to catch in the air and slowed down, decoded, and read at Bragg.

At the conclusion of the two-week Pisgah exercise it felt quite strange to have been away from Army routine so long. On that day, the sergeants called together all the teams at a meeting place on the Kistler Highway. With everyone present or accounted for, one instructor began: "Listen up men. I want ever' one of you mustered in that Table Rock parking lot by 0900 hours tomorrow." He raised his arm in its crisply starched fatigue blouse to indicate a break in the tree line to the right of Table Rock. The gazes of the thirty-odd men around him settled on that landmark, then traced an imaginary line which descended the east side of the canyon, passed over sheer cliffs, paused at nigh impassible masses of shrubs, crossed the wavery white line of the boulder-choked river, and rose again to the forested west side on Linville Mountain where we stood. We were contemplating one hell of a walk. The sergeants' truck left us in a cloud of white Kistler dust.

We held a hasty consultation, during which I, as a former trekker of the gorge, urged them to seek out one of the Forest Service trails to the river. We wasted about a quarter of an hour scouting the road north and south for trailheads. A few self-appointed leaders then plunged down the banks and the rest followed. Down and down we slid and scrambled, fighting our way through the infamous "hells" or laurel thickets, with their limbs catching at our feet or clutching at the equipment we carried. One man's canteen slipped from his grasp during a break, and I remember how it tumbled out of sight down the slope. By late afternoon we had reached the river, which we crossed single-file holding our looped web belts. I took a brief dunking with the result that my photos were water-stained. On the other side, the party lumbered up through the dense dog-hobble between tremendous boulders, mostly speechless from fatigue. At dusk, everyone simply hit the dirt and collapsed for the night with no attempts at dining or radio messaging. Early the next morning, still damp to the waist, we continued, until eventually we emerged right alongside the bluffs of Little Table Rock and hastened down to the parking lot. There, at 0900 hours, a sergeant casually said, "Now keep on going and we'll see you on the shore of Lake James." Down the dusty Forest Service road we trudged, insects rasping and buzzing in the trees, and the completion of the course nearing with every step. Scents of roasting phone poles exhaled the tangs of Carolina creosote. Big migratory warblers sang in the whirring brush. Later in the afternoon we were greeted by cool lake waters below red clay banks and the welcome sight of truck transport.

At one of the boat ramp picnic areas at Lake James State Park the sergeants were all waiting with our "B" team support crew from Franklin's Restaurant; with them they had brought cases of ice-cold sodas, cool ripe watermelons, fried chicken with cole slaw and potato salad, cake and ice cream. We swam and gorged ourselves while the instructors briefed us on our grades. Students who had sent out nonsensical rather than military-style communiques were lucky to have those counted as legitimate radio traffic. Finally, the Deuce-and-a-half diesel trucks rumbled up to take us back to training brigade at Bragg. Just as with Outward Bound, it took a day or two to acclimatize to the tempo and complexity of domestic routine.

NOTE: The Special Forces radio operator skills required in the late 1960s pall beside today's complicated tasks, which range from complex computer programs to satellite communications. The radio operator in the Vietnam War era needed proficiency in radio-telegraph procedures peculiar to special forces operations, such as sending in Morse code at eighteen words per minute and receiving at twenty words per minute. He needed a grasp of cryptography or encoding, the ability to transmit on high and ultra-high frequencies, and handiness at making and operating field antennas.

In a review of the first edition of *River of Cliffs* posted on his Linville Gorge Yahoo! Group site on Monday, July 4, 2006, Bob Underwood recalled his own encounters with the Green Berets training in the Gorge. His complaint about lack of Gorge cave coverage is addressed in the second, following a letter by North Carolina spelunker Dr. Cato Holler.

I chanced upon Christopher Blake at the [Famous Louise's] *Rockhouse Restaurant this past weekend and we shared an animated but all too brief conversation about things Linville.*

Blake has recently published a digest of various historical and fictional references to Linville Gorge. He quotes extensively from the journals of the 1800s early explorers. Then he reprints parts of Jules Verne's novel, Master of the World, a successor to the more famous Twenty Thousand Leagues under the Sea. Blake recounts his adventures as a trainee in the Special Forces back in the '70s [1969] *as they scrambled through the gorge. He also records his diary notes from a month at Outward Bound. Blake and I have travelled similar paths; I know some of his O.B. instructors: John Lawrence and David Mashburn. Lawrence once said of the Rockjock Trail* [created by Underwood in the 1960s in the southwest gorge]*: "It is a genuine work of Art." I also encountered one of the U.S. Army Special Forces sergeants, Perkins, who found a rope I had left hanging near The Camel back where there were no trails to the North Carolina Wall. I returned for the rope four days later, shocked to find it gone. Eventually, after asking some of the S.F. troops about it, I contacted Sgt. Perkins and enjoyed his hospitality at his home in Fayetteville—and got my rope back.*

I believe some S.F. units trained quite differently from others. Most of the time I would see them stationed near the trailheads—I wonder if they really saw anything of the area they were camped on top of—but occasionally I would find military gear in places like The Amphitheater—so I know that at least a few of them got a good look.

Another addition to the book could be the list of Linville caves compiled by the North Carolina Cave Survey. Some members of the survey were active in the search for [Eric] Rudolph a few years back and out of their catalog of 2000? Caves I'd guess about twenty are found in the Linville wilderness.

Blake covers the original accounts of the murder of Linville by Indians in the 1700s but does not cover the more recent murders on Spence Ridge Trail a few years ago by an "Eric Rudolph wannabe."

We discussed the latest news on the Old Lead Mine legend (which has many variations).

River of Cliffs is painfully short of photos, but I guess that if it sells well, the coffee-table picture book of The Grand Canyon of the East would make a fine second addition.

Blake considers Linville Gorge a sacred place; so do well all!

"Special Forces Training in Linville Gorge Area," an article by Thomas Ditt, turned up in my gorge archives, with no indication of source, place of publication, or date. It is included for its peep into late '60s Green Beret operations in the gorge and Falls area. Unfortunately, it breaks off as a sergeant is answering a question of Ditt's.

With the coming of warmer weather, many McDowell Countians will make an annual pilgrimage to Wiseman's View to watch the Brown Mountain Lights and get a spectacular view of Linville Gorge.

In addition to these two area attractions, the visitor might get a glimpse of olive-drab clad figures and trucks moving in the area. Don't be alarmed; we are not in the midst of another "mock warfare exercise" like last summer.

The men are part of a communications trainee group from Fort Bragg's Special Forces Detachment training in the area.

The 34-trainees and three instructors were scheduled to parachute into an area north of Morganton Tuesday of last week, but due to bad weather were forced to drive in.

Base of operations is in a small frame house back of the Linville Falls Post Office and in a room over the Linville Falls Restaurant.

One of the instructors, Sgt. William Bridges, said of the training, "This is an exercise on unconventional guerilla warfare. We have 7 four-men teams deployed in the field and one four-man team in the room over the restaurant. They are communications teams and try to communicate with Fort Bragg."

Sgt. Bridges, Sgt. Dale Magee, and myself visited one of the field camps Friday afternoon. The camp was located approximately 50 yards off the Wiseman's View road on the Babel Tower Trail.

The shelter housing the radio was made of eight ponchos tied together. The radio is a 15-watt transmitter.

"The trainees receive and send messages to Bragg and this is the way that they get their food. Each camp is moved every so often. The A-teams are in the field around the Linville Gorge area and along Kistler Memorial Highway, and the B-team is in the restaurant. Bragg will radio us (the instructors) and then we will take the food (C rations) to an area and leave them for the team to pick up," said Magee.

"Linville Gorge is a very rough area and an ideal place for training. It would compare to the areas of Greece," noted Bridges.

Not only are the trainees getting trained, but they are performing a valuable service for the U.S. Forest Service.

Says Grandfather Ranger District Ranger John Kennedy, "The group polices the gorge every day and are on call to help us fight fires. They leave the area in better shape when they leave than when they come in. We're glad to have them."

This group will leave the area April 19 and a group of Marines from Camp Lejeune will come in then for training.

After visiting the field camp, Sgt. Ernest Bryant and myself visited the B-team camp over the Linville Falls Restaurant.

On one side of the room two trainees manned a bank of radios, while others stood by. In one corner of the room two medics matched wits over a chess board.

In answer to a question, Bryant said, "No, this wouldn't be the best place to be because this team in the... [source breaks off]

25

"LINVILLE GORGE CAVES"

In reply to the editor's question about caves in the wilderness, North Carolina Cave Survey director and former Marion, North Carolina dentist Dr. Cato Holler sent me the following concise overview of the gorge speleology. His brief résumé includes writing the guide, with his wife, Susan, to the Linville Caverns and membership in the Explorer's Club. He is an active member of the Jules Verne Society, hosting a 2012 conference in Marion where he lectured on Verne and the Brown Mountain Lights. He poses inside Hole Rock, a deep pothole on the Linville River south of Babel Tower, in my Arcadia Images of America volume *Linville Gorge Wilderness Area* (2009).

Hi Chris,

It's nice to hear from you. Sounds like a fascinating project. We'll be looking forward to the release of your new book. On the subject of caves in the gorge: it's true that due to the lack of limestone, we have never seen any karstic (or solution) caves (such as Linville Caverns) in the gorge. On the other hand, the gorge abounds with other cave types. Rock shelters of various sizes are quite numerous. Generally wider than deep, these features are found weathered out along weak zones in cliff faces. Tectonic (or fissure) caves are large cracks caused by fracturing of the rock. Boulder (or talus) caves develop along stream beds and at the base of cliffs.

Another small cave type is the eroded "pothole" caused by swirling water action. There are a couple of good examples of these in the gorge. The caves are significant for a number of reasons. For many generations, people have camped or sought refuge in rock shelters such as the large well-known Conley Cove Rockhouse. The caves also serve as important habitats for some fascinating biota. Bats, salamanders, and pack rats are sometime found in these underground retreats. Several undescribed species of invertebrates such as white, cave-adapted flatworms and amphipods have been observed in shallow pools. The caves are a vital part of the natural history of the gorge and as such, should be respected. If you are fortunate enough to come across one of these in your explorations, please abide by the motto of the National Speleological Society, "Take nothing but pictures; Leave nothing but (carefully placed) footprints.

As director of the North Carolina Cave Survey, I always enjoy hearing from hikers who might have come across a new cave in the gorge. Some of these can be of significant scientific interest as well as one of the many natural curiosities of the gorge.

Hope the above comments will be of some help.

Here are a few comments about myself:

Dr. Cato Holler Jr.
Director, North Carolina Cave Survey
Recently retired dentist, having practiced for 38 years in Old Fort, N.C.
Founding member and Chairman Emeritus of Flittermouse Grotto of the National Speleological Society
Fellow Emeritus of the Explorers Club
Co-author (with wife Susan) of *Caves of South Carolina*
Co-author (with wife, Susan) of *Hollow Hills of Sunnalee, The LinvilleCaverns Story*
Director of the North American Jules Verne Society
Active member of the Brown Mountain Lights Research Group

26

MOUNTAIN YARNS, LEGENDS AND LORE

"A Trip to Linville Gorge" appears among these yarns in which J. Alex Mull, writing sometime in the early 1970s, offers us "modest tales of fact and fiction, which in the opinion of the author, are typical of the early days in the Blue Ridge Mountain country." Born in Morganton in 1909 of Scotch-Irish and Dutch parentage, Mull's maternal forbears founded the Swannanoa Settlement in Buncombe County—as he puts it, "the first white out-post west of the Blue Ridge." He was owner and developer of the Gingercake Acres Community. The wager footrace up the Gorge, described here in the first of the four Mull pieces, has inspired Mountain Park author Allen Hyde's Franklin Challenge Marathons in recent years.

A Trip to Linville Gorge

It begins (the river, that is) with clear, cold, bubbling springs on the sides of Sugar Mountain, Grandfather Mountain, and nearby peaks east of Tennessee Divide; forks around the City of Linville into Lake Kawahna at the foot of Pixie Mountain; comes nearly full circle around the camps of Linn Haven and Carolina on its way through the old Anthony Lake bed; meanders through Pineola, then rushes in a narrowed bed between Snakeden Mountain and Locust Knob; begins to change pace around Crossnore where it winds through the Sam Brown Bottoms [near the North Carolina Division of Forest Resources training facility], making a big loop on its way to Linville Falls.

All along its course can be found clear, placid pools reflecting the profuse rhododendron and overhanging hemlock trees, interrupted at intervals by swift shoals and roaring rapids. Then suddenly it plunges precipitously in two drops about 200 feet into the most rugged gorge east of the Rocky Mountains.

My first experience in the Gorge came at age 15, when I was summoned by Mr. Willie Wise, fire warden, as follows: "I hereby summon you to be on top of Dogback Mountain in the morning at six o'clock to 'fit' far'" (meaning to fight fire).

This was an exciting adventure to me since I had heard so many stories about this area, but I didn't realize then just how exciting it was going to be.

Within a few hours about 8 to 10 men (and one boy) gathered for the trip. To take us part way was an old Model T Ford truck....This "Paul Revere" of the Hills was not suited for mountain climbing since the gas tank was under the seat with a gravity flow to the carburetor. Therefore, whenever a steep hill encountered you had to "back up" so the gas would flow to the motor. Still, it was better than walking.

We quickly gathered our provisions (rakes, sandwiches, shovels, and axes) and started for Dogback Mountain, where the forest fire was out of control. The old Model T made it about half way up the mountain and we walked about eight miles further, to an abandoned saw mill camp, where we "bedded down" until dawn.

I was awakened by a companion, complaining that he had slept with a rock in the middle of his back. When I told him how comfortable I rested, he said, "Well, I reckon so, with your head on a pile of horse manure." (If you have never tried it, I can assure you it makes a comfortable bed...especially on top of a mountain fighting fire.)

Now firefighting in those days was all hand labor....There were no dozers, chain saws, sprinklers, or other modern equipment; only rakes, hoes, axes, and shovels [similarly at Outward Bound]. The theory was to hack, rake, and clear a trail ahead of the fire, then set the woods afire between the trail and the forest fire itself. The "backdraft" caused by the suction of air toward the big fire would cause the little fire to burn upwind, clearing a strip of land ahead of the blazing inferno...causing it to slow down. That was the theory!

My duty was to patrol this trail up and down the mountainside to keep the little fires from starting another "big fire." Well, Mister, if you have ever tried to mind 400 mischievous children at one time over a thousand-acre playground, you have an idea of my problem.

Finally, with my tongue half dragging the ground, I discovered that the "big fire" didn't believe in theories! It had jumped the trail and was roaring down the mountain as if the Devil was after me. (I thought for a while he was gonna catch me too.) So I ran and staggered all the way down that steep mountain to the river before I caught up with the rest of the party. When informed that we were cut off from the only road, we were all proud that some bear hunters were with us who knew the Gorge and where the trails were. This was my introduction to Linville Gorge, and Brother, whatever you may have heard—either ridiculous, gigantic, or absurd—you can believe it!

There are boulders larger than houses with water swirling on all sides… saw-briars that can take your arm off [*Smilax,* also known as cat-briar and wait-a-minute vine]…Laurel "hells" and pot holes, with the solid rock walls of the canyon heading straight up toward the sky.

And that river! It's a miniature Grand Canyon gone plumb wild…so swift in places that it can actually take a man's pants off in waist deep water! It's hard to imagine the breath-taking beauty of this wilderness area, it's so wild and different…surrounded by rugged mountain peaks and virgin forests, you'd think you were in another world. I don't know how many snakes we may have run over. Since we were more afraid of the fire than rattlesnakes… but I do know that they are there, which reminds me of a tale I heard:

A mountain man named Franklin, well-known for his reckless as well as other spirits, took a dare and a bet that he could go up the Gorge in one day…a trip that usually takes three to four days. Well, he started at Beach Bottoms, just above Lake James; tied his pants legs to his boots; stuffed his pants with dried leaves until he looked like a Dutchman in pantaloons; drank a pint of "white lightning" and started up the Gorge.

A companion who had followed him said that before he got two miles up the Gorge, he had three copperheads and one rattlesnake stuck to his britches like barbed wire around a fence post. But he won the bet…with his leather boots and pants full of leaves, he didn't have to worry about snakes.

On our firefighting trip, we were led out of the Gorge by a man named Jim Gray, a true mountaineer and bear hunter. He led us up over cliffs that seemed to be straight up and down, called the "Bear Den Cliffs" that looked impossible for a man to climb, but he knew where each crack and foothold was located.

Reminds me of the song, "Rock of Ages, Cleft for Me"…he knew where the "clefts" were.

GINGERCAKE MOUNTAIN

Sitting on the porch of a 150-year-old, hand-hewn log cabin, on the rim of a mountain as old as time itself, and looking out into the haze of the distance over a veritable ocean of mountain peaks as far as the eye can see, gives me a feeling of awe and serenity; a feeling of humble faith in something greater than man; a sense of promise for the future that the daily news of man's actions threatens to destroy; a belief that things will come out all right somehow, sometime, and renewal of the spirit of body and soul.

Old Gingercake rises to a height of only 4,000 feet and is surrounded by the most majestic, unusual, and famous collection of mountains in this hemisphere. To the north, only eight miles away, is the oldest mountain in the world—Grandfather; to the west is Mount Mitchell, the highest mountain east of the Rockies; southwest are Table Rock, Hawksbill, Sitting Bear and the only [with Shining Rock] "Wilderness Area" (Linville Gorge) in the Eastern United States; east is Blowing Rock, Chestnut Knob, Brown Mountain (with her mysterious light) and range after range, peak after peak (tumbling over each other as if in a hurry to get somewhere) of blue and green mountain tops, blending into the distant sky like stair steps into heaven.

I started, though, to tell of Gingercake—of the hermit, the "thresh rock," the "old timers," Cindy's Gap, and the legends and true stories of a mountain that has more to tell than any I know. So I will commence, not in the beginning with heaven and earth, but with man—THE HERMIT.

The stories I have heard agree substantially with the account of an expedition, published in 1848 and entitled *Letters from the Alleghany Mountains* [see chapter nine], and later published in *The State* magazine.

In this book the mountains were referred to as "Alleghany," whereas now they are called the "Blue Ridge Mountains." If you would take a look at the rainfall map in your geography book, you will notice that the heaviest rainfall is in the section now called the Blue Ridge Mountains. This name is very descriptive since the moisture in the air gives the distant hills a very blue color.

The Gingercake Mountain derives its name from a singular pile of rock on the extreme summit [incorrect, for one can look down on Sitting Bear's top from higher up on Gingercake]. There is one huge boulder 32 feet in length and about 8 feet thick balanced precariously on a pyramid shaped stone, 30 feet in height and now called "Sitting Bear Rock." Geologists say it's been sitting there for thousands of years. Which reminds me of a little poem I learned as a boy.

I wish I wuz a little rock,
A 'settin' on a hill;
Not doing nuthin' but just sitin' still.
I wouldn't eat, I wouldn't drink.
I wouldn't even wash—
I'd just set there a thousand years
And rest myself, by gosh.

"Sitting Bear" was so named because, from a distance, it looks exactly like a huge bear on its haunches. The mountain was named by a hermit named Watson who died and was buried there in 1816.

Our hermit lived in a small two-room log cabin, entirely alone, and, though peculiar and eccentric ("tetched in the haid" by local standards) was noted for his amiability and loquacity.

He had given up the world because of a disappointment in love, and one of his most peculiar traits was his utter contempt for females. Whenever ladies were in his presence he treated them politely, but never spoke another word to a woman 'til the day he died. Furthermore, he even went so far as to burn the top rail of any fence they straddled, and covered with dirt any place they sat.

He never molested the wild animals around him and the deer, squirrels and foxes considered him their friend. His hobby, or avocation, was the raising of peacocks, a very loud-mouthed fowl that were better than watchdogs when visitors approached. They are also credited with killing snakes of all kinds, which would be a comfort to me in this area. All his clothes were trimmed with peacock feathers, and his best suit was covered almost entirely with these beautiful spots of color. For some unknown reason he referred to his suit as his "culgee" and was locally called Culgee Watson. To this day he is still spoken of by that name.

The location of his cabin was undoubtedly in the gap between Gingercake Mountain and Hawksbill Mountain (so called because of its resemblance to the bill of a giant bird) and now known as the McKinney place. The United States Forest Service now has a camp and picnic area near the spot [which is also close to the Devil's Hole Trailhead].

The two mountains mentioned, Gingercake and Hawksbill, together with Table Rock Mountain and Shortoff Mountain, form the east wall of the Linville Gorge Wilderness Area and are among the most picturesque and unusually shaped mountains in the world. According to the geologists, these rugged peaks were formed by a tremendous glacier during the Ice Age. They are now part of the Pisgah National Forest.

One of the first tales I heard when I built my log cabin for a summer home on Gingercake was of the "Thresh Rock" This is an immense outcropping of stone—the backbone of the mountain—with numerous depressions or cups chipped in the rock, where the early settlers (and Indians before them) used to "flail" their small grain. When the wheat, oats, rye or buckwheat was harvested (always with hand reapers) it was brought in sheafs to the "thresh rock" and there flailed or beaten with brush or small sticks. [On the contrary, the cavities were not chipped but formed by untold eons of geologic action, namely wind spinning small stones in a quartzite pocket to form the crater in which rainwater still gathers.]

The rock is located on the rim of the mountain where there is most always a breeze [possibly the bluff overhanging Highway 181 at the entrance to the Table Rock Road]. So like the passage in Scripture: "Like chaff which the wind driveth away," the breeze would blow away the chaff and leave the grain in the holes or depressions cut into the rock. This was seldom a time for celebration as it was very hard work and serious business.

Another ghostly, but true, story about this rock concerns the McKinney family who lived some three miles down the trail at the foot of Hawksbill Mountain. As told to me, the head of the household failed to come home when expected, so a search was started. Now mountain folk are perhaps more superstitious than most, so when one of the search party saw a stiff, cold hand sticking out of the leaves on top of "Thresh Rock," they took off like scared "haints" [haunts] to find the law.

When the group, with reinforcements, finally returned, the hand (and supposed body) was not there. Now in fact, the murdered body of McKinney was later found buried below a spring about one half mile away; and to this day, how and by whom he was killed, or how his body was spirited away has never been revealed. Many of the natives have knowin' looks when telling of this episode, but true to the "code" of the hills, not one has ever told the true story.

Cindy's Gap is another spot on the Mountain that has always intrigued me. The stories are true; as numerous residents can testify. There were two homes at the Gap, one in the "flats" occupied by Bo Franklin (of whom more will be heard later), and another down the mountain-side near a spring, which was known as Cindy's Place. Here was the gathering place for the Saturday night "hoe downs," "jamborees," and "frolics" that are still the talk of the old timers.

These are only a few stories and legends about old Gingercake. And now where the "frolicking" and episodes of violence used to be common, there is a new resort community, dedicated to modern enjoyment of the peace and serenity of these beautiful hills. Occasionally, the "plinkin" of the banjo is heard, but usually at the Recreation Club, far, far from Cindy's Gap.

Note: Mull's scriptural reference is from Psalm 35, verse five of David, who calls on the Lord to blast his enemies: "Let them be like chaff before the wind, with the angel of the Lord driving them on."

Dan the Mountain Man

There is one real "character" of all the mountain people who stand out in my memory above the others. This man we will just call Dan, which is what everyone else calls him. The tales about this gent are too numerous to document; and like stories about most characters, some are true, and some are untrue. The following accounts have been repeated so often, by so many different people, that one can't help but believe them.

Dan's father was an excellent business man, having accumulated over the years many acres of valuable land, mica mines, and mercantile interests. He was determined that all of his children get a first class education, and so they did—all but Dan. He had the opportunity, and it looked for a while that we would do as well, if not better, than his brothers. He became interested in art and sculpture, attended one of the Ivy League universities, and had so much talent that he won a scholarship in France. There the lures of Paris and the beautiful live statues in the night clubs and Follies intrigued him more than the cold, cold marble, and the silk and mascara brushes more than the canvas and camel's hair brushes.

The story goes that he fell in love with an actress and after following her all over Europe, finally wound up broke, spurned, and heart-broken in Rome. This completely cured him of art and artists of all kinds. It is said that from the time he wired for money to come home to the present time, he never touched chisel or brush again.

It is like the "Twilight Zone" for our hero…he jumped back 100 years in time to the days of his ancestors. To this day he wears high boots, a slouch hat or coon skin cap, tight levis, a frontier jacket, and looks and talks like a man who had never seen a train, ship, or city. He prefers a horse for transportation, but will settle for a beat-up truck for longer trips.

Dan will stay out in the woods or along the river just as long as his "rations" hold out…fishing, hunting, or just settin' and looking. His true love is bear hunting above all others, though a few tow-headed Dan Juniors, scattered throughout the hills, attest to a sport he learned too well in Paris.

Dogs and kids all love Dan as he loves them…loyally, totally, selflessly, and completely. The following story of a bear hunt shows what he thinks of his houn' dogs:

It was in November, just after "Bruin" had loaded up chestnuts, acorns, and other delectable bear "tid bits" that prepared her for her winter's nap. The dogs had trailed a good part of the day until everyone was exhausted except Dan. He always got more excited than even the dogs, and was credited with having a better nose than they did.

Finally, way down in Linville Gorge, he could barely hear the pack baying, which was a sign they had either "treed" or "cornered" the varmint, and that it wasn't a deer they had been trailing. (A true bear hunter despises deer because they sometimes side-track the dogs.)

Realizing what a she-bear will do when cornered, and that his most beloved bear dog, "old Belle," was in the pack, Dan took off his coat, propped his gun against a tree, and started running with only a hunting knife at his belt for protection against the strongest and meanest beast in the mountains.

When he finally stumbled to the scene of the battle, three of the pack were already dead, his own true love was bleeding from a nasty shoulder wound, but still fighting valiantly along with several other dogs. Now "bear dogs" in the mountains are so called, regardless of breed, because of the bravery, tenacity, and size. They fight in a pack like bull dogs teasing a bull; a quick lunge forward with teeth bared, then back out of reach of the 600-pound chunk of dynamite. At the same time, others of the pack are nipping at the flanks and sides in an effort to get the beast off balance and get at her throat. Even a sizeable pack of first-class dogs are no match for a full grown bear without assistance from their masters. In this battle, with only a few dogs left, and one of them wounded, it would only be a matter of times before all the dogs would be in "dog heaven."

Dan hesitated only enough for the bear's attention to turn before he leaped plumb straddle of that bear's back and started jabbing his hunting knife at her heart and throat. This distracted the she-devil just long enough for the remaining hounds to close in; and with a tangle of bear, dog, and Dan, succeeded in winning the war. Dan escaped with only one gash in his arm, delivered in error by one of the dogs. When the rest of the party arrived on the scene, they found Dan bleeding like a stuck hog, trying to bandage up "old Belle" with his shirt (in November).

By modern standards, with his education and talents, he is a "drop-out" who could have been famous, wealthy, and happy. Happy? He wouldn't leave his mountain retreat for all the wealth in Boston. If you would like to meet this no good, lovable gent, go to the Linville Gorge section of North Carolina during bear hunting season, and look for an excited old man in his 70's (who looks 50) with snow white hair wearing tight levis, a slouch hat, high boots, and a hunting knife on his belt.

If the dogs are running, you will see an expression of joy and happiness on his face that would make "the man who broke the bank at Monte Carlo" look like an undertaker.

The Ridge Where Jonas Froze

Most mountain peaks, ridges, or knolls were named for the original owners or residents, such as Ben's Knob, Carpenter's Knob, Walker's Top, Baker's Mountain, etc.; or for their shape, like Table Rock, Grandfather Mountain, Hawks Bill, Short Off; or for their coloring, like Black Mountain, Blue Ridge, etc.

The mountain ridge in this story, however, has a different twist.

I am indebted a great deal to the late Mr. Martin Barrier of Jonas Ridge, a very fine gentleman and leader in his community, for much of my information. The story as told to me concerns a man by the name of Jonas (Jonas Braswell) who was in or resided near the community now called Jonas Ridge, North Carolina.

It seems that Mr. Jonas went bear hunting down in the Linville Gorge area in the fall with one companion. Now it so happens even today a blizzard can come up with very little warning, with the temperature dropping 20, 30, and even 40 degrees within hours. That is what happened on this day, so the two hunters started back for shelter across the highest ridge in Burke County.

Near the summit Jonas developed what was called "stomach cramps," or colic, and could go no further; so his companion left him in a cave and went for help. Dwellings then were mighty far apart and the blizzard didn't help any, so when finally his companion returned with help, they found poor Mr. Jonas frozen to death…stiff as a board. Hence the name, the "Ridge Where Jonas Froze" and finally just "Jonas Ridge." [See Charles Preston Arthur's *History of Watauga County* in chapter 27 below, for a variant source for Jonas Ridge.]

According to my information, the Barriers were the first permanent settlers in this area, and today are the most numerous inhabitants. A story told me by the Honorable Frank C. Patton concerns one reason why Jonas Ridge has, for the most part, been a Democratic stronghold in a predominantly Republican region. It seems that the first Mr. Barrier was well educated for the times and somehow received copies of the old *New York World*, a very partisan newspaper. This paper, together with his own personal convictions, helped to influence his family and neighbors to such an extent that, until recent years, one could count on a sure Democratic vote in the Jonas Ridge Township.

This section of the mountains, until very recently, was almost inaccessible, with no decent roads. A lawyer in Morganton who wanted to attend Court in Newland (County seat of Avery County, only 36 miles away) had to catch the Southern R.R. train from Morganton to Marion; change in Marion to the C.C.&O. for Spruce Pine [see note at end of this chapter]; then change again on to the East Tennessee and Western Carolina Railway ("Tweetsie") for Linville; and then take a hack from Linville to Newland. Some journey for a day in court!

In the early days, the Loven family, who lived at the foot of the mountain near Steele Creek Park (another branch of Lovens lived at the top of the mountain and operated the Loven Hotel at Cold Springs) decided to open a wagon road up the mountain to Jonas Ridge [present-day Highway 181].

This was a back breaking task since there were no tools to work with except hand—pick and shovel, but they cut a wagon trail up over Ripshin Mountain. I was told that to remove the large outcroppings of stone, huge fires were built on top of the rock and let burn for several days until the rock was "hot as fire," and then cold creek water was poured over the stone, causing it to split into pieces of rock small enough to handle. After opening this wagon road, the Lovens erected a gate, charging a "toll" of ten cents per horseman or twenty-five cents for a team and wagon.

In this community today are many descendants of the early settlers… Barriers, Lovens, Franklins, who could tell many tales if so motivated.

Mr. Salem Franklin (known as the Squire of Jonas Ridge) was a community leader and postmaster for many, many years. Back then most folks made a little "likker"….It didn't seem wrong for a man to grow his own corn or apples, on his own land, and make a little brandy or "corn squeezings" for himself and friends. The Revenooers looked down on this practice, however, so a code was evolved that worked and still works for most mountain folks… "You don't tell on me and I won't tell on you."

This system worked very well until a gent by the name of Bo Franklin moved into the community in 1925. [Of whom we will hear more later.] Now Bo was quite a controversial character, to say the least, with a following who liked him and an equally large group who feared him. They say that he did pretty well and was right good-hearted until he got drunk, but then he became plumb mean. He was convicted and served three years about 1926 or 1927 for killing his own son-in-law, in what was described as a drunken brawl. I had it from the late Mr. Hansel Singleton, Forest Service interpretive host at the Information Cabin on the Kistler Highway, that, "Bo beat him to death with logging chains." Hansel paused a moment to reflect, "No, sir—you did not want to get on Bo's wrong side"]. He was charged with a number of other crimes but never convicted.

Arthur Causby, who was custodian of the County Jail at the time, said of Bo, "If he liked you, he would do most anything for you, but if he didn't like you, better stay away from him. When he was drinking, he would try and get even with his enemies.

Stanley Moore recalls one instance when Bo was incarcerated in the local jail, when the prisoners got hold of an old guitar and were having a regular "jamboree" inside that attracted quite an audience across the street. Stanley said, "He (Bo) is the only person who ever dedicated a song to me, so I can't help but remember him kindly."

Bo Franklin is buried in the cemetery at Jonas Ridge, and on his tombstone is his photograph and the inscription "A sinner saved by the grace of God." [Mr. Leroy Rose of Ridge explains Bo's photograph set in the tombstone as meant to confront anyone looking out from the church windows, particularly the ones among the congregation whom he hated.] He left many legends and stories unanswered and was perhaps blamed for some things he didn't do. A number of his children still reside in the Jonas Ridge area, and to my knowledge are mighty fine citizens and a credit to the community.

Note: The *New York World* ran from 1860 until 1931. Staunchly Democratic, the paper was purchased by Joseph Pulitzer in 1883. In his rivalry with William Randolph Hearst's *Journal American*, Pulitzer pushed his sensationalist reportage into the era of "yellow journalism."

The Carolina, Clinchfield & Ohio Railroad, or Clinchfield, crosses the Appalachians from Elkhorn City, Kentucky, to Spartanburg, South Carolina, a span of 277 miles. It passes under the southern end of Linville Gorge, by Linville Mountain, before winding up in the Blue Ridge at Altapass. Created to haul coal from the fields of Kentucky and Virginia to the South Carolina Piedmont, the line offered passenger service from 1909 to 1954. Today, the CXS line shuttles coal cars southward many times daily.

27

A HISTORY OF WATAUGA COUNTY

A second candidate for the origin of Jonas Ridge's name is one William Jonas Braswell, a hero of the Revolutionary War, whom Charles Preston Arthur venerates in his 1915 book on Watauga. Avery County historian Michael Hardy points out that the name "Jonas" is found in the area before the appearance of William Braswell. Preston lived from 1851 to 1916, practiced law in Asheville until 1898 and wrote a history of western North Carolina. He is a source for the Civil War iron forge operating upstream from Linville Falls until it was raided by Union colonel George Kirk in 1864.

William Jonas Braswell, Hero.—In a lonely field now owned by W.H. and Harstin Ollis, under two hickory trees, a third of a mile above the old Gen. Albertus Child's place on Three Mile Creek, is another one of those "monuments" at the unveiling or dedication of which our great government occasionally invites its citizens to be present. It contains an even more economical inscription than that of poor Edward Moody. It follows:

WM. BRASWELL,
N.C. MIL.
REV. WAR.

"That's the crap," as our farmers say in derision of a small offering. This was unveiled to the light of day and to the indignation of all right-thinking people in 1913, the crowd in attendance numbering nearly five hundred. That seems to be all this great and powerful government could find out about this dead hero, now without a vote. But others remember something else of him, John Wise, born May 9, 1835, relating that Braswell lived on Lower Creek in Burke County, and hunted through the country lying between that locality and Black Mountain, in what is now Yancey. He had relatives in Pensacola, near Big Tom Wilson's old home, "under the Black" [Mount Mitchell]. When a very old man, Braswell, his wife, and a girl named Yarber started late one fall from Lower Creek to Pensacola to visit people named Mace, relatives of his wife, probably. They had to spend the night in a camp under a rock on a high ridge leading up from Burke to the Linville country, then and now a much used highway for local travel, a wagon road now replacing the former trail. They could not procure fire, and a cold-snap coming on, the old man "froze down," to use Captain Wise's forceful phrase. When the chill morning dawned his wife and the Yarber girl met Jacob and William Carpenter at the ford of Linville River, to which point they had hastened through the darkness, seeking aid. The women went on to Carpenter's house in the meadow in front of Captain Wise's present residence, while the two Carpenter men hastened on to the camp rock, where Braswell was found, very low, but still alive. Placing him on a horse, they managed to keep him there by walking on each side of him and holding him in the saddle till they reached home. There he died after having revived for a short time, and was buried where the so-called "monument" now stands. His name was William Jonas Braswell, but to have spelled all that out on a tomb-stone would have required, at five cents a letter, at least fifty cents more! Hence, etc. The present wagon road does not pass very near the old camp rocks, but they are still remembered, while the high ridge on which they stand have preserved that part of a hero's name which a niggard nation consigned to oblivion, for it has been called ever since "Jonas's Ridge."

28

THE LOST AIRMEN OF JONAS RIDGE

On May 15, 1943, in Burke County's worst aviation disaster, eighteen young airmen of the Army Air Corps died in the crash and explosion of a Douglas C-47 on the side of Gingercake Mountain. For a day or two, the story made world headlines and then faded from public memory in the wake of news of ongoing campaigns of World War II. The lost airmen were to have joined in the Normandy invasion, having been trained as glider pilots at their home base at Fort Benning, Georgia. Tom Armstrong, adopted son of Courtney Armstrong of Knightstown, Indiana, mother of a casualty of the accident, Flight Officer James C. Armstrong, twenty-five, has kindly made available to me copies of his papers on the crash, including the local media coverage, aircraft clearance form and accident report. The account I give is a composite of news accounts, military records and information supplied to me by Mr. Armstrong.

At the second of impact, the hands of a wristwatch belonging to one of the dead airmen stopped at 4:35 p.m. Upon Flight Officer W.B. McBroom filing his instrument clearance for a take-off from Maxton Army Air Base, his C-47D transport plane had departed at three o'clock on the afternoon of May 15, 1943, bound for Cincinnati, Ohio. The army later ruled the crash time at approximately 5:00 p.m. Normal flight time for the 160-mile journey between Laurinburg-Maxton Army Air Base and Jonas Ridge should have been a little over an hour. The army inferred that McBroom had made 360-degree turns in zero visibility before attempting to clear the mountain. This accords with reports by witnesses in the area who had heard the plane circling above them in the pea-soup fog. The crash, however, must have occurred some half an hour before five o'clock.

Rocky Knob lies in the vicinity of Gingercake Mountain, which, with an elevation of 4,450 feet, is the highest point in Burke County. Human error melds with an act of God and Nature in that the flight clearance papers allow an altitude of 3,500 for pilot McBroom, who suddenly encounters a dense fog blanket mantling the crest of the Blue Ridge chain. He circles vainly, not gaining sufficient altitude, then tries to pull up at the last moment at a slanting granite slab on the side of Rocky Knob. The plane struck this rock at an angle, with trees on the bank soon shearing off both wings as it ploughed into the hillside. The nose and tail sections broke clear and parts of the craft such as the piston rings, wiring harness and manifold gauge were widely scattered over the scene. Exploding fuel tanks turned the area into a hellish scene as burning and mutilated airmen who had not been killed by the initial crash died in the flames spread by the deadly fireball of the explosion.

The Charlotte Observer of Monday, May 17, 1943, published an account of the disaster under the headline "Find 17 Bodies in Gingercake Mountain Crash." Ultimately, the eighteenth body was never located. To this day, there is literally a "lost airman" on Jonas Ridge. Early reports made factual errors such as reporting the plane as a bomber with Morris Field in Charlotte as its destination and the lives lost as numbering fourteen. The army, however, announced on May 17 that eighteen airmen had died and that the C-47 from Fort Benning's Lawson Field had been temporarily based at the Laurinburg-Maxton air base in North Carolina and had left Saturday on a routine training flight to Cincinnati, Ohio. Burke County sheriff R.C. Chapman told the Charlotte paper that seventeen bodies had been removed from the scene and that searchers were still looking for the eighteenth.

Area residents told first responders that they had counted fourteen bodies, strewn with the wreckage of the plane around an area of five to six hundred feet. An army detachment of black G.I.s arrived some hours after the crash to post guard and await army investigators. And now Bo Franklin reappears, for he lived some two hundred yards from the crash site. Franklin told Burke chief deputy sheriff W.R. Patton he saw the plane flying northward through the heavy fog. According to Franklin and other locals, the plane approached the mountain suddenly and tried to pull up but crashed. Bo Franklin reported hearing a loud "whooshing" noise that followed the initial impact:

the fuel explosion. The C-47 topped saplings before its right wing struck a large white oak tr/ee, twenty to twenty-five inches in diameter at the break.

Franklin stated that when he got to the crash site, he found the wreckage still in flames so that he could not get near to the men. According to the *Valdese News*, Franklin and family members "carried water to extinguish the blaze...particularly to a number of the bodies which though not in the midst of the bulk of the broken plane were ablaze."

Mrs. Franklin raced on foot to the home of her husband's brother, Deck Franklin, who made a two-mile trip, running most of the way, to the nearest forestry telephone, located on Chestnut Mountain (3,400 feet), where he called the forestry station at Mortimer. From this point the call was relayed to the Burke sheriff's office, which received the message about five o'clock. Deck's foot relay of the news is crucial to the timing of the events, for the air force sets the crash time at 5:00 p.m., around the same time the sheriff's office is getting the alarm call from the forestry telephone in Mortimer. A collision time of 4:35, as indicated by the frozen watch, allows for the two-mile footrace to the nearest telephone by 5:00 p.m.

Chief Deputy Sheriff W.R. Patton, rural policeman C.A. Fox and jailer Jim L. Smith left right away for the scene, accompanied by a reporter from the *Morganton News-Herald.* They arrived at six o'clock to find part of the wreckage still burning and a number of local children still bearing water to a small group of men of the neighborhood who had promptly made their way to the scene.

To Mr. Patton, the plane appeared to have started rising at what he estimated to be a thirty-degree angle before it crashed into a white oak tree, which it cut in two about thirty feet from the ground.

"The detached wings lay near shattered trees, while the bodies of the dead were strewn over an area estimated up to five hundred feet. Not over a third of the victims could be seen from any one point on the slope. Bodies lying further away seemed to have been burned less. While severely mangled, the bodies of most of the men could probably be identified by military authorities without too much difficulty," the sheriff's deputy concluded.

Chief Deputy Sheriff R.C. Chapman wrongly concluded that "death for the men had been instantaneous." Hansel Singleton and Leroy Rose were youngsters on the scene carrying water. Men were dying, screaming in the flames, which must have imparted a nightmarish glow to the spectral murk on the ridge. From a flight jacket caught in a tree above him a detached arm fell beside Rose. Perhaps this limb had the telltale watch attached to it and had escaped burning. Now, not having arrived until around an hour and a half after the crash, other officers held to the mistaken belief that probably "none of the men even had time to know of their danger, except possibly the pilot, who may have seen or felt the plane brushing over the tops of the smaller trees and attempted for a second to lift the craft in a steep climb but failed in the face of the rising slope before him." Chief Deputy Sheriff Chapman observed that an additional hundred feet in height might have saved the plane, while others pointed out that at the height the transport was maintaining it could have passed over Franklin's house and through what is known as Cindy's Gap if it had been flying two hundred yards to the west.

The dense fog afforded a visibility of little over zero. The first county officers to arrive estimated that a motorist could distinguish an object in the road ahead for only a hundred feet, a meaningless distance for a plane probably traveling between two hundred and three hundred miles an hour. Today, the dense fogs arising along Highway 181 from Morganton to the Gorge are notorious traffic calmers, especially where the old toll road (twenty-five cents a vehicle) crests the Ripshin Ridge. One is truly lost in the clouds

Initial reports of the accident told of fourteen bodies having been found, counted by residents of the area who were the first to arrive and who hinted that others might be dead. County officers, who found the plane too scattered to give them any clues as to the identification of the craft, reported by radio to the sheriff's office, which then notified the air force in Charlotte, but the army was unable to offer an immediate aircraft identification from that distance away from the scene.

Throughout upper Burke, the news of the tragedy spread like wildfire. Some Morganton residents first learned of it on Saturday night in news broadcasts coming over from radio stations as far away as Chicago.

The first of the curious onlookers came largely from Jonas Ridge township, but by Sunday morning cars started streaming into the area from more distant points, autos from two states being seen parked all along the roads in the vicinity, snarling the free automotive passage on the state highway

Sergeant C.R. Duncan, who was in charge of state patrolmen on duty there, figured that on Sunday between four and five thousand people came to the crash area, which was closed off with barbed wire and rope, with military guards patrolling to keep out the public.

A detachment of seven officers and men from Fort Benning arrived at mid-afternoon Sunday; they drove to Jonas Ridge from Hickory airport in a jeep they had flown up with. They found the traffic congestion so severe that they were forced to walk almost a half mile, instead of being able to drive to within two hundred yards of the secured site. They completed their investigation late Sunday night, and were supposed to have agreed with the theory, locally held, that while one body had not been discovered, no one who was on the plane escaped alive. What the media referred to as "The death plane" was huge, the kind normally used to carry up to forty men. In India, the Burke reporters understood, up to seventy-two men have been carried in an aircraft like this. Primarily a cargo plane, the C-47 could carry passengers on aluminum frame and nylon webbing benches ranged down each side of the fuselage. Below, I give air force specs on the C-47D.

"Salvage crews came up to the Gingercake Mountain from Morris Field late Saturday night and were busy all the next day with recovery of parts and remains, while helmeted black guards held back curious onlookers. Except for personal papers that escaped the flames and were removed earlier, little of value appeared left from the crash."

The *Morganton News-Herald* of Friday, May 21, reported the follow-up to the incident as the U.S. Army Air Force completed its investigation with the dynamiting of the plane's two large engines. Damaged beyond repair, they were blown up as a "precautionary measure" said the report, leaving minor wreckage scattered about. On May 25, the Morganton paper reported that army salvage crews had carried away the last pieces of the plane in what amounted to eight truckloads of wreckage taken to Morris Field in Charlotte for further salvage work. Workers used acetylene torches to cut up larger pieces of the plane, but onlookers noted that the bulk of the craft had already been shattered into little pieces. With the removal of the armed guard detachment, the abandonment of the search for the eighteenth victim and the release of the names of the dead, the army inquiry board posted a brief narrative of the accident, attributing 80 percent of the cause to the weather and 20 percent to pilot error.

The army report notes that "nothing at the scene of the crash indicated that anyone was expecting difficulty. This is borne out by the fact that the only body that was not thrown clear of the plane was found in the lavatory near the tail section. None of the passengers or crew were wearing parachutes at the time of the crash."

The story of the Lost Airmen of Jonas Ridge does not end here, however. Sometime in the early 2000s, a heavy equipment operator, digging utility lines in the crash vicinity, uncovered a cache of buried uniforms and footwear. Someone had stripped the bodies of most of their valuables and concealed their clothing—local suspicions settled on the man first on the scene, Bo Franklin. The backhoe operator contacted

Tom Armstrong in Indiana, who then visited the site to take charge of the discovery. I accompanied Armstrong and Jonas Ridge local Leroy Rose to the crash site on May 15, 2007, where Armstrong sketched a map of the collision for me and Rose collected pieces of wreckage with the aid of a metal detector. Scraps of windshield and fuselage had remained jammed under rocks, and a rubber shoe heel caught my eye. These remain in the Armstrong collection with the recovered clothing and a graduation photo of the airmen. Armstrong also recovered military-style barbed wire and k-ration cans from the scene, informing me that army barbed wire differs from that used for containing livestock.

To this day, there is no memorial to the lost airmen. Until such time as one is placed, this volume must serve as a tribute and memorial to the glider pilots, average age of twenty-three, who died near Linville Gorge less than a month before their scheduled participation in the June 6 Allied invasion of Europe at Normandy, codenamed "Operation Overlord."

1943 Crash Victim List

W.R. McBroom (Pilot) F/O Age 20
Son of: Mary Etta McBroom
Corvel City, Texas

Edward T. Russell (E) T.Sgt. Age 23
Brother-in-law: Glenn A. Magott
Bellville, Ohio

Robert C. Mack (Pilot) 2nd Lt. Age 25
Son of George Mack
Birmingham, Alabama

William B. Goddard (R) S.Sgt. Age 24
Son of James Goddard
Cincinnati, Ohio

Gerald J. Sutherland (E) T.Sgt. Age 22
Son of Arthur J. Sutherland
West Duluth, Minnesota

Francis P. McMahon (X) S.Sgt. Age 26
Son of Elizabeth McMahon
Portsmouth, Ohio

Kester J. Kruchar (R) S.Sgt. Age 23
Son of Joseph Kruchar
Chicago, Illinois

Guy A. Partridge (X) S.Sgt. Age 22
Son of Martha M. Partridge
Marion, Indiana

Donald D. Lewin (Pilot) 2nd Lt. Age 22
Son of Mabel E. Lewin
Huntington Park, California

Melvin F. Mulinax (R) Sgt. Age ?
Son of Mabel Mulinax
Decatur, Illinois

James H. Valentine (P) 2nd Lt. Age 21
Son of Mrs. H.H. Valentine
Cincinnati, Ohio

William T. Templeman (X) Pvt. Age 20
Son of Alice Templeman
Chicago, Illinois

Morten M. Katz (X) 1st Lt. Age 24
Son of Mrs. Herman R. Katz
Cincinnati, Ohio

Thomas B. Oskendahl (Glider Pilot)
2nd Lt. Age ?
Houston

James E.R. Lauderdale (Pilot)
2nd Lt. Age 25
Son of Mrs. W.C. Hughes
Artemisia, New Mexico

Orville M. Bucheit (Glider pilot)
F/O Age 23
Son of Mrs. L.C. Bucheit
Greencastle, Indiana

Joseph E. Plaza
Son of Emmett Plaza
Elks, Nevada

James C. Armstrong (Glider pilot)
F/O Age 25
Son of Courtney Armstrong
Knightstown, Indiana

Douglas C-47D "Skytrain"

U.S. Air Force History Support Office

Few aircraft are as well known or were so widely used, for so long, as the C-47, or "Gooney Bird," as it was affectionately nicknamed. The aircraft was adapted from the DC-3 commercial airliner, which appeared in 1936. The first C-47s were ordered in 1940; by the end of World War II, 9,348 had been procured for U.S. Army Air Force use. They carried personnel and cargo; in a combat role, they towed troop-carrying gliders and dropped paratroops into enemy territory.

After World War II, many C-47s remained in U.S. Air Force service, participating in the Berlin Airlift and other peacetime activities. During the Korean conflict, C-47s hauled supplies, dropped paratroops, evacuated the wounded and dropped flares for night bombing attacks. In Vietnam, the C-47 served again as a transport, but it was also used in a variety of other ways, including flying ground attack (gunship) missions [when it was dubbed "Puff the Magic Dragon, ed.], reconnaissance runs and psychological warfare.

Specifications

Span: 95 feet
Length: 64 feet, 5 inches
Height: 16 feet, 11 inches
Weight: 33,000 pounds loaded
Armament: None
Engines: Two Pratt & Whitney R-1830s
Horsepower: each engine 1,200
Crew: Six
Cost: $138,000

Performance

Maximum speed: 232 mph
Cruising speed: 175 mph
Range: 1,1513 miles
Service Ceiling: 24,450 feet

29

A NATURAL HISTORY OF NORTHWEST NORTH CAROLINA

Biology professor Stewart Skeate's lavishly illustrated naturalist guide to the mountainous area centering on Boone and Banner Elk, North Carolina, runs in its coverage from the New River in the north to Linville Gorge in the south. I know of no better specialized guide to the Gorge terrain than Skeate's, sadly now out of print. Dr. Skeate informs us about the violent geological formation of the Gorge and its ridges in the late Carboniferous and Permian periods some 325 to 250 million years ago, when Africa collided with the southeastern United States. He covers features from balds to bogs. Here, I excerpt Dr. Skeate's natural survey of the Linville Gorge Wilderness biosphere. Dr. Skeate teaches at Lees-McRae College in Banner Elk.

The 10,975 acres of the Linville Gorge Wilderness Area are located in the Pisgah National Forest in Burke County. A designated wilderness area is managed to maintain its natural character, and while hiking, hunting, fishing, and camping are allowed within its borders, road, timber harvesting, and mechanical vehicles are prohibited. Linville Gorge is located on the edge of the Blue Ridge with elevations ranging from 1,300 feet on the lower end of the Linville River to 4,120 on Gingercake Mountain. Uplift of the surrounding mountains and millions of years of carving by the Linville River have produced one of the deepest gorges in the east. The eastern rim of Linville Gorge consists of a series of rocky peaks, running from north to south. These include Gingercake Mountain, Sitting Bear Mountain, Hawksbill Mountain (elevation 4,020 feet), Table Rock Mountain (elevation 3,920 feet), The Chimneys, and Shortoff Mountain. The western rim consists of the long Linville Mountain. Two forest roads access the eastern and western side of the gorge, Kistler Memorial Highway on the west and Forest Service Road 210 on the east.

An excellent view of the scenic east rim can be seen from Wiseman's View off Kistler Memorial Highway. Linville Falls, located at the northern end of the gorge, is accessible either from Kistler Memorial Highway or the Blue Ridge Parkway. All of the peaks and the river are accessible by an extensive trail system, and possession of the Linville Gorge Wilderness map is highly recommended before embarking on any trip within the gorge. Be warned, however, many of these trails are poorly marked and steep.

The diverse topography, wide elevation range, rocky peaks, and river ecosystem produces a great diversity of plant communities, including Mixed Oak Forest, Cove Forest, Dry Ridge Forest, Rocky Outcrop, Mountain Bog, and Riparian communities. The steep terrain hindered logging and old growth forests are still common along many of the lower slopes. The forests along the rims are Dry Ridge Forests with Chestnut Oak, White Oak, Scarlet Oak, and Northern Red Oak. Pines are also common, including Pitch Pine, Virginia Pine, and White Pine. Carolina Hemlock, Sourwood, Black Gum, and Red Maple are also found in these dry forests. The herb layer includes Galax, Wintergreen, Indian Cucumber Root, and Trailing Arbutus.

Down the slopes of the gorge, Cove Forests take over. American Basswood, Sweet Birch, Eastern Hemlock, Cucumber Magnolia, Fraser Magnolia are mixed with Northern Red Oak and Chestnut Oak. The herb layer becomes more diverse and includes Fire Pink, Small's Penstemon, False Solomon's Seal, Bloodroot, Crested Dwarf Iris, Whorled Loosestrife, Heartleaf ginger, Sweet Cicely, and Bluebead Lili.

Along the Linville River Sycamores appear and Eastern Hemlocks shade the bank of the river. Tag Alder lines the river and Ninebark, Common Elder, and Yellowroot also appear. Eastern Phoebes and Acadian Flycatchers are common along the river. The Conley Cove Trail off Kistler Memorial Highway passes from Dry Ridge Forest to Mixed Oak Forest to Cove Forest, to Riparian Forest and is an excellent way to experience some of the common habitats of the gorge.

The open rocky outcrops and peaks of Linville Gorge are popular due to their outstanding scenic value, but are also fascinating communities in themselves. Scattered trees include Chestnut Oak, Sourwood, Pitch Pine,

Eastern Hemlock, Carolina Hemlock, and Serviceberry. Table Mountain Pines are restricted to these rocky outcrops, often perched picturesquely on exposed outcrops. Shrubs include Catawba Rhododendron, Punctatum Rhododendron, Mountain Laurel, Male-Berry, and thickets of Black Huckleberry. Low-growing mats of Sand Myrtle and Dense-flowered St. John's Wart are also common. Accessible rocky outcrops include Babel Tower and Wiseman's View on the western rim and Table Rock and Hawksbill on the eastern rim.

In 2003, a wildlife platform was opened on Pinnacle Rock on Kistler Memorial Highway, just outside the wilderness area. This platform offers a spectacular view of the southern end of the gorge and is an excellent viewing point for the fall raptor migration.

In the fall of 2000, a fire swept through the eastern side of Linville Gorge, burning thousands of acres. The fire began on the Cabin Trail and traveled south to the lower end of the gorge. The fire moved from the rim down to the river in many places, even jumping the river in several spots, although the western side was for the most part left unscathed. The fire was primarily restricted to the ground, with relatively few trees killed, but many shrubs were charred. The regeneration of these burned areas has been rapid and impressive. Pine seedlings and rhododendron and Mountain Laurel root sprouts are abundant while herbaceous plants are taking advantage of the open ground layer. These dry oak communities are clearly fire adapted and many species appear to benefit from the occasional fire. Linville Gorge is an excellent place to observe first-hand the ecological process of fire succession.

Contact:
Grandfather Ranger District
PO Box 519, Marion, NC
(828) 652-2144 or www.cs.unca.edu/nfsnc.
Maps: USFS Linville Gorge Wilderness; USGS Linville Falls, Ashford.

30

"LINVILLE"

Tom Patterson's report of a 1970s adventure in the Gorge complements Dr. Skeate's biodiversity report (chapter 29) with its attention to vivid detail and its lively literary flair. The article appeared in *Brown's Guide to Georgia* in November 1978. The author went on to pen some of the first articles about famed Georgia folk artist Howard Finster. His "Linville" recounts a day hike down Spence Ridge Trail on the Gorge's east side, a river fording and a passage up the west side to the distinctive Babel Tower. The rotting paperback carried along is the 1959 novel *Naked Lunch* by Beat author William S. Burroughs, the publication of which was the occasion for the last literary censorship trial in America, in 1965. In 1984, I published Burroughs's short story "Ruskie" as a limited-edition chapbook.

The yellowjacket had appeared without warning, without even an audible buzz, and, before I knew what was happening, had lit on my right elbow, where he planted his stinger. I brushed him off and uttered an obscenity, but the damage was already done. A small painful knot was rising quickly around the red spot on my arm. Charlie, one of my two hiking companions, took a bit of chewing tobacco from his jaw and slapped it on the wound as we paused on the trail. Not a very auspicious way to begin a long hike, I thought, but as we resumed our descent down the east side of Linville Gorge, I soon forgot about the insect and became absorbed in the interplay of light and shadows among the lush greenery through which we were walking.

The past week had brought a good deal of rain to this section of Western North Carolina, and though the sky had been clear earlier that morning, clouds were beginning to converge from several directions as we set out on Spence Ridge Trail. Our plan was to hike down the trail to the river, which we would cross and follow northward to a rocky peak known as Babel Tower, which offers one of the best views of the entire gorge. We had stored our supplies and camping gear in a car on the other side, and we planned to camp near the rim if the weather was nice that evening.

The path dipped and curved as we moved deeper into the gorge, and the trees became thicker and more tropical-looking, reminding me of forests I had hiked through in the Guatemalan Highlands. Here the ground was covered with thick patches of bright ferns, and the path littered with delicate pink rhododendron blossoms. Large clumps of moss at the bottoms of trees and on stones seemed almost to glow when the sunlight caught the tiny beads of water that had collected on them like thousands of little jewels.

Soon the sound of running water reached our ears, and a small rocky stream appeared on our right. The trail followed this stream for a while, then curved and crossed it at a cool, shaded spot, where we stopped to drink. The water was clear and cold. I knelt on a rock and let it flow over my face and into my mouth. A small green-and-black striped newt, disturbed by my presence, slithered out from under a rock and moved quickly downstream and out of sight.

We resumed our walk and, nearing the river, found ourselves under the shade of several huge spruce trees. Suzanne, my other companion on this hike, marveled at the size of these, pointing out that two of us could barely encircle one of the massive trunks with our arms.

By this time we could hear quite clearly the rush of water from the river below. Within a few minutes we emerged from the wall of rhododendrons onto a huge slab of stone sloping gently downward to the bank of the Linville River. The waterway stretched out before us, its course punctuated by flat-faced boulders such as the one on which we were standing. These pieces of the cliffs on either side of the gorge had been torn off by the forces of gravity and the weather, bit by bit, over the past several million years. I felt a strong sense that this process was still going on—that at any moment another of those stones could rip loose and come sliding and tumbling down on top of whoever and whatever happened to be in its path. [Gorge guidebook author Allen Hyde often refers to the Linville canyon as "a slow-motion rockslide."]

The clouds overhead had been building steadily all day and had massed into a gray smokescreen above us, obscuring the blue sky and sun. But as we walked out onto that deck-like rock, extending out into the middle of the riverbed, the clouds parted and the sun came into view, its light flooding the gorge, striking the pale stones and shimmering in reflection on the surface of the turbulent stream.

Though the river had been swollen by the rains, the gigantic rocks that scattered its length indicated that finding a place to cross would be fairly easy. For the moment, though, we were in no hurry to resume our walk. This was an ideal place to stop for a while. A steady cooling breeze drifted downstream with the river, drying the sweat on the hot surface of my skin. There was a rush of sound from all directions, an effect perhaps of the river's echo bouncing back and forth off the cliffs. It sounded like the roar of several jet planes, except that it was sustained and did not fade out. We sat silently for several minutes, lighting cigarettes and watching the smoke carried downstream in the wind.

A ruby-throated hummingbird appeared suddenly in the air a few feet in front of me. He hovered over the rushing water for a moment, then darted over to the west bank and began sucking nectar from the bright red blossoms of a cardinal flower. I pointed him out to Suzanne and Charlie, and we watched him until he disappeared into the green curtain of the forest.

A small fir tree, the earth below which had been worn away, hung upside down by its roots from a steep rock face on the east bank, opposite the red flowers where the bird had been feeding. I walked over to the rocks to this inverted sapling and, reaching it, startled a flock of yellow swallowtail butterflies that had been resting on the bank below the ledge from which the tree was hanging. They took to the air and fluttered around me like brightly colored bits of paper in a sudden gust of wind.

We could have stayed all afternoon there on the rocks at the bottom of the gorge, but the clouds were moving in, blocking out the sun once again, and we wanted to see how the area looked from higher up on the west side. So we decided to move on. Upstream a short distance, we found a place that offered a promising bridge. Two of those gigantic flat-topped rocks lay on either side of the river, approaching each other within a few feet at the bottleneck they created near the center. A thick, water-worn log, barely long enough to span that space, lay wedged between the two slices of cliff. Testing it out, I found it sturdy enough to cross. [Patterson is writing twenty-eight years before the installation of a U.S. Forest Service footbridge on Spence Ridge Trail in July 2006. Some seven years later, the span crossing from river center to the west bank was swept away by high waters.]

We wanted to avoid falling in at this point, as the extreme narrowing of the river here created a deep slit in the stone, with enough force behind the current that rushed through it to dash one against the rocks without mercy. I straddled the log and slid across it, the river roaring in my ears the whole time. Suzanne followed in the same manner, but Charlie, always the daredevil, walked nimbly across.

Once across the river, we picked up the Linville Gorge Trail and began to follow the river northward. We heard the rumble of thunder behind us, and looking back through the leaves, I could see the clouds rolling and swirling around Hawksbill and Table Rock Mountains, the two peaks whose craggy shapes dominate the opposite rim of the gorge. On our left the ground rose steeply toward the peak called Green Mountain.

We passed a number of spots that looked as if they had been used as campsites—cleared areas under the shade of more giant spruce trees, scattered with the charred remnants of recent campfires. We found only one of these occupied, near the crossing of Sandy Flats Trail [now closed]. The wet weather had apparently discouraged most would-be campers from spending this weekend in Linville Gorge.

On this side of the river I noticed an abundance of bright yellow coral-like mushrooms growing in clusters on the fringes of our path. Damp and thriving in the humid weather, they seemed almost luminescent. Consulting a mushroom field guide later, I found them to be *Clavaria pyxidata,* which are reportedly edible and quite good when fresh.

The rain had brought out a variety of different species of mushrooms, though few were as eye-catching as the bright yellow ones. I found a beautiful specimen of *Amanita verna* [rather, *virosa*], the elegant-looking white mushroom known as the Destroying Angel, near a stone outcropping where we paused to look down on the river, winding below us at the bottom of an almost sheer cliff. This, the deadliest of all the poisonous varieties in the U.S., is also one of the most exquisite mushrooms to look at.

It began to rain a few minutes after we left the stone cliff. The foliage above us was so thick, however, that it sheltered us from the full force of the storm. There were places along the trail where the branches weren't so thick, so we did manage to get fairly wet before reaching the top of the ridge where Babel Tower is situated.

Before we reached the tower, the path began to ascend sharply, winding and twisting its way uphill to the top of the ridge. The rain had been coming and going for the past hour or so, but had let up temporarily when we emerged from the thick bushes walling the trail and found ourselves in a clearing on the crest of a ridge. There, a hundred yards or so to our right, was our destination.

I stood for a moment facing the monumental pile of stones that made Babel Tower the highest point on this ridge. The bend in the river far below us was more pronounced than I had imagined from looking at our map. At the western base of the ridge, the ribbon of water curved sharply northward, then back southward, so that the river's course formed a horseshoe shape around the base of Babel Tower. From my vantage point, unable to see the uppermost crescent of this bend for the tall trees and piles of rock, it was easy to be taken in by the illusion of two separate rivers flowing in opposite directions on either side of the ridge.

Reaching in my pocket for a cigarette, I found that the whole pack was thoroughly soaked with rain and sweat. At the same time, Suzanne was taking from her back pocket a paperbound copy of William Burroughs' novel *Naked Lunch*, which she had brought along in case she had the urge to read. The book too was thoroughly drenched and dog-eared from the beating it had taken in the course of our walk. A few hours before, it had looked like a volume fresh off the bookstore shelf.

"This book really looks like it just wants to stay here and rot," Suzanne commented.

I removed my soggy T-shirt and hung it on a branch, then spread my arms out and felt the soothing breeze on my damp skin. My gaze rested for several minutes on the tower, and I suggested we go climb it and have a look at the river from that high perch.

At just about that moment, from the small scrub trees and bushes at the base of the stone pinnacle, four people emerged and wandered toward us. We greeted them and asked if they had been to the top of the tower. One of the four, an athletic-looking fellow wearing wire-framed glasses and a T-shirt decorated to look like a tie and tuxedo jacket, answered that they had, and that the view from there was well worth the short climb. He described what he considered to be the best course to take to the top and warned us to be careful.

"It's not really that hard a climb," he said, "but there are a few tricky places on those rocks just below the top where it'd be real easy to fall off and die." At this he grinned knowingly and chuckled to himself.

I thanked him for the advice as Suzanne, Charlie, and I struck off along the little path to the top of Babel Tower. The trail skirted the rock formation on its left, then bent sharply upward and to the right. Here it was quite steep, and we held onto the trunks of small trees in order to keep our balance as we ascended. We clambered over some big rocks and found ourselves nearly at the top. There were several gaps and fissures in the rocks between where we now stood and the topmost point, but it looked as though it would be easy enough to make those last few yards over to the peak.

Suzanne, who had once seen a young child plunge off a cliff and break her neck in some mountains not far from here, found a level point and sat down, shivering a little. "I'm cold," she said, watching Charlie and me walking around and hopping from stone to stone. "Please sit down," she begged us, "I don't want y'all to fall off."

As I made my way over to the highest point, the top of the tower, I assured her that we wouldn't fall. Reaching a place just below the peak, I saw that I was only a leap away. Between me and the top was a gap maybe three feet wide. But below me was a sheer drop of at least 30 feet. In order to get across, I would have to jump slightly upward so that I could brace my knee on the ledge-like piece of rock on the other side, a little higher than my waist. Then I would immediately have to lean, or fall, forward on that side and, with a steady grip on the rocks, hoist myself up.

I hesitated, surveying the situation for a moment. Glancing down at the spot where we had emerged from the woods a few minutes earlier, I saw the four people with whom we had just been talking, all watching me intently. They called out their encouragement.

I held my breath and, raising my right knee, pushed off with my left foot, and jumped/fell forward and across. My fingers clutched the weathered lichen-covered stone as I raised myself up from the knee. I had made it. I was standing at the top of the Tower of Babel. Looking down on the four people who had just left this peak a few minutes before, I waved, describing an arc over my head with my outstretched arm.

"Was it worth it?" one of them called out.

I looked out over the gorge, stretching out into the hills to the south, sliced open by this powerful river whose roar was from this high point only a soft rumbling. From here there was an excellent view of Hawksbill and Table Rock. Thick clouds being pushed in from downstream were partially blocked by these two peaks [weather fronts move upriver from Lake James]. The giant smoky plumes broke like slow-motion waves on the peaks and poured from around their edges into the gorge. A thin vapor arose from the greenery below, along the river's edges.

I turned back to look at the four people below. "Yes!" I answered loudly, and my voice echoed back to me on the other side of the gorge.

Turning in the other direction, I could see Suzanne still sitting in the same spot. I called out to her and leaped in the air. She watched me for a moment, obviously unamused, then turned her head, determined not to see if I did happen to slip.

A few minutes later, I slowly made my way back down to where she was. Charlie, who had climbed to the top and back down before me and then wandered off somewhere, joined us, and we set off walking again, along Babel Tower Trail toward the west rim. From somewhere to the south came a loud roll of thunder; and within a few minutes a steady rain was falling once again. The droplets of water felt good on my face and arms. We were all fatigued, but I think we shared an equal sense of exhilaration. There was still a slight stinging sensation in my right arm, but I had all but forgotten where it came from.

Tom's gambol/gamble on the Babel Tower could have seen a fatal spill off the spire; annual crippling accidents and the occasional fatality make the local papers. Let me produce a couple that illustrate the expense and risks of Gorge rescues. From the *Avery Journal-Times* of March 21–22, 2007, comes the story of "Blackhawk Rescue at Shortoff." Lauren Ohnesorge filed the following:

> *Burke County Emergency Services' operations director, Major Ken Anthony has seen a lot of rescues, but none as dramatic as the one at Shortoff Mountain Saturday night.*
>
> *"We made history," he said. That history is attracting national attention. Four climbers were rescued via UH60 Black Hawk helicopter. That alone, has been done before. The fact that the helicopter was deployed at night makes this rescue unique in the nation.*
>
> *"The probability for error and the chance for danger is extremely high at nighttime," Anthony said. The helicopter, at times, was within 30 feet of the rock cliff.*
>
> *"The policy in North Carolina is, they don't do it at night," Anthony said.*
>
> *"I feel like, if we hadn't gotten her out in a significant amount of time, her life status would have been questionable," Anthony said.*
>
> *David and Marla McNeely of Dallas, NC, were climbing with two friends on Saturday afternoon when Marla fell an estimated 25 to 50 feet off the rock cliff.*
>
> *"Once she fell, she had excruciating back pain," Anthony said. Her husband dialed 911 and rescue teams assembled.*

"We attempted for four to six hours to make access," Anthony said. Due to temperatures, water, and ice, the terrain was extremely difficult. The darkness added to the treacherous conditions.

"We just could not get to her," Anthony said. As Marla McNeely's condition deteriorated, action had to be taken.

Anthony felt he had no choice but to contact the NC National Guard for mutual aid, and he does not regret that call. While sometimes it is hard to tell if a life genuinely has been saved by a decision, Anthony does not doubt the importance of what was done Saturday.

"I can truly tell you, I feel we saved her life," he said.

While the helicopter took flight, instructions were given to the group via cell phone. The two other climbers were instructed how to build a fire and keep the McNeely's warm. Rescue workers were able to get a hypothermia bag to the pair, and they were able to get to the McNeelys' location. Both the McNeelys showed signs of hypothermia when rescued.

Marla McNeely, 45, suffered from severe hypothermia, according to Anthony, and was transported to Carolina Regional Medical Center by Blackhawk. She was released Monday and is doing well, thanks to rescue workers.

"It was the absolute most dramatic and high risk incident that I have ever been involved with," Anthony said. The incident may serve as a model for future rescues and research, as the first night rescue using civilians in a military helicopter.

The first day rescue with a military helicopter piloted by civilians happened in Burke County in 1995 near Wiseman's View. Making history has never been more exciting to Anthony.

"I'm still feeling the rush," he said on Tuesday.

Agencies involved included a N.C. Forest Service BRIDGE crew, Burke County Emergency Services, Burke County Special Operations Team, Lake James and Oakhill Fire Departments, N.C. Emergency Management, Burke County React, and the N.C. National Guard.

Caroline Harris reported on a "Linville Gorge Climber Rescued" in the March 12, 2014 edition of the *Avery Journal-Times*, as again the National Guard Blackhawks flew to the rescue.

A climber was rescued on March 10 after a fall in Linville Gorge, according to Burke County Communications supervisor Beverly

Roland. Communications received a report at 1:10 p.m. that a male subject of approximately 23 years of age had fallen approximately 20 to 40 feet while rappelling at Shortoff Mountain in Linville Gorge.

Burke County EMS, Burke County Special Operations, Burke County Emergency Management, Burke County REACT, N.C. Helicopter and Aquatic Rescue Team, Burke County Rescue, Lake James Fire Department and Chesterfield Fire Department responded to the scene.

Some rescuers were able to reach the climber, but a helicopter was needed to extract him from the Cliffside where he had fallen. NCHART, a taskforce of N.C. National Guard helicopters, flew a Blackhawk helicopter to the scene and lowered rescuers to the injured climber, according to Roland.

According to Roland, the patient was in the Blackhawk by 5:41 p.m. and was transported from the Blackhawk to a Med-Center Air Helicopter that was in a landing zone nearby. From there, he was transported to a nearby medical center.

31

"THE CIRCLE OF LIFE

A STORY FROM LINVILLE"

Gerald Hutchinson's narration of a magical October day south of Table Rock, near The Chimneys, comes from Bob Underwood's Linville Gorge online Yahoo! Group of April 2, 2008. Nature outshone herself on this one remarkable day, which fairly begs for Perry Como's "Magic Moments" as a soundtrack. Radical weather shifts form only a part of the thrills in Gerald's report.

Although I have no pictures to share, for in those days I did not carry a camera, my story is nonetheless burned into my memory in high-definition. It is a story that both removed me from my earthbound existence, bearing me into the far reaches of space and also more fully humbled me as a being on the face of this earth.

The setting is the Linville Gorge Wilderness Area, located in the Blue Ridge Mountains of Western North Carolina. The time is the peak season of autumn in October, when the leaves were showing their most glorious colors for many years: red, orange, and yellow.

The setting is local space, time, and Mother Nature. A climbing partner, who shall be known as Windbreak, and I played chiefly witness roles in the unfolding drama.

Windbreak and I arrived later than we'd hoped at the parking lot below Table Rock about 2:00 p.m. We had hoped to get in a full day of climbing on the North Carolina Wall on the Linville Gorge's eastern side, but needless delays in getting on the road and some navigational challenges had squashed those plans. Now, with only three hours of daylight left, it looked like tonight would be just a campout. Compared with what we had expected, the weather was dismal. The forecast had called for blue skies after the passing of a front, but the trees were dripping from the wetness of a chilly fog that drifted through the gap. Grudgingly we accepted our fate, deciding to continue with our trip. "Maybe it's just the remains of the front," said Windbreak hopefully. We finished packing our food and got on the trail heading south along the east rim of the Gorge.

The trail was carpeted with leaves of many hues: reds and oranges from the maples, yellows and browns from the sourwoods, hickories, and oaks. It provided a cheering break from the grayness of the sky. We hiked in silence, the ridgeline forest in a hushed quiet punctuated only by our footfalls and the occasional exception of Windbreak fulfilling his name.

When we arrived at The Chimneys, we stopped to take a drink of water. The wind had picked up a bit, and we could see west over breaking clouds across the Gorge. It looked like some rain was probably headed our way. More fog drifted by, obscuring our view. Then, the fog broke, and, sure enough, a nasty-looking squall was looming towards us.

Knowing that we would get no climbing done today, and preferring to enjoy our evening in a camp rather than hiking on in the rain, we scrambled for cover. Windbreak found a flattish area between two cliffs. We used some climbing hardware and a stunted pine to anchor a tarp line and pitched a nice shelter, protected from the weather. And the winds picked up, suddenly striking The Chimneys' ridgeline with a whooshing gust. Rain began flying. It made it hard for us to hear each other as it beat its arrhythmia upon the tarp. Snug inside, we threw our pads and sleeping bags on the ground, pulled out the stove, and brewed some tea. We chatted indifferently and listened to the varying intensity of this storm that had hampered our plans.

After an hour or so the rain let up. Then, in what seemed like an instant, the sun broke though! We poked out our heads to be greeted by a perfectly clear sky overhead. The light of late afternoon lent a beautiful warm-yellow cast to the wet rocks and colors of a splendid autumn. We were amazed at how fast the rain cleared out. That system moved fast! It only took a couple of minutes for us to scramble to the top of the ridge. From our aerie perch there we could see the retreating storm out to the east. And underneath the slate-gray backdrop of clouds was the most amazing double rainbow! They were perfect half-circles of light that glowed with an intensity that made it seem as if they themselves were the source of the light, rather than merely refracting the light of the sun.

We both high-fived at our good fortune in seeing this spectacle. The depressing delays in getting to the mountain were forgotten and forgiven by us now and seemed as if they had been fated to allow us to witness this glorious vista.

As the storm roared rapidly east over the foothills of North Carolina, the rainbows persisted for perhaps fifteen to twenty minutes. We savored every moment of this scene that seemingly had been painted by the brush of the Creator more than the art aficionado relishes the sight of a work by Monet.

Neither of us had ever seen such perfectly formed double-arcs, nor had we ever been in a position to see them from end to end. It was truly phenomenal! As the storm receded into the distance the rainbows diminished to mere small and irregular arcs as the rain pattern changed. We turned to clamber back down to our camp.

We could tell that this was the cold front that we had expected to have cleared out by midday. Better late than never! With nothing better to do, we decided to have an early dinner, "cowboy-camp" where we were, and get an "alpine start" (pre-dawn) for the North Carolina Wall. We enjoyed a simple dinner of pasta and cheese, apples and crackers, and a flask of wine. Because our camp was near the ridge, we also got to look across the Gorge and witness a beautiful sunset over Mount Mitchell and the Black Mountain Range as they lumped up against the golden-orange rays. The entire western sky was an orange wash punctuated by sparse trailing clouds. Windbreak suggested we could see the fabled "green flash" that occurs when the sun sets on the horizon. I had heard of it from sailing, and thought it was only visible at sea.

As the sun touched the horizon, we scrambled back to the top of the ridge for a better view. And as we got there, out to the east, a flat and full harvest moon greeted us! We could not believe our good fortune. Neither of us had expected this, as we had not kept track of the lunar cycle recently. The moon was a gorgeous cream-yellow, and the Man in the Moon smiled happily at us as we grinned back like fools, struck by the awesomeness of Mother Nature.

We kept glancing back and forth from sunset to moonrise, our view unimpeded by any obstruction. Our perch allowed us to witness the turning of the earth. Never before have I so fully experienced the fact of the earth's circular rotation. The celestial bowl above us began filling with stars, while tears filled my eyes at the grandeur before me. I have never felt so humbled by the massiveness of space as I did then, knowing that I am but a speck of life in the immensity of the universe. Though the wind was not strong, it was quite chilly, and our hands and ears began suggesting that we return to our camp. And so we did. Since we knew no more rain would come, we took down the tarp. The rocks around us provided sufficient protection from the wind. We had nice down-filled sleeping bags to guard us from what would be a frosty night, and we snuggled down inside them with a blanket of stars over our heads.

We set the alarms on our watches for half an hour before dawn. We wanted to get going early—but not TOO early—in what would surely be a chilly start to the day.

In the middle of the night I had to get up to pee. I opened my eyes, looking for the moon to get an idea of what time it might be. I had to search, and finally I found it, directly overhead. Only it wasn't a full moon anymore; it was a thin red crescent. That meant it was being eclipsed by the earth! After taking care of my business, I woke Windbreak to show him.

The wonderful scenes had just kept piling up for us. First the rushing of a squall line followed by perfectly clear skies. Then double-rainbows. Sunset. Moonrise. Lunar eclipse. What else would we witness? We enjoyed the show for a while, but lunar eclipses move slowly, and I fell back to sleep.

When the alarm went off, we roused ourselves up and looked west across the Gorge. The full moon was at the horizon, fat and white. We knew that the sun would be rising as the moon set, so after dressing in some warm clothes and getting our water heating on the stove, we climbed back up the ridge, where we were again grateful witnesses to the double feature of a moonset and a sunrise. The spectacle of the earth's rotation and the orbit of the moon around the earth and the earth around the sun had a more profound meaning now.

I thought of the shepherds and seafarers and the farmers and the fishermen who, for millennia, had witnessed such events on a regular basis, unencumbered by electric lights and the conveniences of industrialized civilization. They knew the beauty and the grandeur of nature, and worked with her rhythms of light and dark, of the days and seasons turning, and the humility of standing alone before such creation. Now I too shared in some of this humility.

As the warming light of the morning sun became more intense, our view of the Black Mountains and the Roan Highlands became more distinct, and the shadow of The Chimney ridgeline crept down the western wall of the Gorge. We breakfasted on oatmeal and coffee, then packed up our camp. Soon we would be climbing Bumblebee Buttress, just two specks enjoying a carefree day on the crags of Carolina. Rock climbing, the whole point of our journey, had been upstaged by the very circle of life in which we exist.

32

THE LAST OF THE MOHICANS AND LINVILLE GORGE

Spectacular Linville Gorge and Falls scenery are some of the settings for action-packed scenes in 1992's *The Last of the Mohicans* by director Michael Mann and starring Daniel Day-Lewis as Hawkeye, Wes Studi as Magua and Russell Means as Chingachgook. Colonel Munro's two daughters, Alice (Jodhi May) and Cora (Madeleine Stowe), are saved from certain death near Linville Falls by the hunting trio's heroic rescue. Standing in for James Fenimore Cooper's western New York State of the French and Indian War era, the Linville Gorge appears in the following three scenes: 1. The First Ambush; 2. The Canoe Chase; 3. Uncas's Farewell, Prayer to Great Spirit.

THE FIRST AMBUSH

Sadly, it may be remarked that this motion picture gives one of the clearest records of the former old growth of hemlock trees at the Linville Falls, devastated by the arrival from Asia of the hemlock wooly adelgid shortly before the movie was filmed. Today's National Park Service's Falls View trails, on the Gorge's west side, pass giant stumps and acres of open air of deforested slope. In *Mohicans*, however, there passes through a shady hemlock corridor a party of Redcoats and Huron warriors accompanying the Munro daughters to their father, the British commander of Fort William Henry.

This ambush scene clues viewers to the treachery of the lead guide, Magua, and then introduces the backwoodsmen rescuers, Hawkeye, Uncas and Chingachgook. Some fifteen minutes into the film, as the company of red-coated infantrymen escort the mounted sisters down a forest path of towering hemlocks and clusters of rhododendron, the mounted white officer wants to stop and rest. "Do you understand me, Magua?" Magua barks back at him in Huron: "Magua understands white man is a dog to his women.…[H]e puts down his tomahawk to feed their laziness." These words foretell his sudden brutal assault on a soldier marching along in rank; planting his hatchet in the man's heart, Magua signals to his war party to spring from ambush. The bloody skirmish is ended by the rescue and by the instant disappearance of Magua from before the bead of Hawkeye's rifle into a wisp of mountain mist that clocks out the scene around seven or eight minutes.

It's easy to get there from the Blue Ridge Parkway, a mile north of the village of Linville Falls and the intersection with U.S. 221. Beyond the parking lot and Park Service Falls Visitor Center, one crosses the Linville River on a footbridge, walking downriver on a gravel trail. A few yards before one reaches the main intersection with the U.S. Forest Service Falls Trail on the right, one climbs a curving bank under a long, drooping tree limb. From behind that trunk poured the attackers.

The Canoe Chase

After the British surrender of Fort William Henry to French forces, soldiers, scouts and their dependents march in a long dusty column into the second key ambush scene of the movie. Young Lieutenant Heyward joins the three male leads and the two daughters in escaping from the bloodbath by canoe. They shove off into the waters of Lake James, created by the Duke Power Company in 1922. As Duncan paddles furiously in the bow of the lead canoe, Shortoff Mountain appears in all its sheer blunt beauty hanging over the distant shoreline, viewed at around the one hour and twenty-one-minute mark in the film.

Suddenly, we are lofted above the Falls to a pool on the Linville where the river is parted by a great boulder and falls some six feet into a broad basin: the Upper Falls. The men are shoving the canoes back into the waters, where they plunge over another waterfall at the one hour and twenty-three-minute mark. Look sharply, for the editors crosscut between two distinct falls.

This location is sited comfortably close to the scene of the First Ambush; simply proceed on the park service path, beyond its junction with the forest service, or Gravel Parking Lot Trail, to the intersection with a cement bench. Turn left to take the trail down to the Upper Falls viewing area with its newly opened geological interpretive displays and, beyond, a tiny footbridge. Besides reliving scenes from *The Last of the Mohicans* one can visit a dramatic geologic window into the plate tectonics resulting from the collision of the southeastern part of the present United States with Africa.

UNCAS'S FAREWELL, PRAYER TO THE GREAT SPIRIT

With the line spoken by Russell Means as Chingachgook—"Great Spirit and Maker of all Life"—the last of the Mohicans commends his son Uncas (Eric Schweig) to the afterlife, standing on an exposed rocky ridge south of Table Rock Mountain known as The Chimneys, near where Gerald Hutchinson and a friend witnessed Nature's grand display. The characters played by Daniel Day-Lewis and Madeleine Stowe, sole survivors, join the prayer as they gaze to the setting sun, falling down the Gold Coast area of the Linville ridge, along the west gorge a mile away, burning low over Humpback Mountain and beyond to the Roan Highlands, farther and farther into the blue haze of Eternity over the rippling waves of hills. As the camera pans, Mount Mitchell and the Blacks are clearly visible on the left of the frame at nearly twice the height of Table Rock.

The stirring final sequence, with its sunlight, breezes and Table Mountain Pine, begins at the one hour and forty-eight-minute mark.

From the U.S. Forest Services's Table Rock Parking Lot, reached from Forest Road 210 off of U.S. 181, a trail leads south from a picnic area toward The Chimneys and Shortoff Mountain. You will know these chimneys by their fantastically weathered and sculpted buttes and stacks, a paradise for beginners, top-rope climbing and an Outward Bound training area. Views look down on grand monoliths and narrow rock blades such as Sphynx Rock, The Mummy and The Camel.

33
JANE BLALOCK HOLTSCLAW, CHEROKEE WISEWOMAN AND HEALER

Women have been conspicuously absent from the pages of this book as leading role players in the Linville Gorge. We have Lydia, the fainting bride under the Falls, the runaway woman mythologized as a Helen of Troy; Suzanne cringing at the sight of Tom Patterson's daredevil leap; and Jessie Bicknell, who lived with her husband, Frank, in a white cottage over the Falls. But the story of the full-blooded Cherokee shaman or healer, Jane Blalock Holtsclaw, leaves us with a vivid portrait of a Native American original, a dynamic, self-sufficient woman fully at home in the wilderness canyon.

She was born in 1848, a significant year for the eastern band, a mere decade after the infamous removal of the Cherokee people westward on the "Trail of Tears." Some fourteen hundred Cherokee remained behind on lands they owned or received for helping in the roundup. Fugitives hid out in the Smokeys. Gorge explorer Charles Lanman visited the Cherokee the year Jane was born and depicts a thriving, happy people with flourishing agriculture and animal husbandry, textile and clothing manufacture, courts of law and sexual equality: "Their women are no longer treated as slaves, but as equals; the men labor in the fields and their wives are devoted entirely to household employments." In July 1848, the U.S. Congress passed an act for taking a census of all Cherokee in North Carolina—in fact, all of them living east of the Mississippi—in order to induce each individual to take up an offer from a "removal and subsistence fund" of payment of $53.33 for relocation to the Cherokee Nation in the west. The census registered Cherokee then residing in North Carolina,

Tennessee and Georgia and was completed by the fall of 1848 with a total number of 2,133. Some opted for the payment; most of the North Carolina band remained in or near the Qualla Reservation. The western band protested the payment, claiming census figures were "enormously exaggerated." Was baby Jane among that 1848 statistics, or was the count solely of male householders? Spurning the offer of Oklahoma western lands, the Blalock family trekked east, perhaps past Sylva and Maggie Valley, to ford the French Broad and reenter the Blue Ridge chain. They passed Mount Mitchell, the highest peak in the east, before reaching present-day Mitchell, Avery, McDowell and Burke Counties. The wild territory that the immigrants found was a favorite summer hunting ground for both Creek and Catawba tribes, though certainly Cherokee war and hunting parties ranged this far east. As Governor Tryon remarked, the marauding attackers of the Linvilles moved directly from Linville Gorge to attack Cherokees living in the Smoky Mountains.

Jane's move to McDowell County, North Carolina, is unclear; her home at Ashford is far distant from the traditional Cherokee lands west of Asheville. But here it was that she settled and married David Holtsclaw in 1870. At the time of the 1910 census, they were still living together, but in 1920, she is shown as living alone in McDowell County. The couple's first child, Aaron, was born in Mitchell County in 1871, followed by William (born around 1873), Nancy (born 1877), Mamie (born 1879) and J. Bryant (no date).

Ashford, North Carolina, as D.R. Beeson and Artie Green Laws have reported, was the site of the former Linville Falls Railroad Depot, nestled at the base of Linville Mountain. My informant, Jane's great-great-great niece, Kayla Holtsclaw Wilson, describes how Jane went medicine gathering by climbing to the crest of Linville's ridge then picking her way down into the Gorge, before any trail system existed. She took along a piece of fatback, some line with a hook and a pan for the trout she'd be catching. For weeks, she would be away collecting in the traditional way, dressed in the heavy skirts and boots of mountain women with a great homespun apron. Night-sheltering under the cliff walls, she could swathe her head with her apron to ward off mosquitos and the dew.

Her solitude puts one in mind of Culgee Watson. Infuriated by men hastening in to check on her and trampling the plants, she resorted to ancient curses and stone-throwing to drive them back from her "space." Back at her cabin, she would prepare the medicines the way she had been taught, for all the old herbal lore had been orally transmitted and passed down among the women.

Jane had heartbreaking disasters strike her family. One night in 1920, she was camping in the Gorge with her twelve-year-old granddaughter Mary Magdalene ("Maggie") when Mary's clothing caught fire in the night. As Mary raced in panic toward the river, Jane caught up with her and forced her to the ground to smother the flames. After Jane had spent many sleepless vigils tending her patient, the girl died.

The other disaster occurred with the flood of July 1916, which wrought destruction all over western North Carolina. Avery County historian Horton Cooper says of this storm, which swept up from the Gulf of Mexico, that it brought the greatest rainfall and stream flow that had occurred in this part of the country for five hundred years or more. For the first two weeks of July, rain had been steadily falling when, on July 14, a front centering on the Blue Ridge between Grandfather Mountain and Gillespie Gap poured torrential rains into the Falls and Gorge area. On July 15, reports Cooper, "all streams rose very rapidly, and before nightfall they went out of their banks, still rising rapidly. On the mountainsides, scores of landslides burst out where the complete saturation of pockets on top of rocky faces occurred. Livestock, houses and some persons were washed away."

In Ashford, Jane sat on a hilltop under a blanket in the rain watching the house float away; nearby, her sister's family with nine children huddled on the roof of the barn that was to become their new home. Jane was loved and appreciated in the expanded family, which knew her as kind, giving and sympathetic. She laid hands on the sick to take the fire out of them, to ease suffering and "the sting of the pain," as Kayla puts it. "Folks from Mitchell, McDowell, and Avery counties all benefitted from her Cherokee medical skills and the remedies she found in the gorge."

Jane died in 1929 and is buried in the English family cemetery at Ashford.

James Mooney's 1891 study, *Sacred Formulas of the Cherokees*, depicts a wisewoman or shaman subtly attuned to the secret life of the natural world—what some philosophers have called the "sacramental view of reality." As an example, Mooney describes the rites attending the ceremonial picking of ginseng in which the healer addresses the mountain as "Great Man" and asks leave to take a piece of his flesh (the plant). Mooney adds, "In searching for his medicinal plants the shaman goes provided with a number of white and red beads, and approaches the plant from a certain direction, going around it from right to left one or four times, reciting certain prayers the while. He then pulls up the plant by the roots and drops one of the beads into the hole and covers it up with the loose earth." Mooney concludes that it's likely the bead is to compensate the earth for the violation of tearing plants from her body. Cherokee medicinal plant gathering was incomplete without dancing, prayers and gestures; herborizing was as much a spiritual practice as a harvesting one. Jane's collecting brought profound meditations on the life of plants and on their powers to combat natural afflictions as well as those caused by witches, ghosts or hostile spirits. Her Linville Gorge was a holy setting and, doubtless, she highly resented intrusions by well-wishing men and their dogs galumphing to her "rescue."

Among the many medicinal plants Jane collected in the Gorge were black cohosh, yellowroot and ginseng. James Mooney lists twenty of the most popular medicinal plants among the Cherokee he studied in the late nineteenth century: snakeroot (*Aristolochia serpentaria)*; beggar's lice (*Cynoglossum Morrisoni*); wild senna (*Cassia marilandica*); life everlasting (*Gnaphalium decurrens*); vetch (*Vicia Caroliniana*); catgut or turkey pea (*Tephrosia virginiana*); milkweed (*Euphorbia hypericifolia*); skullcap (*Scutellaria lateriflora*); maidenhair fern (*Adiantum pedatum*); wild alum or cranesbill (*Geranium maculatum*); Indian physic (*Gillenia trifoliate*); liverwort (*Hepatica acutiloba*); tassel flower (*Cacalia atriplicifolia*); ginseng (*Aralia quinquefolia*, or, in Cherokee, *Atali Kuli*, "it climbs the mountain"; also addressed in the Cherokee formulas as the "great man" or "little man"); meadow-rue (*Thalictrum anemonoides*); ladyslipper (*Cypripedium parviflorum*); cone flower (*Rudbeckia fulgida*); Solomon's seal (*Polygonatum multiflorum latifolium*); queen of the meadow or gravel root (*Eupatorium purpureum*); and shield fern (*Aspidium acrostichoides*).

In her 1969 classic *Indian Herbalogy of North America*, Alma R. Hutchens describes dozens of the native plants with which Jane would have been familiar. I have mentioned black cohosh, yellowroot and ginseng, known locally as "'sang." We can add balsam fir, birch, blackberry, boneset, chaga, chicory root, coltsfoot, comfrey, dandelion, wild ginger, goldenrod, hellebore, henbane, iron weed, larkspur, maple, mint, mugwort, sassafras, slippery elm, willow, wintergreen and yarrow. Nonnative plants such as mullein and pokeberry also lay plentifully at hand. Alma Hutchens describes Jane Holtsclaw's vocation in words that can still arouse a warm response in Gorge visitors today:

> *The Indian art of healing was ceremonial in nature. To us their rituals seem strange and without meaning. They knew physical health often failed without the aid of spiritual means. Dancing, chanting, etc. was conducted, according to conditions, or severity of the patient.... Their health and spiritual source was closely connected with natural surroundings, they of course were inspired by the significance of nature and to the Sun, Moon, Stars, Rain, Wind, etc., that encouraged it.*

Hutchens adds that Indian healer training began at a very early age.

> *Selection was from the family or from signs of devotion, wisdom, and honesty. It was more than a career, as it is of our time; the girl or boy was elected by ability. Trusted with all secrets, rituals, habits and legends of their people, while attending all ceremonial celebrations and critical meetings of the people, he or she was at the side of the leader. The trainee had to know and remember the many herbal species, their properties and uses, for all medicinal plants in the area were used. The flora and fauna differed in each locality, but each knew her immediate supply.*

And Jane Blalock Holtsclaw, wisewoman and healer, knew her Linville Gorge fauna better than anyone.

RECOMMENDED READING

Blake, Christopher. *Linville Gorge Wilderness Area*. Charleston, SC: Arcadia, 2009. The earliest photographs in this Gorge picture book are stereoscope slides made in 1873 by Rufus Morgan, father of famous Appalachian (and Gorge) photographer Bayard Wooten. The majority of the images are from the F.W. Bicknell Collection at the State Department of Cultural Resources in Raleigh. They depict life at the Falls and in the Gorge circa 1910. Many pictures come from National Park and U.S. Forest Service holdings.

Carter, Mark W., Carl E. Merschat, and William F. Wilson. *A Geologic Adventure Along the Blue Ridge Parkway in North Carolina*. Bulletin 98. North Carolina Geological Survey Section. Raleigh: North Carolina Department of Environment and Natural Resources, 2001. This is a detailed description of the Grandfather Mountain geologic window and the Linville Falls fault, with sixty pages of color photographs and charts.

De Hart, Allen. *Hiking North Carolina's Mountains-to-Sea Trail*. Chapel Hill: University of North Carolina Press, 2000. In section two, De Hart's guide to the trail running from Mount Le Conte in the Smokeys to the Carolina coast profiles the Linville Gorge, calling the area "the most difficult and challenging of all the sections of the Mountains-to-Sea Trail." As De Hart updates his volumes on the Mountains-to-Sea Trail, work progresses in the area around Lake James and the south gorge.

———. *North Carolina Hiking Trails.* 3rd edition. Boston: Appalachian Mountain Club, 1996. Hiking directions to the Linville Gorge trail system. De Hart gives U.S.F.S. trail numbers, length, elevation change and distinct features such as views or water sources.

Hyde, Allen. *Linville Gorge and Wilson Creek Hiker's Guide: An Introduction.* Newland, NC: Allen Hyde, 2013. Allen just about says it all in this voluminous spiral-bound yellow manual, which builds on his previous Gorge trail guides with the addition of the Wilson Creek forest area on the lower slopes of Grandfather Mountain; he delves into subjects from genealogy to geology. Some of the Gorge's most secret trails ("unofficial") are laid out "A-to-Z" in this hefty tome that will likely never be surpassed among Linville Gorge guides—what the Romans called the *vade mecum,* or indispensable "take me with you" book.

But, for the record, I did not *kick* the skull I found on Yorick's Trail on October 17, 2005, in the company of Bob Underwood, but instead carefully left the cranium of Philip A. Duane Jr., sixty-eight, undisturbed for the FBI and the U.S. Park Service to investigate. Bertie Burleson quotes me in the *Avery Post* (volume 4, number 24) of October 19:

> *"At first I thought it was an old* [white] *grocery bag lying there, and then I thought it was a big mushroom," said Chris Blake. Looking closer at the object Blake saw that it was a human skull. "I saw a metal filling in one of the upper teeth," he said. His fellow hiker, Bob Underwood, had observed some bones at the same location where the skull was found about a week ago. "I thought it was animal bones," Bob said. They immediately* [no; they delayed reporting until the lowering of the American flag at 5:00 p.m. by the late Visitor Center host, Vivian McKinney] *reported the gruesome discovery to the Avery County Sheriff's Department on October 17th and officers Mike Ellenburg and Allen Wells reported to the Linville Falls Visitor Center and awaited Park Ranger Ben Hansel. Since the remains were in Burke County, the Burke Sheriff's Office was involved. Blake is the author of River of Cliffs (first edition, 2005), and Bob Underwood maintains an online Linville Gorge yahoo website. Philip A. Duane Jr., sixty-eight, had been missing since May 2004.*

Linville Gorge Wilderness: Pisgah National Forest. Recreation Guide R-8-RG4. Revised November 2009. Nebo, NC: U.S. Department of Agriculture, U.S. Forest Service, Grandfather Ranger District., 2009. This is the official trail map and regulations guide for Gorge outings. This map replaces the 1986 version, which shows Sandy Flats Trail open for use; the trail has been closed.

Phelan, Phil. *Linville Gorge Hiking Circuit.* Linville Gorge Adventures.com.

Philyaw, Scott, et al. *The Natural Diversity of Linville Falls*. U.S. National Park Service, n.d. A colorful visitor's brochure giving a varied overview of the site's natural history.

Sakowski, Carolyn. *Touring the Western North Carolina Backroads*. 2nd edition. Winston-Salem, NC: John F. Blair, 1995. Sakowski's guide is a treasure trove of little-known mountain attractions, man-made and natural. She devotes a chapter to a fifty-mile tour to Table Rock and environs from Morganton and back.

Spencer, Marci. *Pisgah National Forest: A History.* Charleston, SC, 2014. This historical guide to western North Carolina's "Wild Treasure" documents the creation of the East's first national forest and the birthplace of American forestry in the Pisgah National Forest. Spencer addresses the Linville Gorge area in her chapter on the Grandfather Ranger District.

WORKS CITED

Arthur, John Preston. *A History of Watauga County North Carolina with Sketches of Prominent Families*. Johnson City, TN: Overmountain Press, 1992.

Beeson, D.R. *A Walking Trip to Table Rock Mountain, July 3–6, 1914*. Unpublished twenty-two-page typescript and black-and-white photograph album held in the Archives of Appalachia collection at the Charles C. Sherrod Library, East Tennessee State University, Johnson City.

Blackmun, Ora. *Western North Carolina: Its Mountains and Its People to 1880*. Boone, NC: Appalachian Consortium Press, 1977.

Blake, Christopher M. *Linville Gorge Wilderness Area*. Charleston, SC: Arcadia, 2009.

———. "Outward Bound—Explore Your Capabilities." *Sky High*. Lee H. Edwards High School newspaper, Asheville NC, Vol. 29, no. 3, November 17, 1967.

———. *Outward Bound Journal, or "How I Skipped School for 26 Days."* Manuscript notebook with author's illustrations. N.p.: October 6 to November 1, 1967.

Bollinger, Cheryl M. "Death Underscores Gorge's Peril." *Morganton News-Herald*, January 6, 2001.

Carolina, Clinchfield and Ohio Railway. *Vacation Days in the Summitlands of the Blue Ridge and Cumberland Mountains*. Chicago: Poole, circa 1909.

Colton, Henry E. *Mountain Scenery. The Scenery of the Mountains of Western North Carolina and Northwestern South Carolina*. Raleigh, NC: W.L. Pomeroy, 1859.

Cooper, Horton. *History of Avery County, North Carolina*. Asheville, NC: Groves, 1964.

Davis, Chester S. "In the Mountains of North Carolina: …The Linville Gorge Country—Wildest and Grandest in the East." *Winston-Salem Journal and Sentinel*, July 10, 1955, 8C.

———. "One Hike to Remember: We Braved the Gorge and Came Out Alive!" *Winston-Salem Journal and Sentinel*, July 12, 1959.

Draper, Lyman C. *The Life of Daniel Boone*. 1856. Edited by Ted Franklin Belue. Mechanicsburg, PA: Stackpole, 1998.

Dugger, Shepherd M. *The Balsam Groves of the Grandfather Mountain*. Banner Elk, NC: Shepherd M. Dugger, 1895.

Harris, Caroline. "Linville Gorge Climber Rescued." *Avery Journal-Times* 56, no. 11 (March 12, 2014): 1.

Hutchens, Alma R. *Indian Herbalogy of North America*. Windsor, Ontario, Canada: 1969.

Hutchinson, Gerald. "The Circle of Life: A Story from Linville." *Linville Gorge Yahoo! Group*. April 2, 2008.

Lanman, Charles. *Letters from the Alleghany Mountains*. New York: Putnam, 1849.

Laws, Artie Green. "The History of Linville Falls." 13-page typescript. 1974.

Michaux, Andre. "Extracts from the Journal of Andre Michaux, 1794." Quoted in Shepherd M. Dugger's *Balsam Groves of the Grandfather Mountain*, 1895.

Mitchell, Dr. Elisha. *Diary of a Geological Tour in 1827 and 1828*. James Sprunt Historical Monograph No. 6. Introduction and notes by Dr. Kemp P. Battle. Chapel Hill: UNC Press, 1905.

Mooney, James. *History, Myths, and Sacred Formulas of the Cherokee*. Asheville, NC: Bright Mountain Books, 1992.

Morley, Margaret W. *The Carolina Mountains*. Boston: Houghton Mifflin, 1913.

Mull, J. Alex. *Mountain Yarns, Legends and Lore*. Illustrated by R.L. Patton. Banner Elk, NC: Pudding Stone Press, n.d.

Ohnesorge, Lauren. "Blackhawk Rescue at Shortoff." *Avery Journal-Times*. March 21–22, 2007, 9.

Patterson, Tom. "Linville." *Brown's Guide to Georgia* 6, no. 7 (November 1978).

Pennsylvania Gazette, October 9, 1766.

Skeate, Stewart. *A Nature Guide to Northwest North Carolina*. Boone, NC: Parkway, 2005.

Spangenberg, Bishop August Gottlieb. *The Spangenberg Diary. Records of the Moravians in North Carolina*. Edited by Adelaide L. Fries. Volume 1, 1752–71. Raleigh: Publications of the North Carolina Historical Commission, 1922. 30–64.

Spencer, Marci. *Pisgah National Forest: A History.* Charleston, SC: The History Press, 2014.

State. "Linville Falls" and "About the Gorge." April 23, 1955.

Sutton, Maude Minish. "Linville Gorge Legends." Edited by Beatrice Cobb. 7-page typescript. 1926.

Tryon, William. *Tryon's Letter Book.* Letter to John Stuart, Esq., of July 30, 1766, from Brunswick, NC.

Verne, Jules. *Robur the Conqueror and Master of the World*. New York: Didier, 1951.

V.W.L. "A Mountain Tramp from Bridgewater to Blowing Rock." *Morganton Star*, August 20, 1886.

Walton, Col. Thomas, ed. "A Terrible Experience." *Sketches of the Pioneers in Burke County History.* Articles written in 1894 and published in the old *Morganton Herald.* Easley, SC: Southern Historical Press, 1984.

Williams, Jonathan. *An Ear in Bartram's Tree.* New York: New Directions, 1962.

Zeigler, Wilbur G. and Ben S. Grosscup. *The Heart of the Alleghanies, or Western North Carolina.* Raleigh, NC: Alfred Williams & Company, 1883.

ABOUT THE EDITOR

Christopher Blake is a retired college English instructor and head of Friends of Linville Gorge, a nonprofit wilderness group based in Linville Falls and dedicated to Gorge preservation and public safety and education. Mushroom forays and stunning vista views are among the free group activities offered by FOLG. Since 2006, when FOLG contracted with the U.S. Forest Service, Grandfather Ranger District's Adopt-a-Trail program, the group has performed year-round maintenance on Devil's Hole Trail, adding Bynum's Bluff, Cabin, Babel Tower and other north Gorge trails in 2014. *River of Cliffs* is a companion volume to Chris's 2009 Arcadia Images of America book *Linville Gorge Wilderness Area*.

Visit us at
www.historypress.net

This title is also available as an e-book